# Grand Junction's JUCO World Series

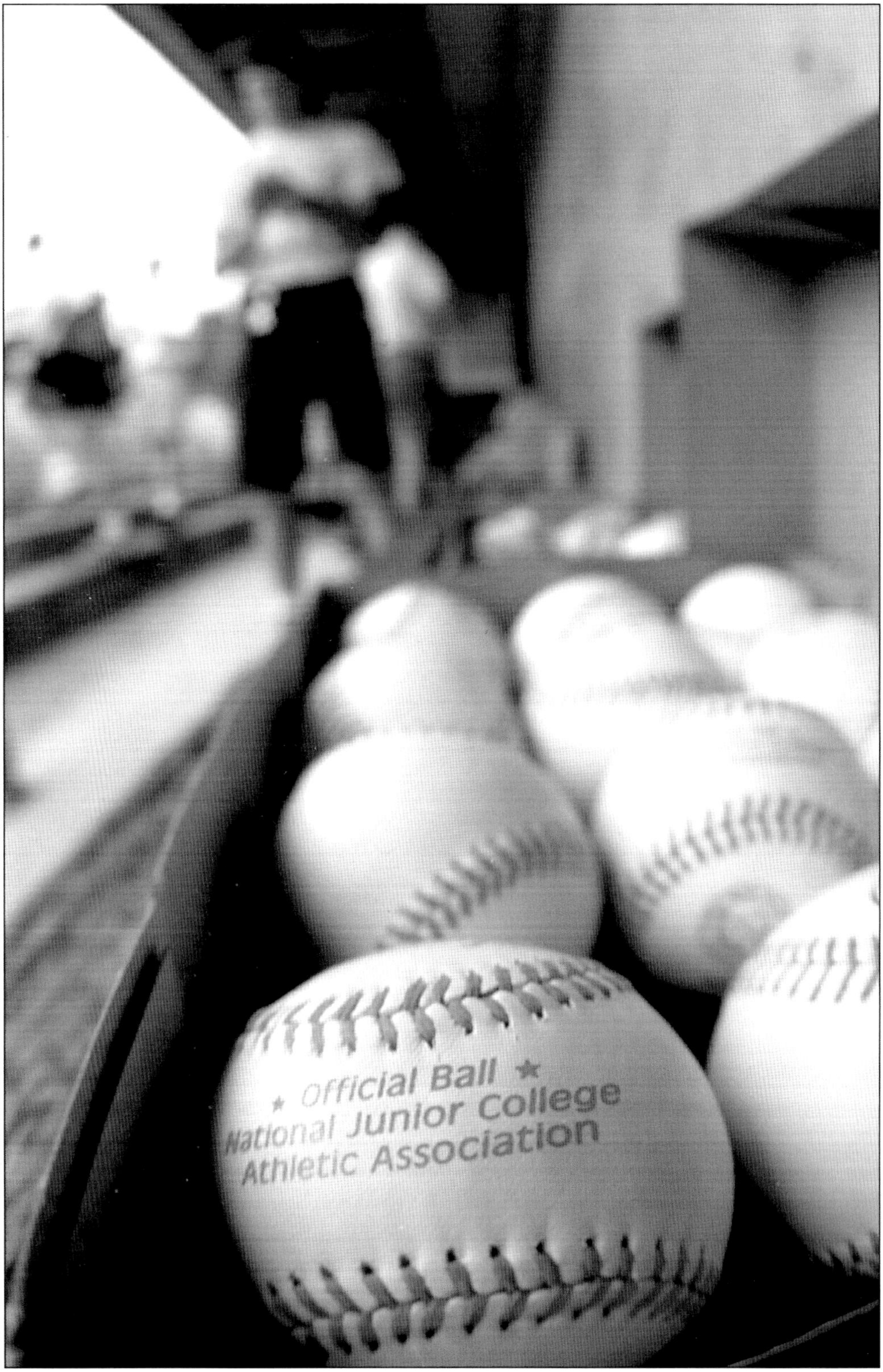
Official Ball
National Junior College
Athletic Association

# Grand Junction's JUCO World Series

Myles Schrag

ARCADIA PUBLISHING

ISBN 978-0-7385-3220-2

Published by Arcadia Publishing,
Charleston, South Carolina

Printed in the United States of America

Library of Congress Catalog Card Number: 2003114742

For all general information contact Arcadia Publishing at:
Telephone 843-853-2070
Fax 843-853-0044
E-Mail sales@arcadiapublishing.com
For customer service and orders:
Toll-Free 1-888-313-2665

Visit us on the Internet at www.arcadiapublishing.com

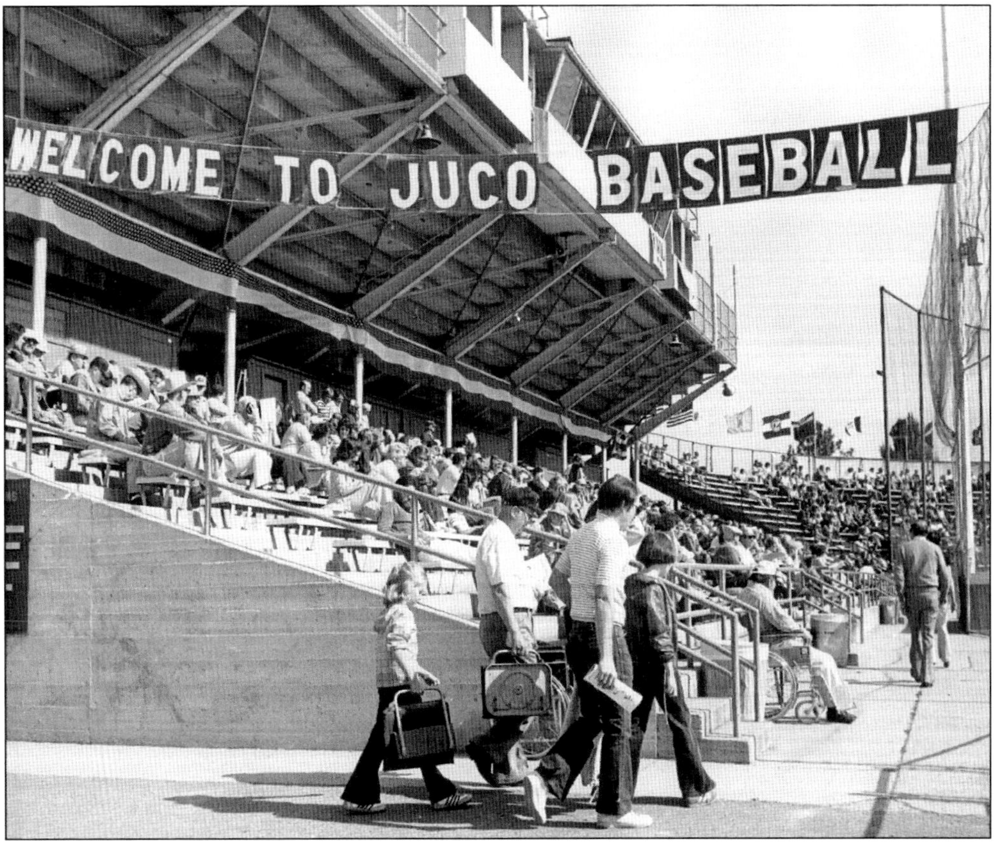

# Contents

# ACKNOWLEDGMENTS

I am the fortunate beneficiary of tremendous amounts of work by people in Grand Junction that have not only made this wonderful tournament occur every spring, but also have made sure there is information available for those of us that came late on the scene about how much the JUCO World Series means to the community. This book is only possible because they understood how important it was to document this event in words, photos and records from the very beginning.

Thank you to Judy Prosser-Armstrong at the Museum of Western Colorado for opening the archives there for me. I am grateful to Chuck at Alpine Bank and JUCO office manager Rojean Wells for working with me to help make my search through the JUCO committee's collection possible. Thanks also to tournament director Jamie Hamilton for granting me a good chunk of his busy time leading up to the tournament and during it.

A huge thank you is necessary for every journalist, photographer, writer, and volunteer that has chronicled the JUCO World Series and whose work has found its way to the JUCO committee headquarters at the Alpine Bank building in Grand Junction. Aside from the two photos on page 13, the photos that make up this book came from the JUCO collection housed there. The most significant voice among these is Ray Coca, whose comprehensive articles, quizzes, and insights in the annual programs were essential in researching the tournament. The *Grand Junction Sentinel* staff writers over the years have clearly taken pride in covering the event, and I appreciate their thorough information to draw from. Likewise, photographers made many of these historic photographs that are now part of the JUCO committee's collection possible. Christopher Tomlinson deserves special mention, but other shooters made valuable contributions as well.

Most of all, thank you to Sam Suplizio, whose vision has guided this tournament almost from the beginning. He is a true community leader that grants respect to all—including a pain-in-the-neck writer wanting to talk baseball and dig through the JUCO committee's files.

I don't deserve to have the author's by-line in this book, considering how many talented and hard-working people have been involved in this tournament over the years. I only hope the joy and respect I have for the JUCO World Series as both a community tradition and a baseball event is evident to those deserving people as they read this book. Likewise, I want to acknowledge the thousands who make the event happen each year through extensive volunteer efforts, through the excitement they bring as fans to Lincoln Park, and as hard-working participants and coaches. You have helped to create a tradition that deserves to be put into book form.

When I wrote *Diamond in the Desert*, my book about Farmington, New Mexico's relationship with the Connie Mack World Series, I felt no other place could match that town's enthusiasm. I won't compare the two here right now. Suffice it to say, I'm honored that these two cities in the Four Corners—one of my favorite regions in the world—show baseball the great respect it deserves.

# FOREWORD

The National Junior College Baseball World Series is an event warmly referred to simply as "JUCO" here in Grand Junction, Colorado, where it has been conducted since 1959 in our beautiful part of the world. Grand Junction is a community nestled in the foothills of the Western Slope of the majestic Colorado Rockies. More formally JUCO is known as the Alpine Bank National Junior College Baseball World Series after our major corporate sponsor, Alpine Bank of Grand Junction.

Every spring the Grand Junction baseball committee begins working in earnest to make certain that the details of our winter meetings and the plans laid out are put into motion and addressed for the upcoming World Series.

The committee is the backbone and strength of JUCO. The 50 volunteers that chair the working committee along with their 300-person work force really get JUCO underway each year. Committees in charge of hosts, programs, banquet, medical service, housing and the Hall of Fame, to name just a few, are all made up of local volunteers.

Now co-sponsored by the city of Grand Junction and the Grand Junction Chamber of Commerce in conjunction with the National Junior College Athletic Association, JUCO was first brought to Grand Junction thanks to the efforts of Mesa Junior College's Jay Tolman in 1958. He felt that our city, known as a good baseball community, might support and make a success of this fine baseball event. The first JUCO was held in Miami, Oklahoma, and had just failed in its initial effort there. An eight-member baseball committee was formed and immediately all of the service clubs in Grand Junction agreed to come on board as hosts. The Lions, Rotarians, Kiwanis, Elks Lodge, Jaycees, Optimists, Sertoma, and others volunteered to host the teams from all over America who qualified for the national tournament. The service clubs' involvement from the beginning, along with the hard-working baseball committee and solid fan support, helped assure the early success of JUCO. Mesa State College, then a junior college, made up the host team for the first decade. The Mavericks were always very competitive and were an enormous help in drawing fans during that period. One has to emphasize that in JUCO history, from the beginning up until the present time, the fans from Grand Junction and the surrounding area have guaranteed the success of JUCO. The World Series truly belongs to our wonderful and supportive citizens here in the Grand Valley. They have been our lifeline.

Banquet speakers have included many baseball greats: Tommy Lasorda, Stan Musial, Bob Gibson, Willie Mays, Paul Molitor, George Brett, Bobby Valentine, and many, many others who have added class and prestige to JUCO, and we are grateful to every banquet speaker that has appeared here over the past 45 years.

Hundreds of heart-warming stories of local people helping out financially those teams that were here on a shoestring budget, friendships between players, coaches, and local families have lasted for years and are as special as having your team win the championship.

Local residents open their arms and their homes to visiting JUCO teams and invite them in as family. Our people have always been there to help where needed. One could write all day about the contributions of our fans, our city, our chamber, our college, our service clubs, our JUCO committee, as well as our other boosters: Major League Baseball, Rawlings Sporting Goods, the National Junior College Athletic Association and the many local corporate sponsors. Each is worthy of a book of their own for their many contributions to JUCO. As important as all of the above mentioned support is, we would be remiss if we did not mention that JUCO has taken all of its profits over the years and used the funds as seed money to raise matching dollars, allowing JUCO to complete over $9 million in local recreation projects, scholarships, and facility improvements in our community for use by young and old alike.

JUCO itself is first and foremost for young athletes who make up the many teams that participate in the national tournament. Hundreds of these players have signed professional baseball contracts because of the stage Grand Junction has made available to them each year. Our heavily scouted event allows players to be seen in the best of competition. Many have starred in the major leagues, including Curt Schilling, Chad Curtis, Kirby Puckett, Rick Langford, John Lackey, Eric Gagne, and Mark Grudzlelanek. Hundreds of other players have been given baseball scholarships to four-year schools so they could finish their last two years of college and receive their degrees.

We here in Grand Junction, Colorado, consider ourselves fortunate that the NJCAA saw to it that JUCO remained in our community for the past 45 years and will remain here for years to come.

Through baseball, young people are given the lofty goal of trying to reach a national championship. Think of it: With the game as the vehicle, coaches take young boys, teach them to take a round ball and a round bat, and hit it square, to catch it and throw it, and in the process they turn our young boys into men who one day we pray will become good citizens and make their own contributions toward making our world a better place in which to live.

For me personally, the highlight of the week of play is to observe how JUCO signals the end of the school year and the beginning of summer as fans come out in large numbers to the baseball stadium, which is their meeting place. It's a terrific coming-out gathering for all of our local citizens. What a beautiful sight it is, each year at Suplizio Field, observing our fans picking their favorite team and cheering it on to victory. Our citizens meet the players and coaches, sharing the hospitality of our wonderful city with all of our out-of-town guests. It is impossible to describe the warm feeling one has as we observe the true magic of the game of baseball in a stadium filled daily with everyone enjoying each other. Friends meet friends and visitors become friends with our local baseball fans. It's a wonderful sight to behold.

I've been blessed by baseball and more than anything I've been blessed just being a part of JUCO for 45 years and working with the great people of our community.

This is the JUCO story.

– Sam Suplizio, December 2003

*Sam Suplizio was tournament director starting with the inaugural tournament in 1959 and was general chairman from 1970 to 2002. The Lincoln Park baseball stadium now bears his name as Sam Suplizio Field. He still advises the tournament committee as chairman emeritus, he still culls from his vast network of big league contacts to schedule the annual banquet speaker, and he will forever be considered "Mr. Baseball" in the state of Colorado.*

# PREFACE

Back in 2000, I was working on a book about the Connie Mack World Series, which has been held in Farmington, New Mexico, since 1965. There was so much to the Farmington baseball story that seemed right to me: the way that the town embraces the tournament, the communal building of the ballpark, the enthusiasm of volunteers and host clubs for the visitors, and the participating visitors being sincerely grateful for the reception given them. I felt that Farmington's long-time job as host to a national baseball event needed some context, so in that book I gave a brief history of the only cities that had managed to keep an amateur baseball tournament longer than Farmington.

I knew one of those cities was Grand Junction, Colorado, located five hours north of Farmington on one of the most scenic drives you will ever have the good fortune to make. I didn't need much information about the tournament, just a capsule history to draw from. So I decided to e-mail the sports editor at the *Grand Junction Sentinel*. Patti Arnold replied very quickly, and with obvious enthusiasm. As a sports editor myself for some time, I knew this was strange. Journalists are notorious for being skeptical curmudgeons about most goings-on, even if the events are good for the community or entertaining. It's not that sports journalists are unwilling to help their colleagues or even to have a good time, but they don't express excitement about it. And replying so quickly to a stranger? Weren't there daily deadlines to meet?

Turns out Patti, like other outstanding *Sentinel* staffers over the years, truly see what's good about the JUCO World Series. She was thrilled to be able to spread the word about her community's cherished event. She also suggested I call Jamie Hamilton, a long-time JUCO committee member who was being groomed to take over for long-time chairman Sam Suplizio. Jamie also was happy to talk to me, but more importantly, he mentioned in passing that the pre-tournament banquet speaker that year would be George Brett. For a Royals fan that grew up in Topeka, Kansas, during the 1970s and 1980s, this was too good to pass up. Jamie said if I wanted to come up for the banquet, he'd save a ticket for me. It would cost me $20, you understand. Everybody has to pay for a ticket, he said. Everybody. I put it on my calendar.

I didn't know exactly why at the time, but I knew I would be making more trips up to Grand Junction, and if I were lucky they would be with baseball on the agenda. Even more than I had expected, this was a sister city with Farmington where baseball was concerned. This town was as committed to its national tournament as Farmington was to its national tournament. Both cities suffer from isolation, or rather, they enjoy having something that others don't know much about, be it stunning natural beauty, committed citizens, or a top-notch baseball tournament. As eccentric local adventurer John Otto, who pleaded with public officials in the early 20th century to get the land now called Colorado National Monument near Grand Junction recognized by the federal government: "We have the goods in Mesa County . . . but it takes about five hundred years to educate people to it."

True enough. Luckily, the National Junior College Athletic Association didn't make us wait that long to give Grand Junction a chance at the JUCO World Series.

My book on Farmington was titled *Diamond in the Desert*. Almost four years later, here is the book on the other deserving baseball community that I didn't realize was needed until I experienced the opening-night banquet in 2000. No, this book doesn't have the title my good friend Rick Hoerner of Farmington suggested was a perfect complement to *Diamond in the Desert*: "Gem at the Junction." But I have great respect and admiration for the people that put on the tournament, the many other volunteers that devote their time, and the fans that have shown consistent enthusiasm over decades of baseball. Definitely I recognize what a jewel western Colorado has.

It is easy to look at a success story after it has been established and assume that what happened was destined to work out the way that it did. It's a little harder to look deeper and appreciate the people and the community that actually did the work to make it all happen. But that's where the stories are, and those stories are exactly what make the tradition special. A community event is not unusual, nor is a baseball tournament, but when the two mesh to form a tradition that spans generations, acts as a reunion, is affordable entertainment, and becomes the focal point for community pride, that is reason to celebrate the achievement.

For the record, there are four cities that have held an amateur baseball tournament longer than Grand Junction and Farmington: Williamsport, Pennsylvania (Little League World Series); Battle Creek, Michigan (Stan Musial World Series); Wichita, Kansas (National Baseball Congress World Series); and Omaha, Nebraska (College World Series). All of these cities deserve recognition for the role they have played in keeping America's love affair with baseball alive over the years. This book is about Grand Junction's place in the baseball story. . . .

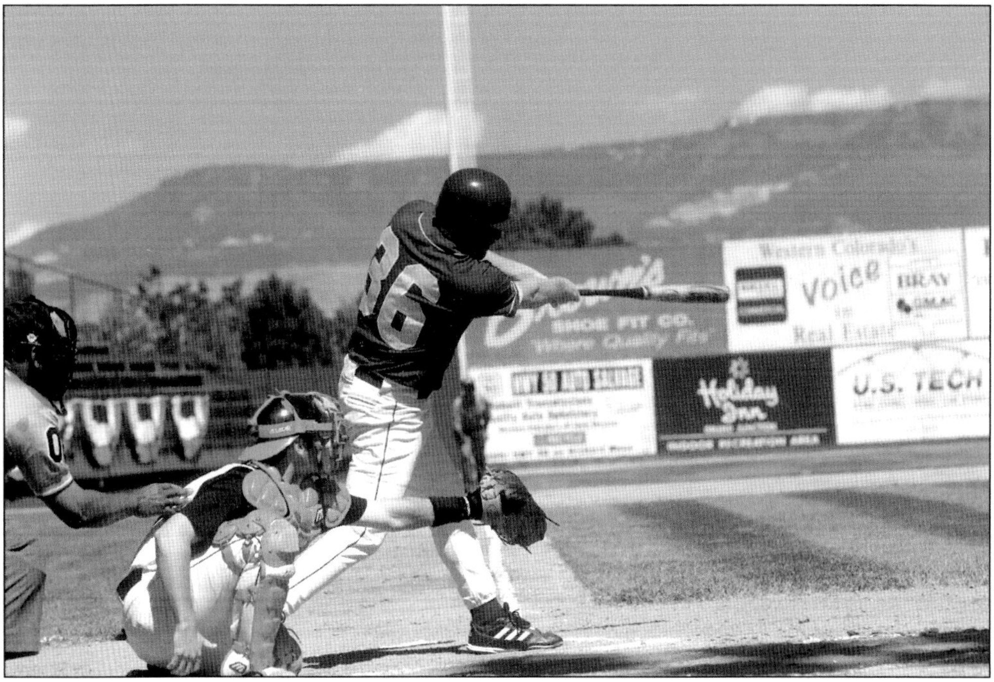


Batters at Suplizio Field swing against a backdrop of the Grand Mesa, the largest flat-topped mountain in the world. It is a majestic site and a frequent destination spot for team hosts to take JUCO World Series players to on an off day when the ballplayers visit Grand Junction. The Colorado community has combined a scenic region with a quirky, lovely stadium and western hospitality to provide one of the longest-running and most impressive amateur baseball tournaments in the country.

# ONE

# *Grand Junction Before JUCO*

Grand Junction civic leaders began plotting to host the national junior college baseball tournament in the summer of 1958, paving the way for the creation of an event that has become one of the most respected baseball tournaments in the country. But it would be wrong to say that baseball didn't already have a high standing in this western Colorado community for years prior to that.

The local semipro team known as the Grand Junction Eagles was a source of civic pride, drawing more than 800 fans a game to the modest stadium at Lincoln Park built in 1949. The Eagles finished the best season in their first 11 years in 1958. Led by future major leaguers Ron Herbel and Max Alvis, the team finished 35-2. Two years earlier, the Eagles had finished fifth at the National Non-Pro Tournament in Wichita, Kansas.

Mesa Junior College began a baseball program after World War II and won its first Empire Junior College Conference championship in 1951 under coach Paul Phillips.

Grand Junction High, like many high schools in western Colorado, began a baseball program after the war. Chuck Cottier helped Grand Junction win a state championship as a junior in 1952 before becoming a big league journeyman. (GJHS lost in the state finals in Cottier's senior year to East Denver, which was led by future Dodger Stan Williams.)

The St. Louis Browns inked Cottier on the recommendation of his American Legion manager Max Carroll in 1953. When the Browns moved to Baltimore, the Milwaukee Braves picked him up on waivers. Cottier later was traded to the Detroit Tigers and Washington Senators.

Prior to World War II, Grand Junction had a fair share of baseball highlights for an agricultural community still young and growing. Baseball was a Sunday afternoon staple during the 1930s, when the Shell Oilers squared off against well-known touring teams such as the House of David and the Negro Leagues' Kansas City Monarchs.

The local Civilian Conservation Corps boys had a team as well. One of its stars was Bill Evans, who went on to pitch for the Chicago White Sox from 1947 to 1949 and the Boston Red Sox in 1951. Prior to that, Grand Junction resident Ray Boggs, who later co-owned Boggs-Fuller Equipment Company in town, was a left-handed pitcher for the Boston Braves in 1928 and 1929.

The legendary "Smoky" Joe Wood even made appearances against Grand Junction town teams in the early 1900s. The future Boston Red Sox star that won three games as a pitcher in the 1912 World Series was a popular young position player for Ouray, Colorado. The August 4, 1905 *Ouray Herald* kidded him after a victory over the Grand Junction nine: "He made the popcorn and soda pop scarce after the game. Must have saved your nickels, Joe." The Ouray newspaper boasted of its squad having easier games against the teams from the north farming country such as Grand Junction, Montrose, and Olathe (Smith 2003).

The mountainous mining towns of western Colorado such as Ouray had more of a baseball tradition established by the time the 20th century began. The first baseball games in Colorado Territory occurred in the spring of 1862 in the relative civilization of Denver (Werner 2003). But the intrepid prospectors that filtered into the rugged San Juan Mountains in the 1870s also brought with them baseball. The game showcased pride in their budding communities and the impression that mining camps could have the entertainment they enjoyed back east in their harsh new environment. Even if the high elevations made level ground scarce and short schedules a necessity, by the 1890s the Western Slope included teams in Ouray, Telluride, Silverton, Durango, and Creede (Smith 2003).

Grand Junction began after mining already had put many of these other towns on the map. The Ute Indians that had inhabited the region were removed at gunpoint from western Colorado in August 1881 and white settlers were officially allowed to enter Ute lands the following month. The Grand Junction town site was chosen on September 26, 1881 and the first fruit trees that would help establish the area's agricultural base were planted in the Grand River Valley the following May. The Denver and Rio Grande Railroad reached Grand Junction in the fall of 1882, which helped raise the town population from 524 people in December 1882 to 2,030 by 1890. That number grew to 3,503 by 1900 and 7,754 in 1910 (Ott 1976).

Baseball was a local attraction by 1910, as can be seen by the dozens of automobiles and horse-drawn wagons parked next to each other along the first and third-base lines and beyond the outfielders during a 1910 game on the edge of town. Like Grand Junction's Peach Festival of the era, America's game brought people together for a chance to see a good cross-section of the community and enjoy public entertainment.

All told, Grand Junction's baseball history by the late 1950s was steady if unspectacular—not bad for a city of 25,000 people nestled between the world's highest flat-topped mountain (Grand Mesa) to the southeast and the stunning red cliffs and canyons of Colorado National Monument at the town's western doorstep. The town had received its name for its location near the junction of the Gunnison and Colorado rivers.

Local leaders, led by Jay Tolman, didn't know it at the time, but the pioneering work they did in 1958 would gradually make their far-flung corner of the world a destination point for baseball teams all over the country. In the process, Grand Junction has thrived at showcasing civic pride through the sport on a scale far greater than the farm country squad Smoky Joe Wood helped defeat in 1905.

Names that would become integral to Grand Junction's baseball history were still quite young in 1958, but already active: Tolman, Walter "Bus" Bergman, Sam Suplizio, Dale Hollingsworth, D.S. Dykstra, Hurst Otto, Wayne Nelson, and many others. Most importantly, they had a community that was just as spirited. The sport in Grand Junction, long established but far too modest to warrant a label like "Baseball Town," was about to become intimately connected with western Colorado's future.

*References:*

Ott, Richard, ed. 1976. *When the River Was Grand: Historical Views of Western Colorado's Grand Valley*. Gazette Press: Palisade, Colo.

Smith, Duane. 2003. "'Nothing But Baseball On His Mind': Smoky Joe Wood Plays for Ouray," in *Above the Fruited Plain: Baseball in the Rocky Mountain West*. Ed. Thomas L. Altherr. The Society for American Baseball Research: Cleveland, Ohio.

Werner, Brian. 2003. "Baseball in Colorado Territory: A Young Game Finds a New Home on the Frontier," in *Above the Fruited Plain: Baseball in the Rocky Mountain West*. Ed. Thomas L. Altherr. The Society for American Baseball Research: Cleveland, Ohio.

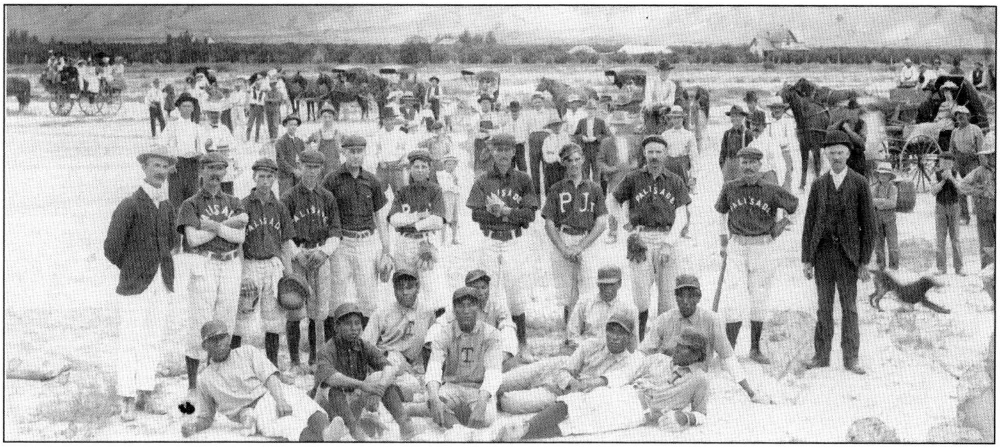

Students from the Grand Junction Indian School team pose with players from the nearby town team of Palisade in this undated photograph. Grand Junction Indian School educated Native Americans from 1886 to 1911, shortly after the Utes were removed by force from western Colorado in 1881. It was also known as the Teller Institute after the Congressman, Henry M. Teller, who promoted the legislation in Congress that led to establishment of the school.

Palisade, known as "The Peach Capital," is a tiny agricultural community located just east of Grand Junction. It has long been known for its excellent fruit and wine, including mention in the 1909 Fruitman's Guide magazine for having peaches that were "the best in the world." Even today, Palisade only has 2,500 residents, but in fin de siecle western Colorado even the smallest towns had baseball teams. (Courtesy of the Palisade Library Collection, Loyd Files Research Library, Museum of WesternColorado.)

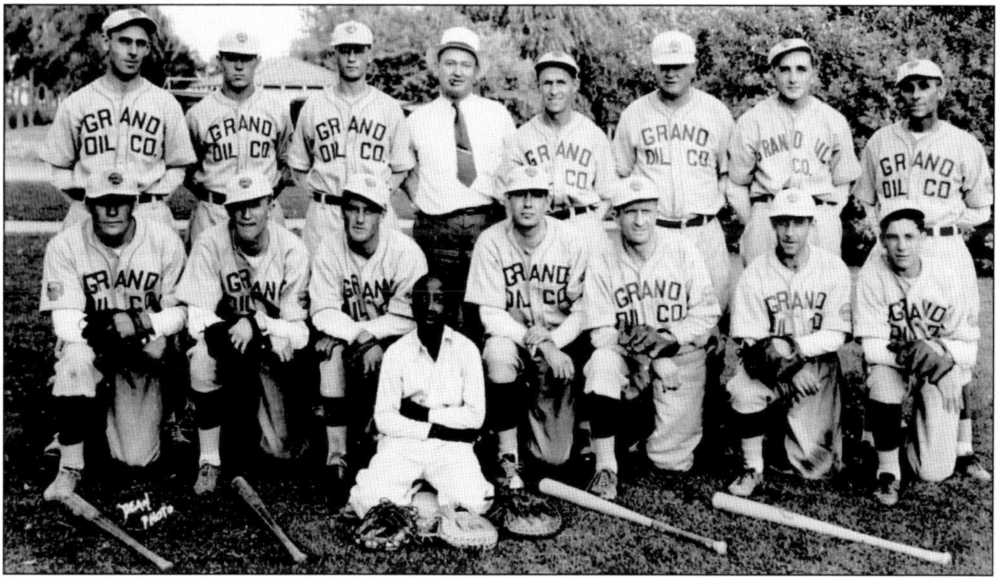


The Shell Oilers provided excellent baseball for Grand Junction fans in the 1930s. One Oiler, Jack Merlino, even signed a contract with the Boston Red Sox in 1938. This photo from the latter part of the decade includes local favorites such as Elmer "Rass" Ingram, Bill Meders, Chuck Hafey, and Bob Evans. Evans came to Grand Junction to work as a railroad machinist in 1930 and ultimately became the local Denver and Rio Grande foreman in 1942. (Courtesy of the Dorothy Evans Collection, Loyd Files Research Library, Museum of Western Colorado.)

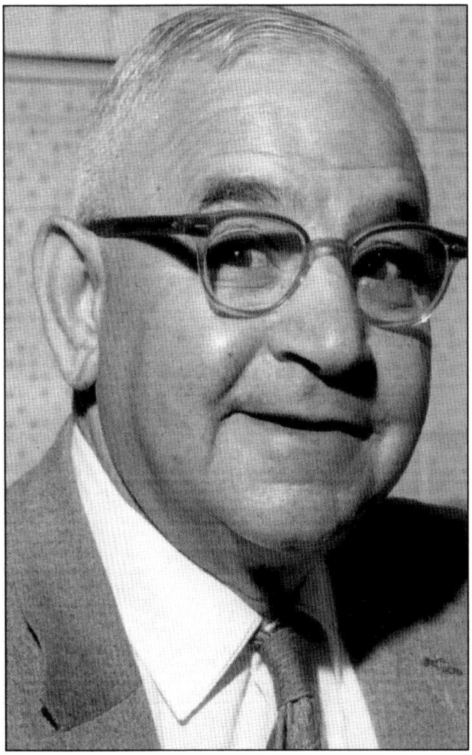

Rudy Susman was the strength of the Eagles from its inception. He was the only member of the team's organizing committee for the Eagles' entire 29-year existence. The beloved Susman served at various times as president, business manager, and secretary from 1948 to 1976, and even initiated "Roll Out the Barrel" as the team's theme song. When Susman, manager Sam Suplizio, and business manager and principal fund-raiser A.C. Corder decided to retire after the 1976 season to pursue other goals, the Eagles program ended its illustrious run.

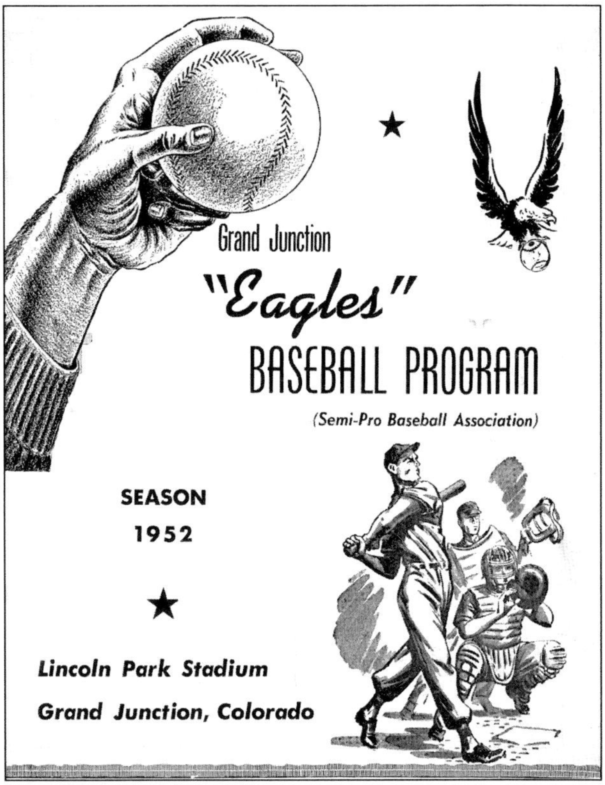


This is the official 1952 Eagles program. In the early years, the Eagles consisted of returning World War II veterans, and local and regional high school or collegiate stars. Later, in the 1960s and 1970s, players arrived from colleges nationwide to join a high-powered summer team in hopes of landing a professional career. Instead of playing air force base teams and local nines from around the West, the Eagles played national powers such as the Boulder (CO) Collegians. They made a two-week barnstorming trip to play the Alaska Goldpanners and the Anchorage Glacier Pilots, a highlight of the schedule starting in 1963.

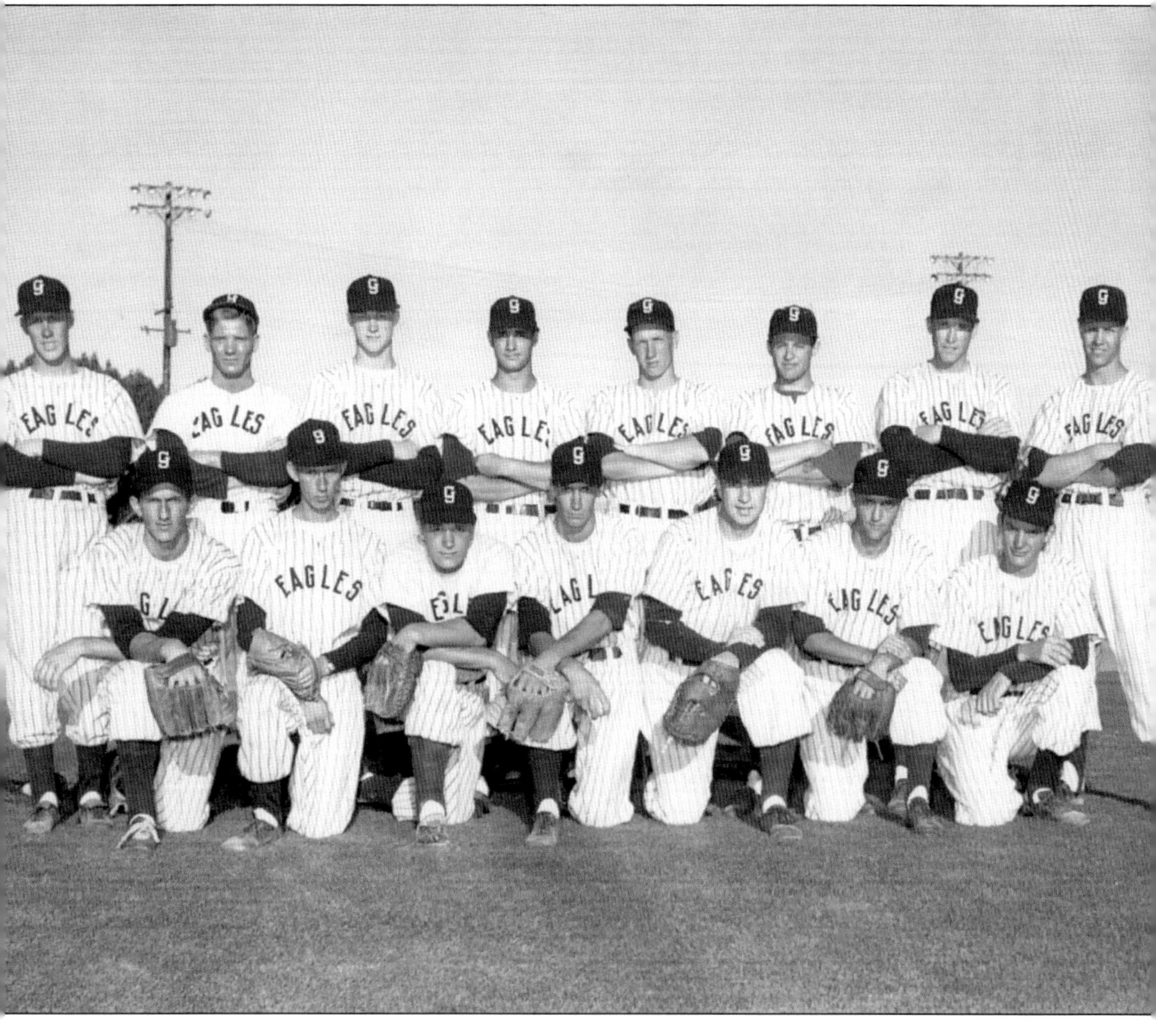


This 1952 team photo of the Grand Junction Eagles is a good representation of whom the famed semipro squad consisted in its early years. This squad had just a few out-of-state players. The Eagles went 31-8 this season and averaged 847 fans a game at Lincoln Park. Pictured, from left to right, are, (front row): Otto Hatcher (from Phoenix College), Ken Coulson (pitched on Grand Junction High's Class AA state championship team in 1952), Gene Taylor (originally from Grand Junction, played for the University of Colorado), Jerry Keith, Ken Murphy (from Pueblo, Colorado, coached at Durango (CO) High School), Gene Haggerty (originally from Denver, played for Mesa Junior College), and manager Walter "Bus" Bergman (He originally came up the Million Dollar Highway from Durango, where he coached Fort Lewis A&M, to pitch part-time for the Eagles in the summers of 1949, 1950, and 1951. This was his first year as Eagles manager after moving to Grand Junction to coach the Mesa JC baseball and football teams); (back row) Jim Payne, John Benson (originally from Grand Junction, played for the University of Colorado), John Roth, Sam Suplizio (at age 19 and still a junior at the University of New Mexico, this was Suplizio's first exposure to the city where he would be so instrumental in the coming years), Joe Pearson (from Odessa, Texas), Lou Tanko (originally from Denver, played for Mesa Junior College), Ed Kinney (originally from Denver, he was a 27-year-old Colorado State University graduate when this photo was taken), and Bill Faddis (from Denver).

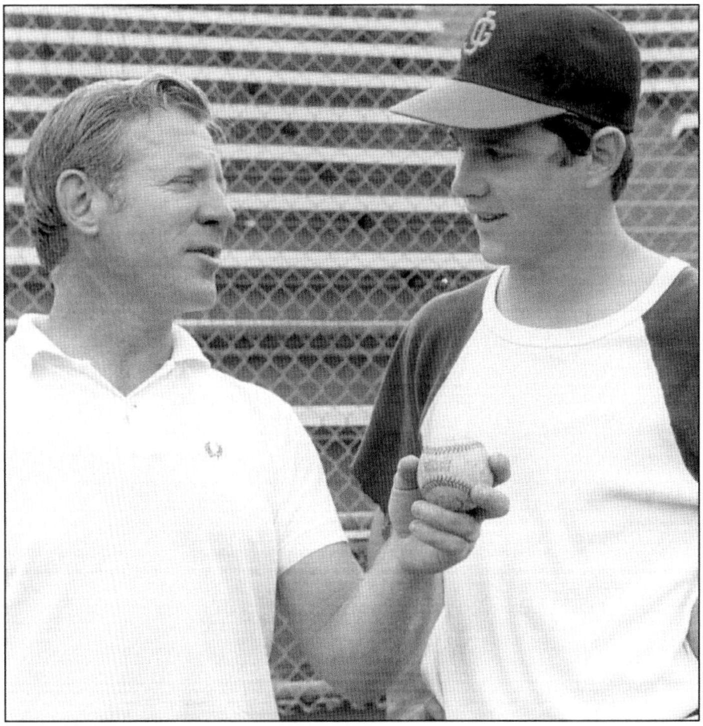

Former New York Yankee pitching star Whitey Ford (left) served as a special pitching coach for the Eagles in 1971 and 1972. His son Eddie Ford (right) was a standout infielder for the Eagles in 1972 and 1973.

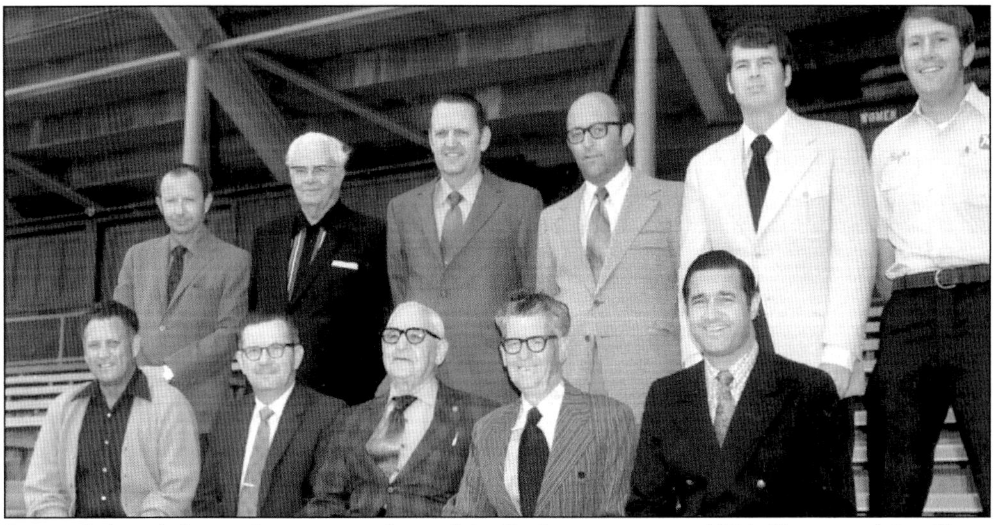

Pictured, from left to right, are members of the Eagles committee, 1974: (front row) Jim Dyer, George Cook, Rudy Susman, A.C. Corder, and Sam Suplizio; (back row) Dr. Hurst Otto, Martin Gaines, Mancel Page, Gene Haggerty, Dr. William Frank, and Tom Dykstra. Committee members not shown: Gene Rozelle, Jim Eisenhauer, Tilman Bishop, Ed DeLucas, Bob Percival, Charles Shaw, and C.A. Smith. The Eagles committee was vital over the years to maintaining contact with the community, keeping the budget, making the schedule, coordinating housing with Mesa JC, and finding jobs for the players, who were required to work 35 off-the-field hours a week during the summer. One of the committee's requirements for players was to "Work daily and protect jobs by working hard, so that the job will be available for a player the following year."

# Two

# *Tolman Forges a Tradition 1959–1969*

The novel idea of holding a national championship for junior college baseball could very easily have died in the muck and apathy of Miami, Oklahoma, in 1958. There was no reason to believe a tournament that attracted few fans and received more hard rain than cheers would live to see 1959. Credit Jay Tolman for seizing an opportunity that would make the national pastime an integral part of life in western Colorado while also giving the national junior college championship idea new life.

The Dean of Men at Mesa (CO) Junior College in Grand Junction, Colorado, couldn't help but think that his town could make a go of a national tournament. Grand Junction's baseball history up to that point had been only modest, not memorable. The picturesque town sat almost a mile high on the Western Slope of the Rockies, a tough road trip for most mid-century junior college baseball programs. But Tolman quickly asked for and received the support of the key players in town he thought were needed if a bid to the National Junior College Athletic Association was going to be successful.

The NJCAA national baseball tournament's arrival in Colorado happened relatively quickly during the course of 1958 thanks to Tolman's vision, Grand Junction leaders' grasp of the potential Tolman was espousing, and unique circumstances that made Grand Junction the right place to rescue the event from oblivion.

A national baseball tournament had been considered by the NJCAA since 1956. The organization saw how a consistent host city had benefited its national men's basketball tournament, which had been held in Hutchinson, Kansas, since 1949. The NJCAA wanted to replicate that success in baseball. Miami, Oklahoma, accepted the job of hosting the NJCAA's first national baseball tournament May 16–17, 1958. Hindered by constant rain, attendance was poor at the event. Tolman, an NJCAA regional director at the time and a member of the NJCAA national baseball committee, saw the conditions in Miami firsthand. When he returned to Grand Junction, he began his sales pitch to colleagues at Mesa JC and town leaders.

He asked Mesa baseball coach Walter "Bus" Bergman if he thought his squad could compete as host team. He queried Mesa basketball coach Wayne Nelson, whose team had just returned from an appearance at the national tournament in Hutchinson, about what the Kansans did to make such an event work. He asked Mesa president Horace Wubben if the college would be willing to make the commitment to host the event. Most significantly, he asked D.S. "Dyke" Dykstra, chairman of the Chamber of Commerce's education and athletic committee, for town support in sponsoring the event. Dykstra in turn talked to chamber president B.A."Boots" Kellogg and chamber director Dale Hollingsworth.

A gathering at Mesa Drug Store on Main Street served as an informal first meeting that included Tolman, Bergman, Dykstra, Hollingsworth, businessman Don Sparn, and Sam Suplizio, a former outfielder in the New York Yankee farm system who was now playing for the semipro Eagles and working for Dykstra at Home Loan.

By the fall, the groundwork had been laid to make an official bid. The Grand Junction Festival Company, a successful local corporation headed by *Grand Junction Sentinel* publisher Preston Walker, agreed to underwrite $3,000 of the $6,000 Tolman estimated would be needed to transport seven teams, feed and house them while in town. By October 2, 1958, when Dykstra acknowledged in the *Sentinel* that the chamber's athletic committee was working on a proposal, Tolman said that there was a "distinct possibility" that a Grand Junction bid would be favorably considered. Later, Coca-Cola offered $1,500 to the bid, but that initial financial commitment from the Festival Company was most crucial in setting the tone for the tournament. It gave Tolman and Dykstra leverage when they took the train to Hutchinson to attend the NJCAA meetings later in October, since it helped mitigate risk that the national organization saw in holding the event in a far-flung locale. It may not have answered the inevitable question from the NJCAA, put so aptly by Dykstra: "Where in the hell is Grand Junction, Colorado?" But it did show that the sentiment of civic leaders was to embrace Tolman's plan. That enthusiasm carried into the following spring. Civic clubs quickly became instrumental to maintaining the upbeat mood. They agreed to act as hosts for teams visiting town. Even today, the role of organizations such as the Lions, Kiwanis, the Elks Lodge, the Jaycees, the Optimists, and Sertoma cannot be underestimated.

Tolman was the only one in Grand Junction with an in-depth knowledge of how the NJCAA worked at the time. It didn't hurt that in addition to his own experience, his brother-in-law, Reed K. Swenson, was president of the NJCAA executive committee and of Weber (Utah) College. When Tolman pooled his own ideas with other leaders in town, Grand Junction was an easy choice for the NJCAA. The bid was officially accepted on October 28, 1958. "Now that Grand Junction's bid has been accepted, as expected, it will be a matter of full steam ahead in preparation for the affair," reported the next day's *Sentinel.*

Building on the momentum generated in Hutchinson was not hard to do, as key volunteers quickly stepped into roles they seemed destined to perform. Dykstra became general chairman, a job he held until 1967. Drs. Charles Lumley and Hurst Otto were co-chairmen. Hollingsworth took care of publicity. Nelson, who had athletic director experience at Mesa, was in charge of housing the players. Local businessman Rudy Susman, the founder of the semipro Eagles, spearheaded the grounds and park committee, while local radio announcer Frank Gibbs of KEXO handled media coverage. Suplizio became tournament director, taking care of issues that arose on the field and making sure the event ran smoothly.

"It was a natural for Sam to get back into the game he loved," Dykstra said. "He still had a lot of contacts at the major league level and with his professional experience as a player and manager he knew how to run a tournament."

Indeed, Suplizio's imprint on the event is everlasting. As valuable as his connections and infectious personality were in securing legitimacy and publicity for the event in the early years, his leadership and foresight have steered the tournament into the future for more than four decades since he first shuffled the rain-soaked schedule during the 1959 tournament.

While Tolman's efforts are rightly praised for seizing an opportunity that opened up when Miami failed as host, it should be noted that Grand Junction had its eyes on a national prize even before the first pitch of the 1958 national tournament had been thrown in Oklahoma. The NJCAA West Regional was held at Lincoln Park Stadium in early May 1958 with Bergman's Mesa squad in the role of host team.

"Northeastern A&M of Miami, Oklahoma, has set up its own NJCAA invitational clambake, which goes off next weekend," reported the *Grand Junction Sentinel.* "The Oklahomans are hoping to make it an annual occasion in their own backyard. But Mesa has other notions. 'If we can show them Grand Junction will support a tournament of the regional caliber in a big way,' said Mav coach Bus Bergman yesterday, 'then we've got a good chance of getting the national here in the future.' "

Of course, not everyone was thinking on such a large scale. The newspaper was thrilled at the conclusion of the 1958 regional tournament and made this prediction on May 14—a prediction that turned out to be rather tepid: "The chance of another regional tournament here next year was considerably enhanced by the mere fact that the affair didn't fall on its nose." Though Mesa won just one of three games in the round-robin tournament that included Trinidad and Pueblo colleges from Colorado plus Weber, the event grossed $993, a profit of $200 that was used to help regional champion Trinidad travel to Miami.

While Lincoln Park Stadium was primitive in the early years of the national tournament, and organizers freely admit that they were learning by trial and error, the event never did "fall on its nose." Improvements to the field and the event were done only as money became available, volunteers always came through before and during the tournament, and crowds always came. A total of 4,700 fans saw the first tournament to be held in Grand Junction in 1959, when the only permanent bleachers were the first-base line seats that formed the reverse side of the football stadium bleachers directly to the west.

The 1959 event faced the same adversary as Miami had the previous year: rain. Despite three rained-out games on opening day of the four-day tournament, Suplizio and other organizers scrambled to keep the schedule on track. Seven games were played on Day 2. Lincoln Park was pushed hard, but the Grand Junction diamond was sturdy enough for the job. Eight teams came, including host Mesa, Northeastern Oklahoma A&M, Wilmington (NC) Junior College, Paducah (KY) JC, Phoenix (AZ) College, Paris (TX) JC, Carbon College of Price (UT) and Trinidad. Trinidad was a last-minute replacement for Montgomery JC of Takoma Park, Maryland, which couldn't come up with its share of money to make the trip.

Paris made a bridesmaid out of A&M for the second consecutive year in 1959. The Dragons belted out a 14-4 win over the Golden Norsemen in the final. The Texans had been a fan favorite from the tournament's outset, as they arrived the night before the tournament began in two full carloads. The Dragons suited up only ten players—one of whom, pitcher Olen Jordan, was out of action with a cast on his arm. They soon earned the nickname of the Iron Men for their determination and grit. Though JUCO lore has it that they were picked to finish last in the inaugural tournament to be held in Grand Junction, this team was full of solid athletes. Tournament MVP Glendell Baker batted .526 and went on to be all-Southeastern Conference at the University of Alabama. Jack Ward and Jim Culpepper starred on the Paris basketball squad that placed fourth at the national tournament in Hutchinson. Ward and Leonard Bell attended Alabama to play baseball and basketball.

The first Grand Junction tournament was also noteworthy for including one feat that has not been accomplished since at the JUCO World Series. Billy DeBruhl of Wilmington tossed a no-hitter in what was an otherwise disappointing trip for the Seahawks, who were considered the most physically imposing team present.

Despite the rain and the host team's early exit, the tournament netted a profit of $137.53, according to the June 12, 1959 *Grand Junction Sentinel*. A total of $3,622.17 in expenses was offset by $3,759.70 brought in by ticket sales, gate receipts, and programs. The host for the 1960 tournament was an easy decision for the NJCAA. The regional directors approved Grand Junction's bid unanimously. This time the chamber's athletic and education committee agreed to underwrite $3,500 toward the tournament.

The first decade of the junior college national baseball tournament in Grand Junction was a gradual success. The community prides itself on the widespread effort that has continued to make it so. But let's not forget Tolman, who died at age 83 in 1996, as the enthusiastic visionary that paved the way. Frank Gibbs wrote a fine tribute to Tolman just one week after the first Grand Junction bid was accepted in his November 4, 1958 "Play by Play" column in the *Sentinel*: "There is no man at Mesa College who has done more to put the Mesa athletic program on a solid footing than Jay Tolman. It is our fervent hope that now that Grand Junction possesses the plum of a national Junior College baseball program—that we expend as much energy, enthusiasm and skill in promoting and carrying out the tourney as Jay Tolman has in getting this classic here."

Many western Coloradoans have heeded Gibbs' call to make the tournament what it is today, 46 years later. For that, the fine baseball town of Grand Junction should be proud.

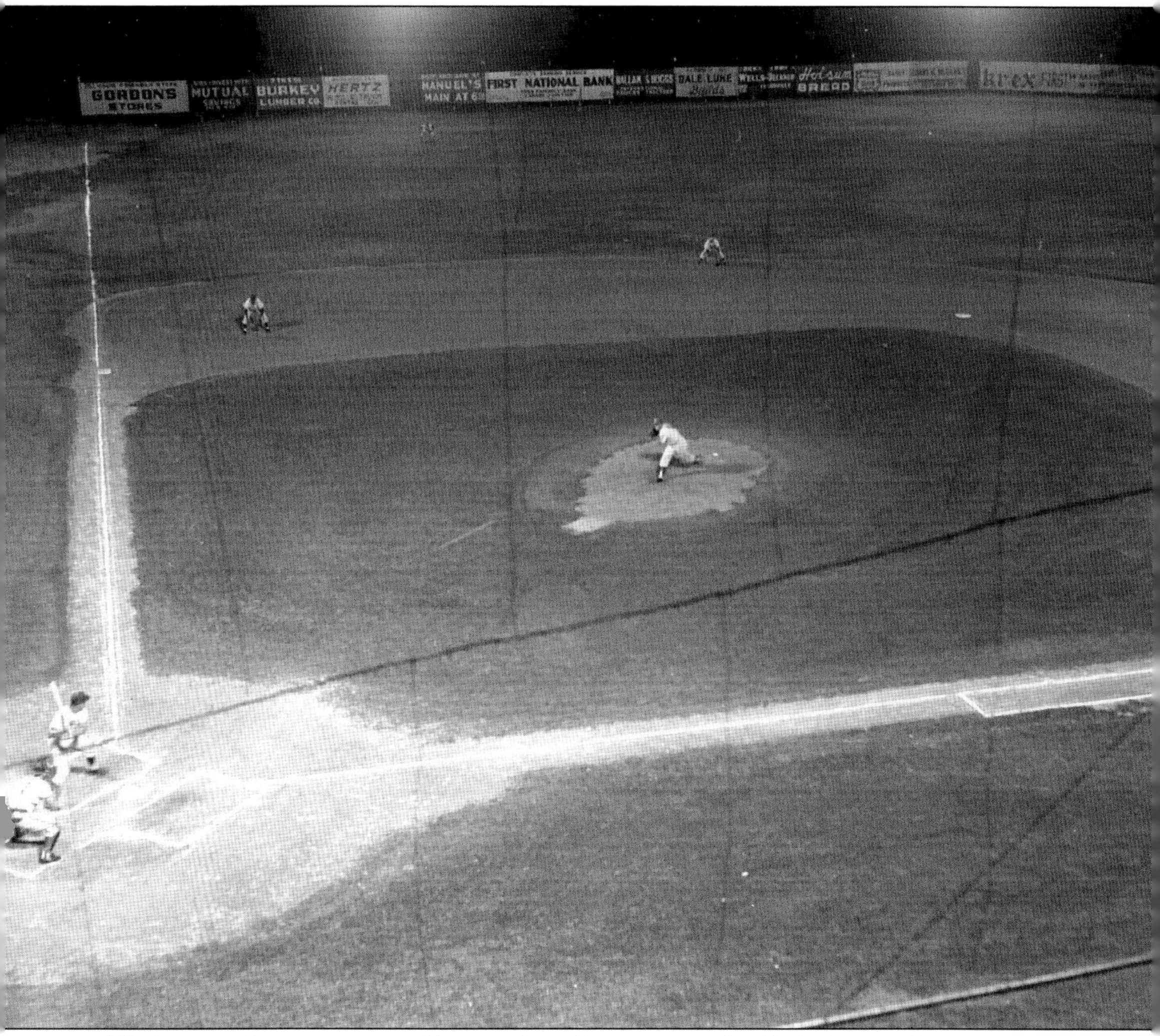


Alkali was such a common problem in Grand Junction in the 1950s for people trying to grow grass and plants that the locals called the area in and around Lincoln Park "alkali flats." The salty substance can be seen in this photo creeping inside the foul line deep in left field during the tournament's early years and killing the grass at the young park. Tournament director Sam Suplizio eventually solved the problem by moving the left-field fence inside the alkali patch, from 351 feet to 302 feet. "Everyone said I did that so I could hit more home runs," said Suplizio, a right-handed hitter who still occasionally suited up for the semipro Grand Junction Eagles in the early 1960s. "But no, I was so old by then I wasn't getting around on the ball. Everything went to right field anyway."

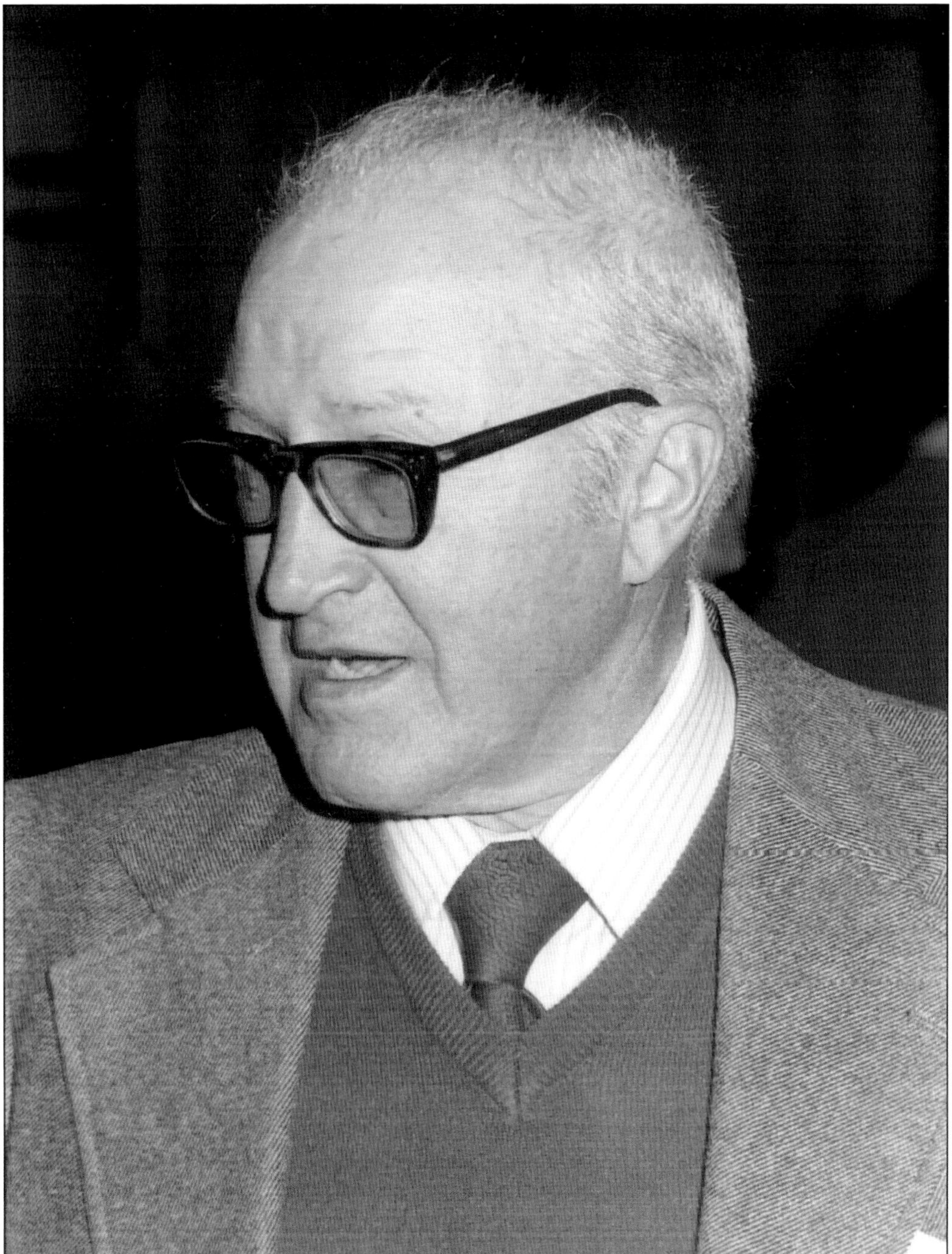

Jay Tolman, quite simply, is the reason the National Junior College Baseball Tournament first came to Grand Junction. His influence was vast in sports even before the event's arrival. After a stellar track and football career at Utah State University and military service as an officer in Europe during World War II, he was a successful coach at Dixie College and the high school in St. George, Utah. At Mesa Junior College, he started the baseball program after the war, coached a variety of sports and taught geology and physical education. Tolman was the first person inducted into the JUCO Hall of Fame.

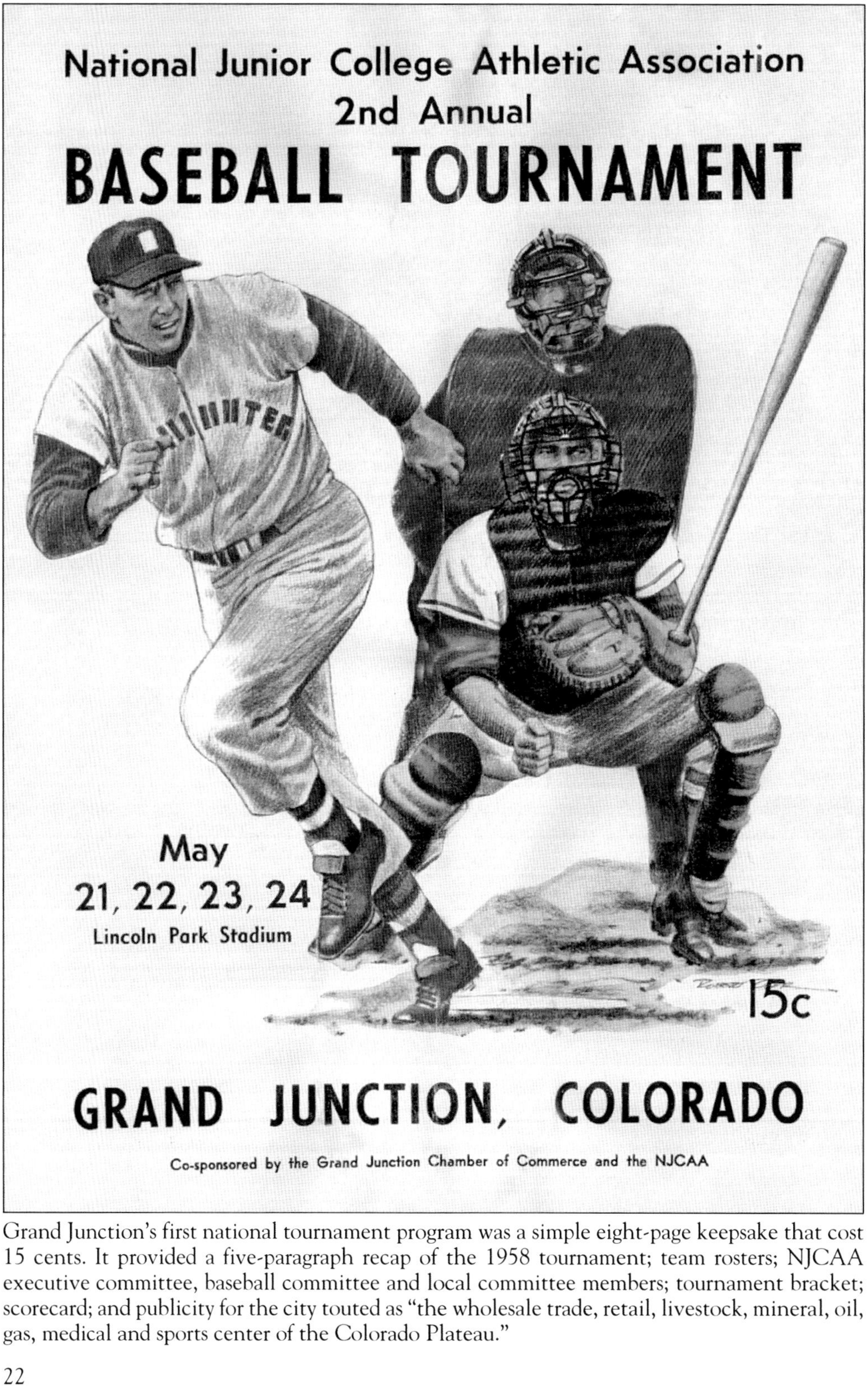


Grand Junction's first national tournament program was a simple eight-page keepsake that cost 15 cents. It provided a five-paragraph recap of the 1958 tournament; team rosters; NJCAA executive committee, baseball committee and local committee members; tournament bracket; scorecard; and publicity for the city touted as "the wholesale trade, retail, livestock, mineral, oil, gas, medical and sports center of the Colorado Plateau."

Catcher Eldon Miller was the first of 18 players from Mesa Junior College to earn all-tournament honors. The Maverick receiver and graduate of nearby Fruita High School was chosen "most likely to succeed" by the scouts attending in 1959. Though Mesa lost its only two games that first year, the squad paved the way for more successful future tournament efforts by the Mavericks.

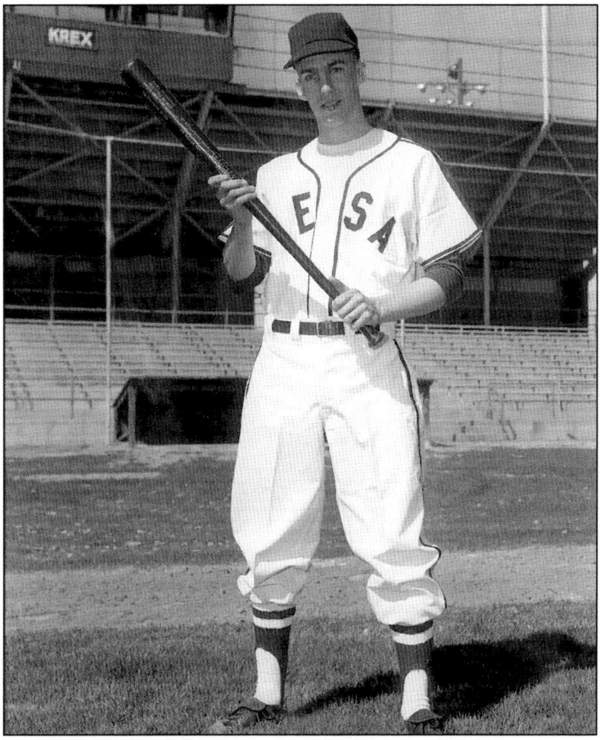


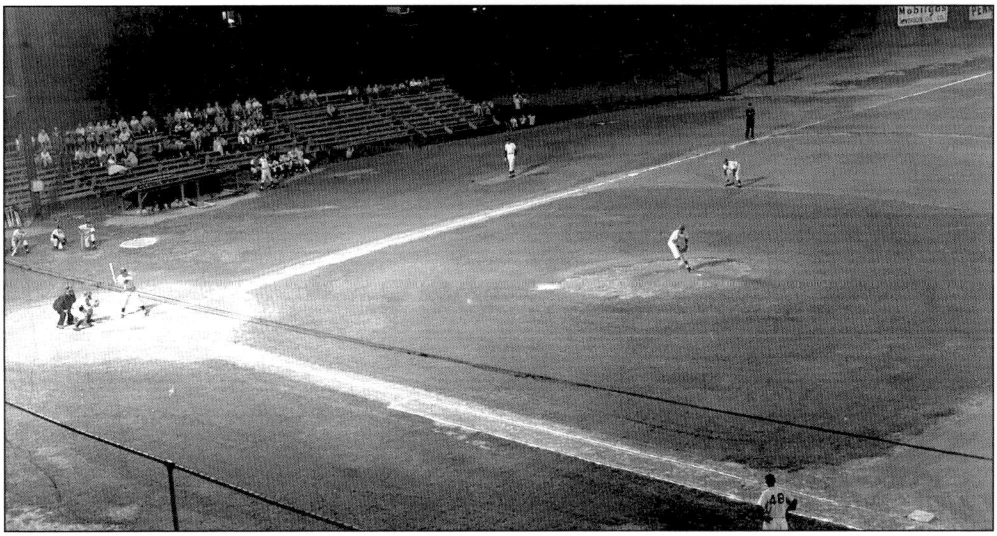

This early tournament photo is a good indicator of how even great things must build slowly. Clearly the tournament was doing well by not losing money, by generating local interest, and by showcasing the city as a hospitable host. But the days of more than 100,000 people for the week were still three decades away. Attendance was considered strong in the early days, but the fact was that the temporary wooden-planked bleachers behind home plate and down the third-base line (along with the permanent seats behind first base) simply didn't hold many fans. Phoenix's 8-4 win over Tarleton (TX) State in the 1960 final came before 500 fans. Wilmington (NC) defeated host Mesa JC in the 1961 final 8-3, which lured 1,105 fans to Lincoln Park Stadium and brought total tournament attendance to 8,000 that year.

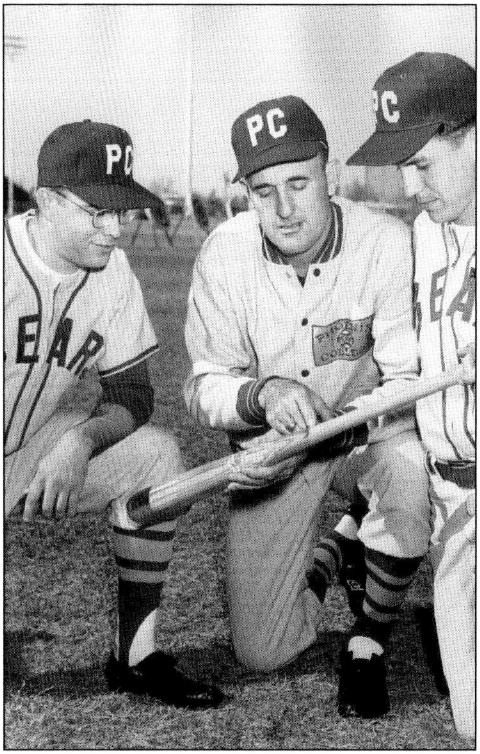


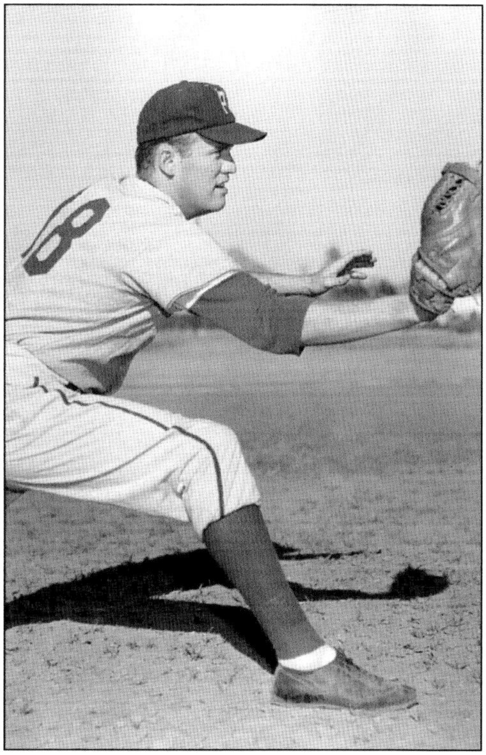

One of the favored teams in 1959 was Phoenix College, coached by Steve Carson (*center in left photo, above*). The Bears took 16 innings to beat Paducah, Kentucky, which was considered one of the weaker squads in the tournament, and won just two games. According to the *Grand Junction Sentinel*, "Phoenix was indicted in some quarters for not 'playing tough.' The Bears were conceded to have the most and the finest personnel—four of them made the all-tourney team—but lacked the drive to capitalize on the advantage." The Bears' time would come. The four named all-tournament were all freshmen: first baseman John Vincent (*above, right photo*), second baseman Larry Brion (*opposite page, left photo*), utility player Kent Olson, and pitcher Rennie Crittenden (*right in left photo, above*). Outfielder Steve Kennedy is on the left. Carson's more seasoned squad won the first of three national titles in 1960. Other championships came in 1962 and 1965.

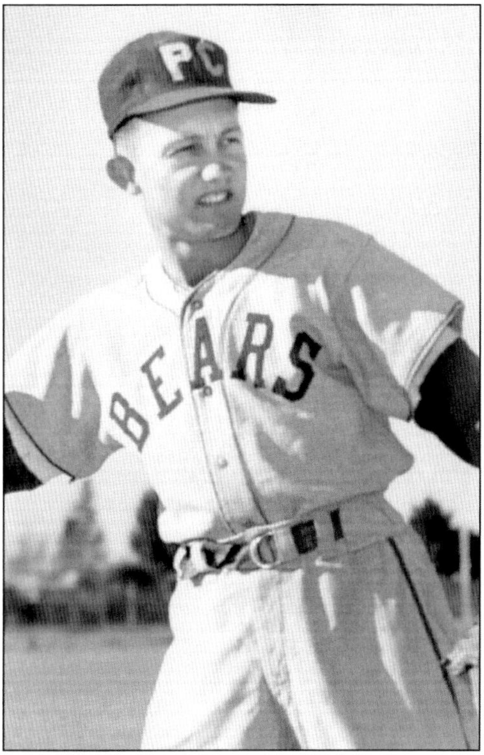

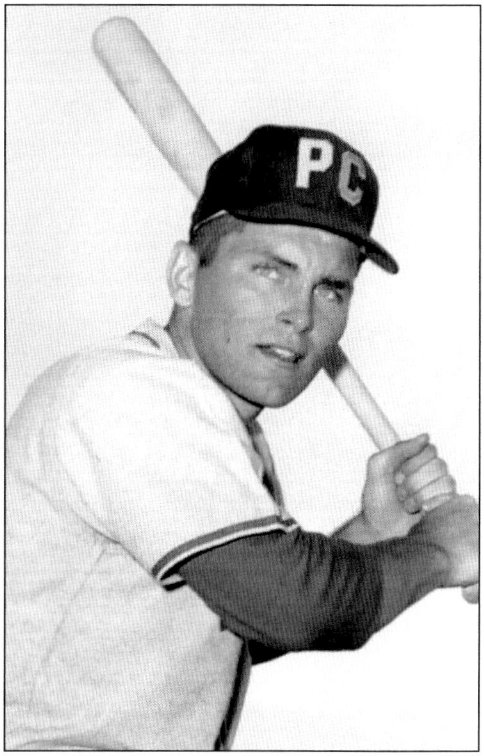

Larry Brion (*left*) was all-tournament for Phoenix in 1959 and was on the 1960 national champion squad. Dennis Starkins (*right*) was a freshman all-tournament outfielder in 1960. The Bears made up for a disappointing first visit to Grand Junction by sweeping four straight victories in the return trip and finish the season with 34 consecutive wins over junior college opponents. Phoenix defeated Tarleton State 8-4 in the 1960 championship game. The Bears also defeated Wilmington 12-1 in the first round and Northeastern Oklahoma 8-2 in the second round. Unlike 1959, when four Bears made all-tournament despite the team's purported lack of toughness, in 1960 the Bears placed only Starkins and third baseman Syd Smith on the honored squad while Tarleton's Mickey Lee took the Most Valuable Player honors. Also of note in 1960, host Mesa earned its first national tournament victories, defeating Long Island (NY) 15-10 in the opener and Wilmington 9-8 in the third round.

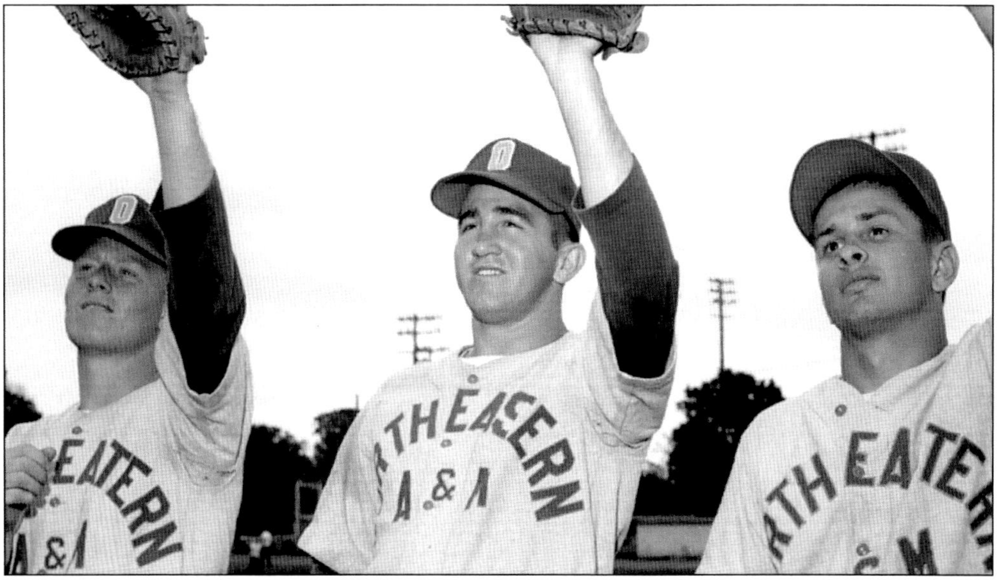

Raymond Porter (*left*), Bob Bruno (*center*) and Robert Johnson played a role in Northeastern Oklahoma A&M's 1961 tournament run. Bruno was an all-tournament outfielder. NEO was the only team to compete in the first four national tournaments (1958–1961), and even though the Miami, Oklahoma school never won it all (placing second in 1958 and 1959, and third in 1960), its place in JUCO lore is secure. NEO hosted the ill-fated first national affair in 1958 and in 1989 suffered the worst championship game loss in tourney history—22-4 to San Jacinto (TX) North. On the plus side, long-time Golden Norsemen coach Homa Thomas was elected to the JUCO Hall of Fame in 1994 after a 17-year career that included more than 300 wins. To his credit, he helped Grand Junction obtain the tournament in 1959 when Miami didn't support it. Today, the sportsmanship award given out each year bears his name.

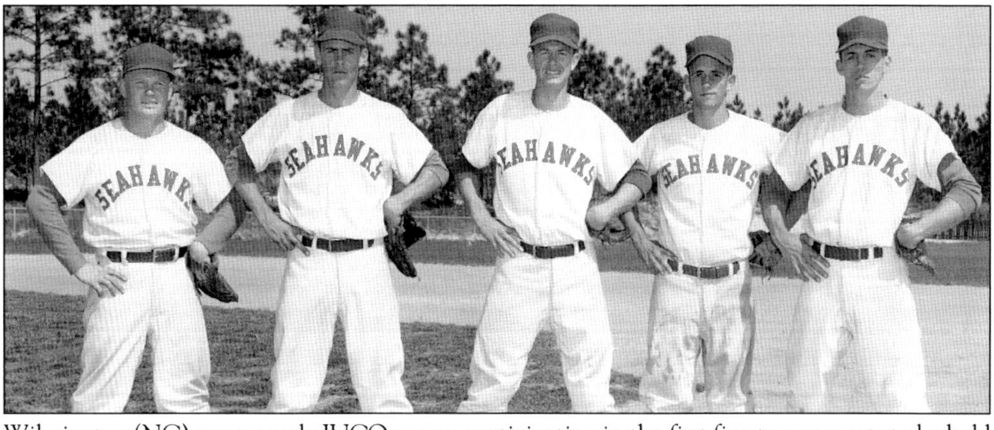


Wilmington (NC) was an early JUCO power, participating in the first five tournaments to be held in Grand Junction (1959–1963), winning two of them (1961 and 1963) and placing runner-up in 1962. Because Wilmington became a four-year college in the fall of 1963, it was unable to return to defend its title. The Seahawks beat host Mesa 8-3 in the '61 final and Manatee (FL) 9-2 in the '63 final. The infield shown here, from left to right, consists of third baseman George Hunsucker, shortstop Bill Harris, second baseman Sterling Coward, utility man Butch Watts, and first baseman Bobby Shipp. Coward was honorable mention all-tournament in 1963 and all-tourney in 1962, when he set a national meet record with five hits in a game. Shipp was all-tournament in 1963.

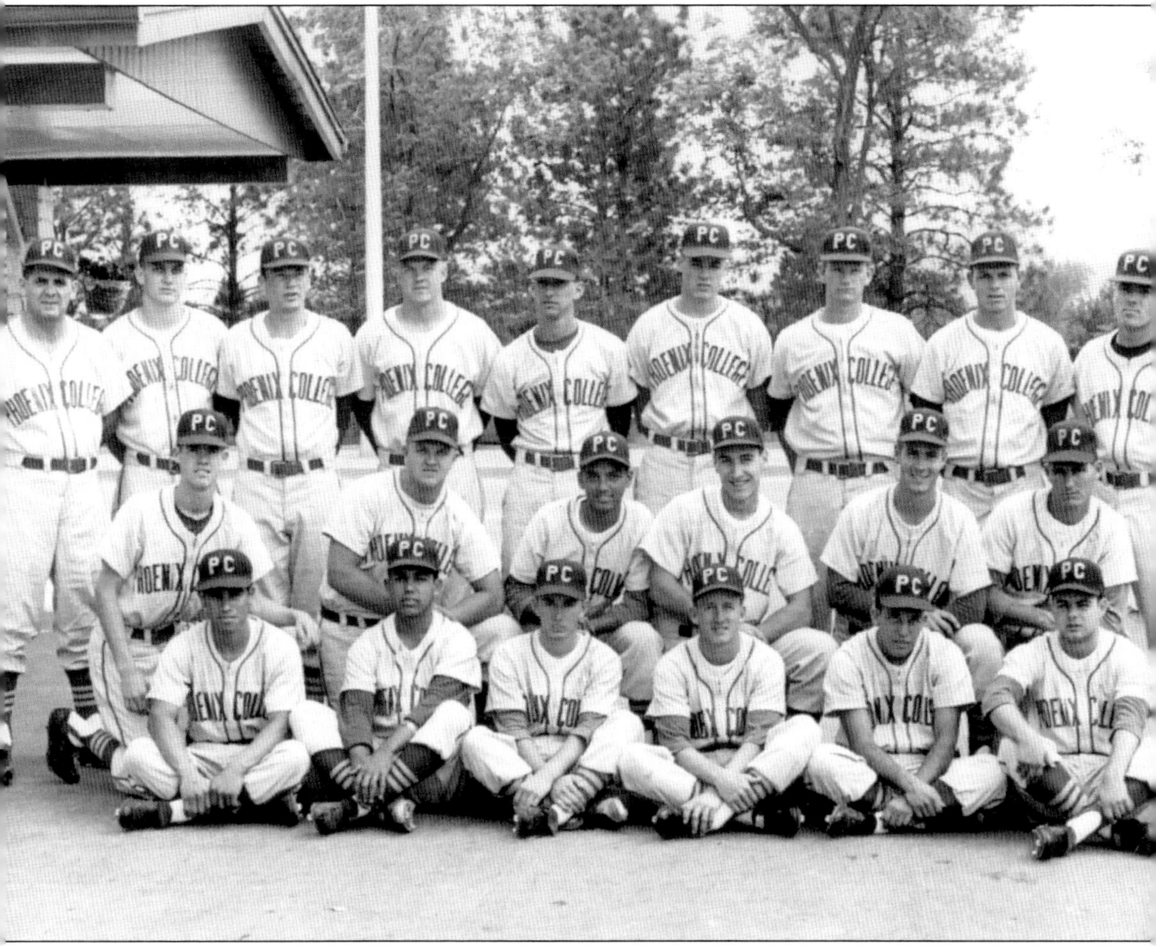

Phoenix College was the closest thing to a dynasty in the first decade of the national junior college baseball tournament. The Bears competed in eight of the first ten national tournaments (1958–1960, 1962, 1964–1967). At a time when teams from warm-weather states in general were the dominant programs and Arizona colleges in particular were the class of the field, the Bears were the most feared. Arizona-based squads nabbed ten of the first twenty JUCO championships (1958–1977). This is the 1962 national championship team that earned the second of Phoenix's three JUCO titles in an offensive-minded tournament. Phoenix finished an undefeated trip to Grand Junction by whipping defending champion Wilmington 13-5 in the final, jumping out to a 7-0 lead in the first inning on three Seahawk errors, four walks, and two hits. In 1965, Tom Burgess led the Bears with a Most Valuable Player pitching performance—three wins on the mound, including 13 strikeouts in the 9-6 final over Gulf Coast (FL). Seventeen-year-old Gary Gentry won two games and was voted most likely to succeed.

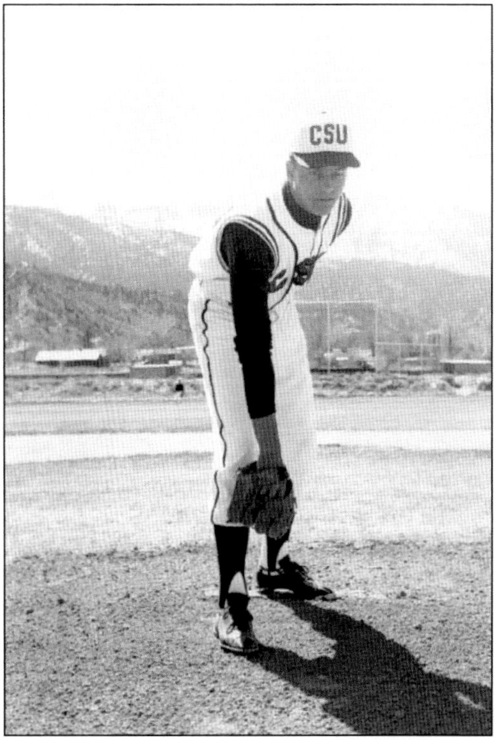


Steve Cahoon was an all-tournament pitcher for the College of Southern Utah in the Cedar City school's only visit to Grand Junction in 1963.

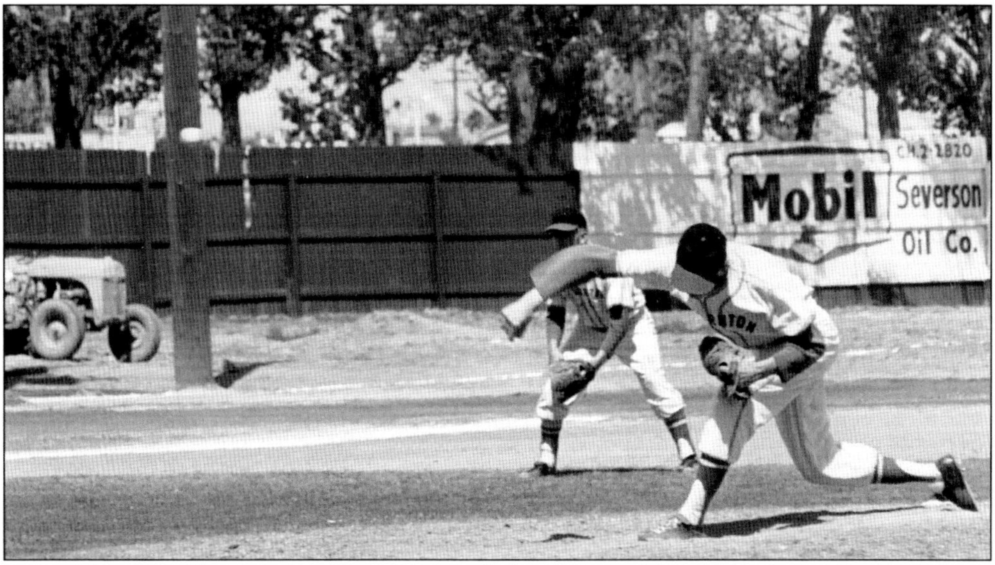


The year 1963 was also the only appearance for Thornton Junior College, which is now called South Suburban College in Harvey, Illinois. This photo is a good indication of how low-key the early tournaments were. A tractor and light standard sit inside the fences, and not even temporary bleachers extend much beyond the third-base bag. Also in the early years of the national tournament, a tree sat inside the fence along the first-base line, forcing infielders that ventured into foul territory for a foul pop-up to watch carefully where they were going. Such quirks prompted New York Yankee great Lefty Gomez, a regular visitor in the early years, to tell tournament director Sam Suplizio that the Lincoln Park Stadium "looked like something Abner Doubleday built."

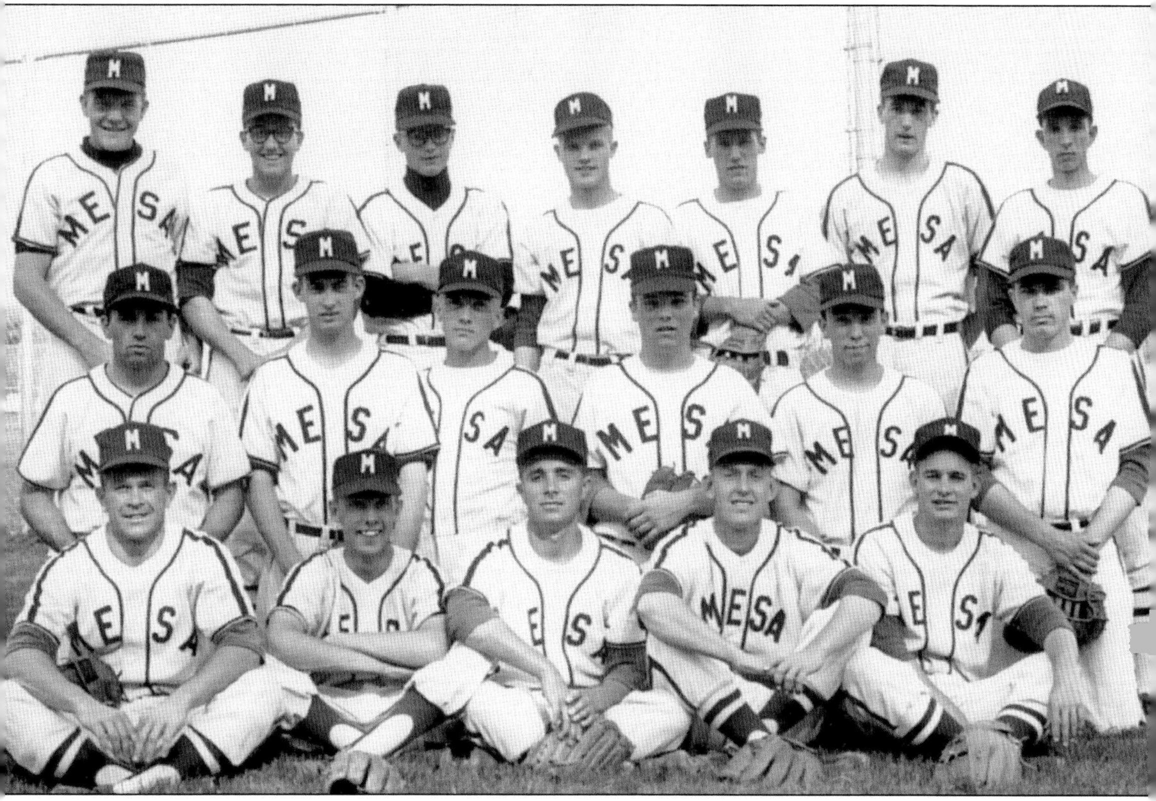

This is the 1963 host team from Mesa. The Mavericks made their presence known in the early years, when the idea of an automatic entry for the host team carried with it a stigma of not having earned a legitimate spot in the national tournament. Coach Bus Bergman's teams proved otherwise, and in the process helped boost attendance at a critical stage in JUCO's development. Mesa won twice in just the second tournament to be held in Grand Junction in 1960, utilized outstanding pitching by Jim Brenneman and Pete Lovrich to place second in 1961, and gave Wilmington its only tough game in the Seahawks' 1963 title run. The 1964 Mavericks, though, were the real breakthrough squad for making JUCO visitors take note of the team whose campus was located catty-corner across North Avenue and 12th Street from Lincoln Park Stadium. Unlike 1961, when Wilmington rolled through the tournament unbeaten, the '64 Mavs and freshman Barry Lersch stunned eventual champion Miami-Dade with an 11-3 win in the first championship game. Lersch, who went on to pitch for the Philadelphia Phillies, fanned 15 batters and all three runs were unearned, plus he had five RBIs in the game. The next night, the Floridians lashed out at six Mesa hurlers for 20 hits and a 19-5 victory, but Mesa had made a valiant stand in forcing the extra game. Mack Gendreau became the only Mesa player to ever win the tournament Most Valuable Player award, as the sophomore left-hander from Boulder, Colorado, earned two complete-game victories, including a 5-1, 15-strikeout performance in a first-round win over Ellsworth (Iowa) College. Lersch, aided by an 11-run second inning, blanked powerhouse Blinn (Texas) 12-0 on a one-hitter in the second round. After a 9-1 loss to Miami-Dade sent Mesa to the loser's bracket, the Mavs rebounded by ousting Blinn behind Gendreau's 3-1 victory. Grand Junction High School graduates Bob Andrews delivered a crucial RBI-single and Tex Tolman (son of JUCO legend Jay Tolman ) had two hits. In addition to Andrews and Tolman, GJHS players Jerry Chick, Bucky Hakes, and Dennis Kelley all played instrumental roles on the '64 Mavs.

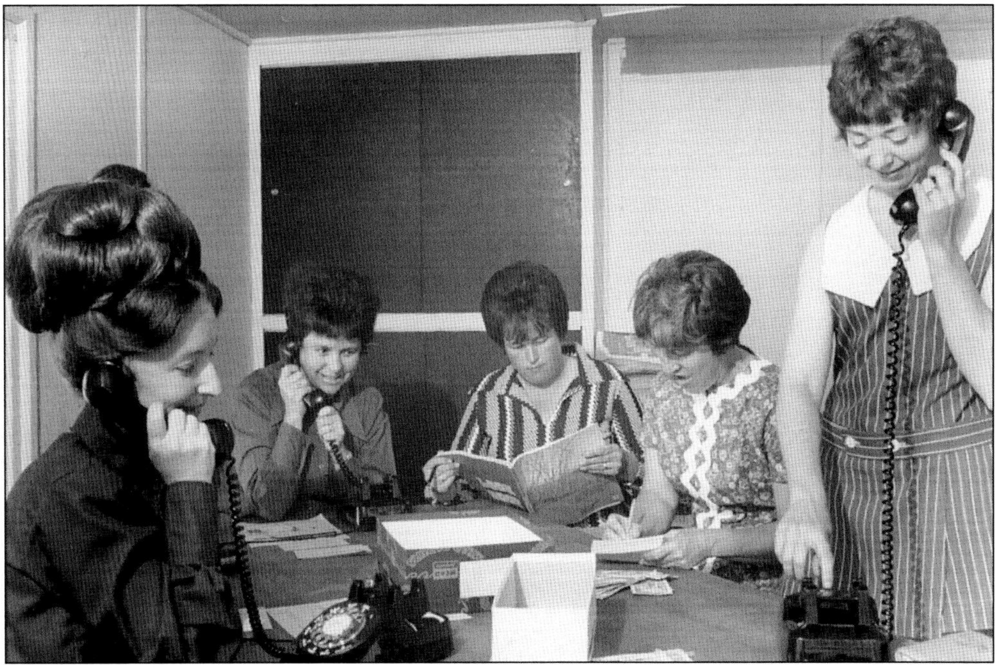

The volunteer effort that has kept the national tournament going in Grand Junction has always included women. Here, a group of local women take care of administrative tasks during the early years. Wives of committee members also helped their husbands paint newly installed bleachers and do work around the stadium as the park evolved.

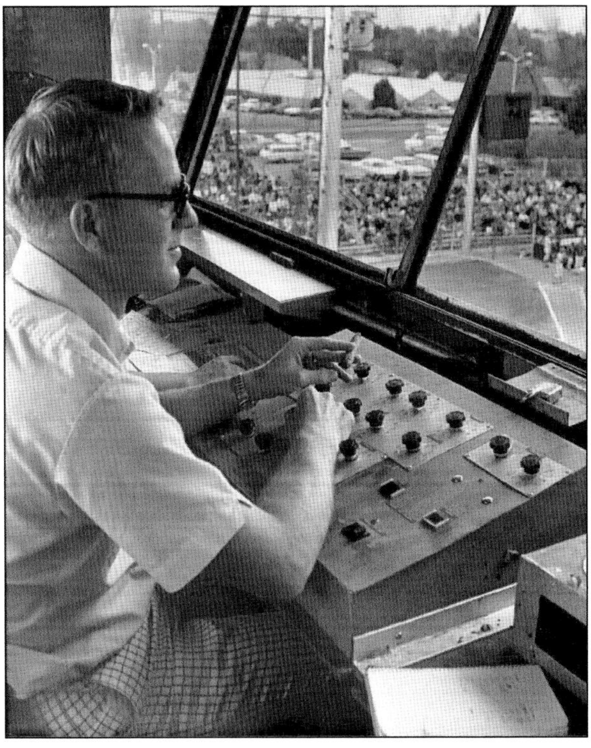

With a stogie in hand, Frank Gibbs mans the scoreboard controls from high above Lincoln Park Stadium in the early days. Gibbs was in charge of getting results to the media in the early days, and like many volunteers, handled multiple jobs in the press box to keep the event running smoothly. Unlike most baseball parks where the press box is behind home plate, the press box at Lincoln Park is located behind the first-base foul line. This is because the press box and the bleachers underneath it form the backside of the football stadium press box and bleachers. The unusual arrangement helps give the Lincoln Park complex its distinctive charm.

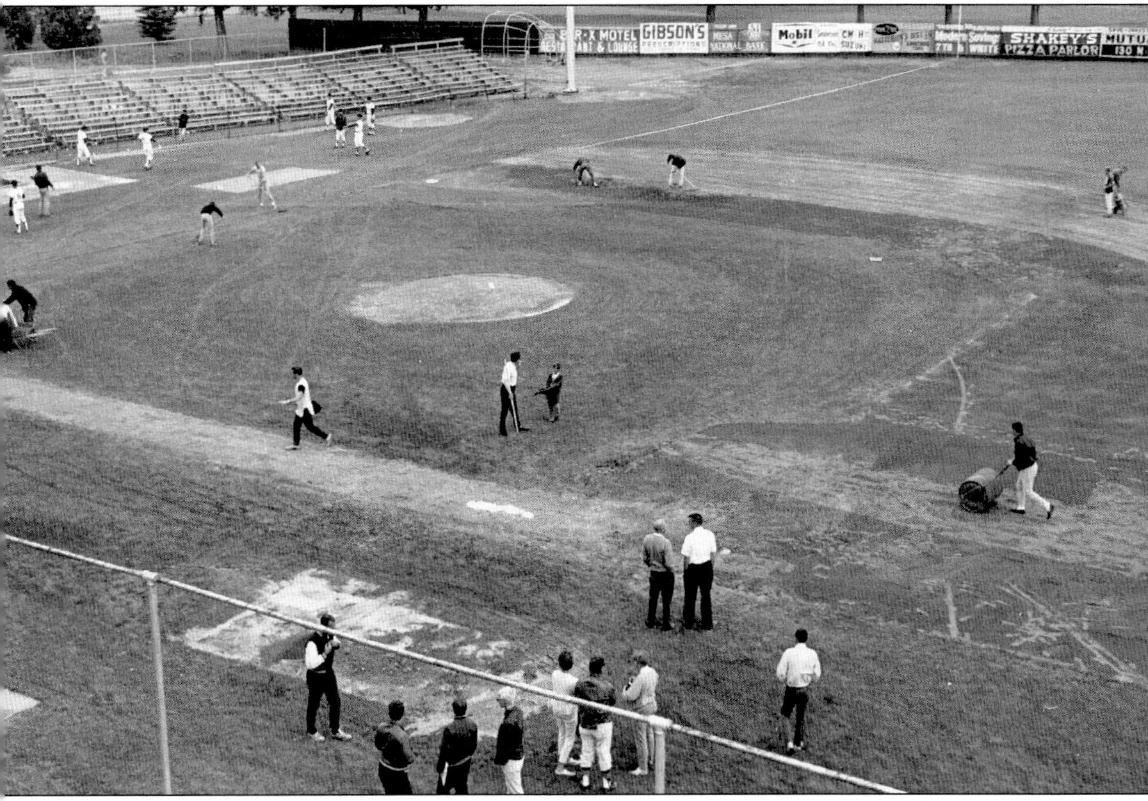


Volunteers have always been willing to lend a hand in Grand Junction. This late 1960s photo is an indicator of that ability to pitch in and get the field ready. This photo also shows some of the park's gradual progress. The temporary bleachers, which are said to have contained more than a few splinters, now extend farther down the third-base line, the wooden light standards have been replaced with metal ones, and the outfield signage extends farther into foul territory on the wooden outfield fence. Included is an advertisement for Bar-X Motel, Restaurant, and Lounge, which served for years as tournament headquarters. A 1969 special tournament supplement in the Sentinel includes a motel ad that says, "Baseball is a game that winds you up! Unwind at Bar X," and touts entertainment by the Cheer Notes, "a vocal and instrumental group featuring guitar and accordion sing-along music."

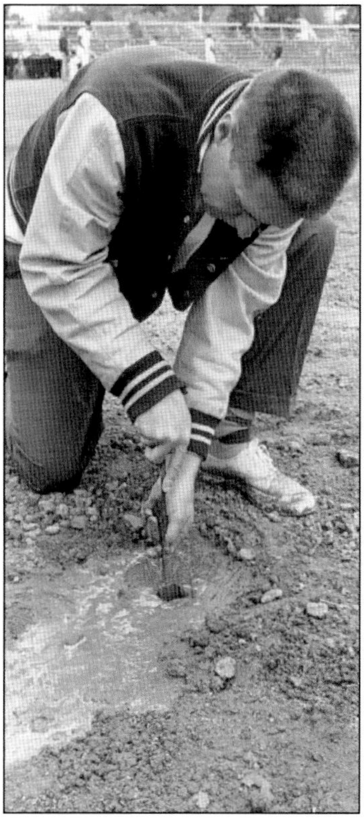

Rain has made its presence felt during the years and thrust the grounds crew into quick action. The 1967 event was among the wettest. The field-drying methods in those days were still rather primitive. Sam Suplizio, the tournament director at the time, remembered one problem they had: "We were burning the field with gasoline and all of a sudden we smelled something like rubber burning. Well, I'll be darned if we didn't catch home plate on fire. Boy, you talk about something funny, that was it."

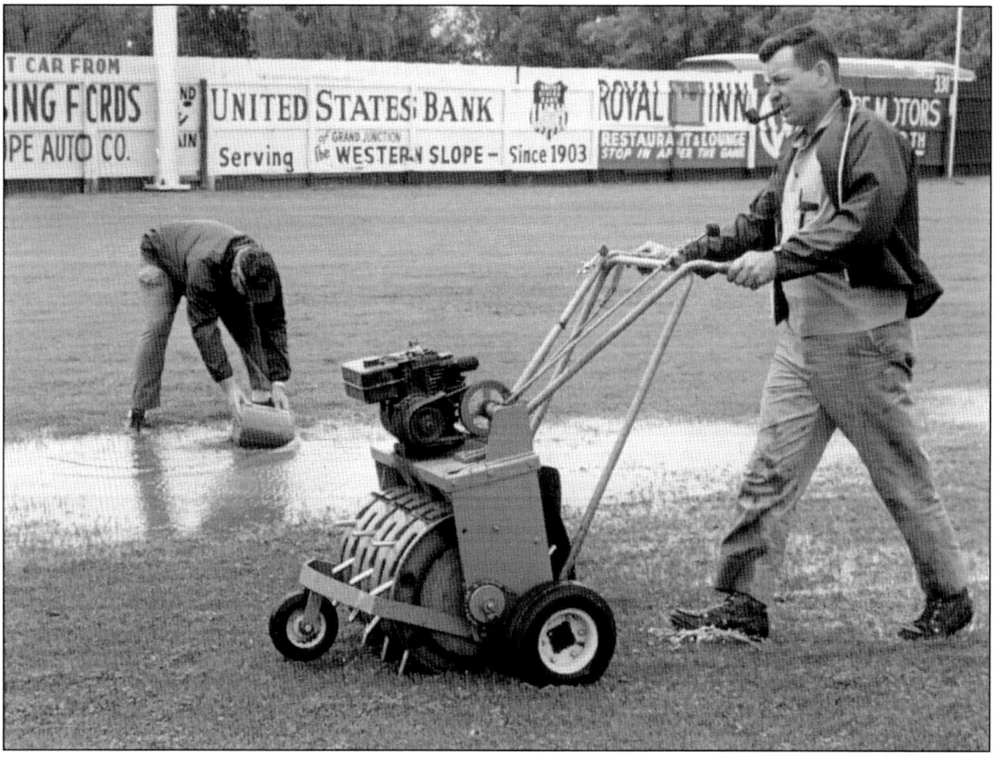

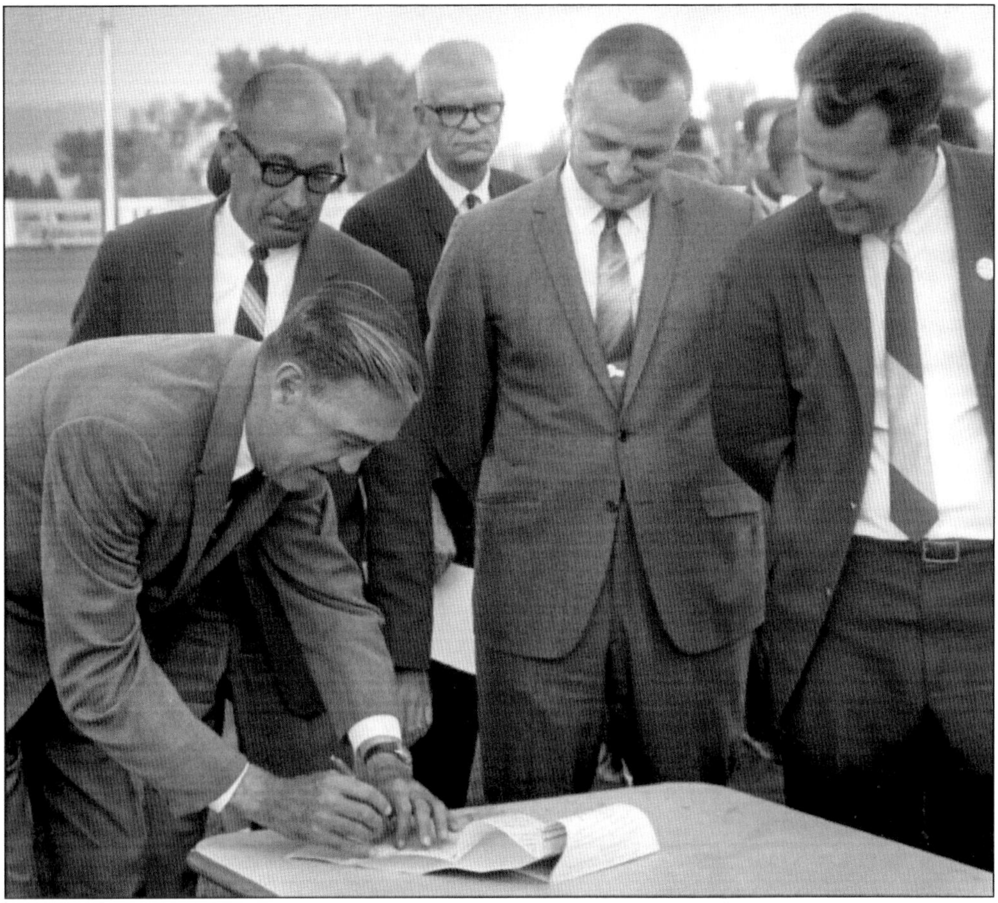

Dr. William Medesy, president of Mesa JC, signs a new five-year contract in 1967 as tournament chairman John McKean (left), NJCAA head George Killian (center), and local committee member Tom Worster look on. The NJCAA rewarded Grand Junction with one-year contracts until 1962, when the local committee first signed a five-year pact.

Attendance wasn't consistently great in the early years, but the quality of baseball was entertaining for fans with plays like this. The committee, boosted by strong support from the local media, generated interest by publicizing the tournament as much as it could prior to the opening pitch. One article in the 1967 *Sentinel* encourages readers to join the Go-Go Juco Club. To be "in the club", a person had to buy a ticket ($5 adults and $2 students, good for all-tournament games). To be on the board of directors, a person had to buy five tickets, which would also allow you to sign a "Go-Go Juco Club" giant cutout baseball that was to be put on display at three local banks.

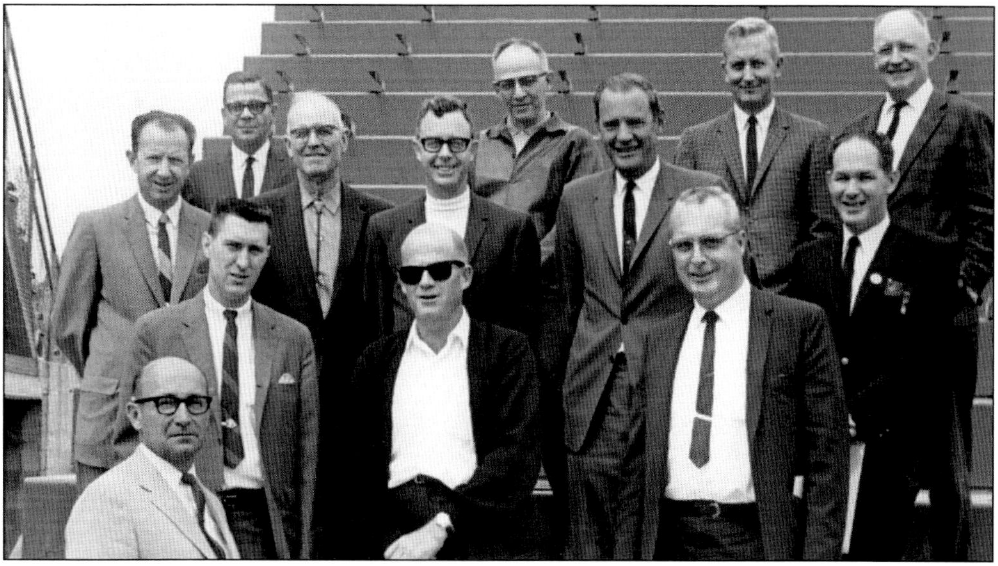

John McKean (lower left) is pictured with members of the 1968 local tournament committee. They are, from left to right: (front row): Dick Reimer, Ed Settle, Bob Quimby; second row: Hurst Otto, Ralph Stocker, Ray Meacham, Bus Bergman, Bert Rosenthal; back row: Charles Love, Max Krey, John Patterson, Wayne Nelson.

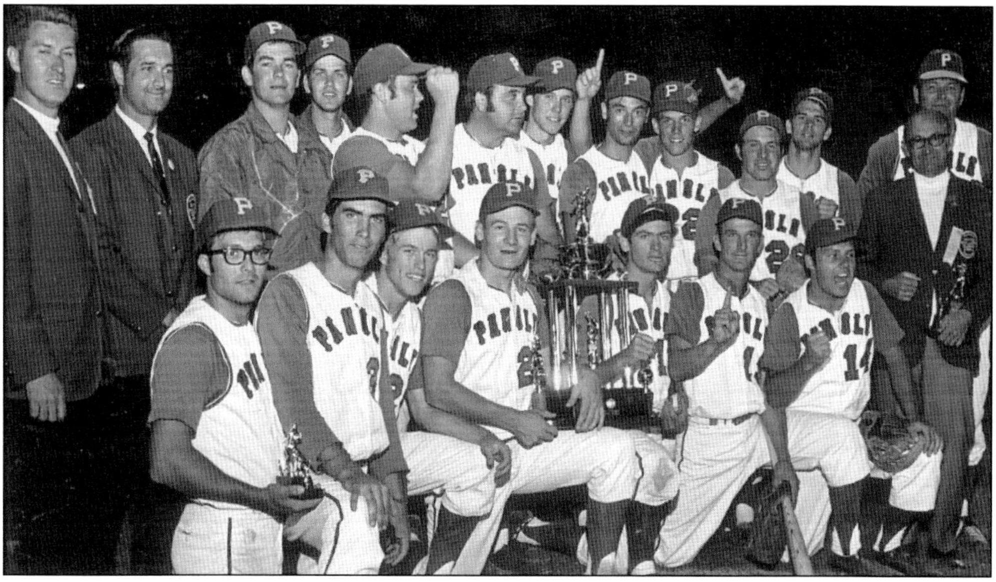

Future major leaguer Doug Ault (second from left, bottom row) led Panola Junior College of Carthage, Texas, to the 1969 national championship. Ault was the winning pitcher in three games and batted .318 for the Ponies. Panola defeated Mesa (AZ) Community College 8-6 in the final on the strength of a six-run fourth inning. Mesa had beaten the Ponies 2-1 the night before to force the second title game. Ault wasn't as fortunate when he led Panola into the 1970 tournament trying to defend its crown. In the first round, again against Mesa, Ault was the losing pitcher when he walked a tournament record 15 batters. Still, Panola led 8-5 in the 13th inning until the HoKams rallied for four runs in the bottom of the inning to win it on their way to their first national championship.

# Three

# *One Mesa In, One Mesa Out 1970–1979*

The first national tournament title game of the 1970s was a pairing of teams with identical names but headed in opposite directions in the junior college baseball world. Mesa Junior College of Grand Junction had been instrumental in giving the fledgling tournament local support and local pride in the early years, while Mesa Community College of Mesa, Arizona, was on the verge of becoming the first repeat national champion in junior college baseball.

When Grand Junction began its second decade as a championship host city, it was on much firmer ground with the National Junior College Athletic Association then it had been at the start of the 1960s. Stadium improvements had been impressive and steady during that first decade, including new ticket booths, new incandescent lights on metal poles, the addition of outdoor booths above the press box, and a continually improving playing surface. Tournament-opening banquet speakers already had included some of the greatest names in baseball history—Stan Musial, Duke Snider, Lefty Gomez—and had been moved from the Bookcliff Country Club to the new student center on the Mesa JC campus.

Grand Junction was a confident and competent host. In fact, the tournament had done so well that the automatic entry given to the Mesa JC ever since 1959 for the expressed reason of boosting attendance was no longer necessary. In 1969, Mesa had to earn its way by winning the regional tournament, which it had done. The Mavericks, led by the esteemed Walter "Bus" Bergman since 1951, accomplished the feat again in 1970—and this time they came close to winning a national crown.

If Mesa JC was a symbol of JUCO's past, Mesa CC was a symbol of JUCO's immediate future. The school didn't even exist until 1963, and Jim Brock began the Mesa baseball program in 1966. By 1969 his HoKams were able to win the brutal Arizona Junior College Conference, represent the Western District in Grand Junction, and finish runner-up in their first trip to the national meet. Mesa headlined a decade of dominance for Arizona-based JUCO teams with their 1970 journey. The Grand Canyon State won four of the first 12 national tournaments from 1958–1969. During the 1970s, Arizona representatives won 6 of 10, with Mesa taking the first 3 in 1970, 1971, and 1972.

So when Mesa vs. Mesa occurred in 1970, it was a case of one school trying to keep alive a tradition while another was just beginning one of its own. The Mavericks weren't able to generate offense in the championship game. They fell to the well-stocked HoKam pitching staff, 7-4 early in the tournament and 8-0 in the final. Jim Otten tossed a three-hit shutout in the decisive game for Mesa CC. Ken Reed finally broke through in the title game for the HoKams. An all-tourney selection at second base in 1969, he was 0-for-23 in 1970 until he belted a two-run homer that started Mesa's scoring in the championship.

Despite the loss, it was Mesa JC's third trip to the championship game in the 12 years the tournament had been held in Grand Junction. The Mavs won no national titles, but surely such a performance was vindication for being granted the host slot. The school of Mesa was growing and by the middle of the decade would be a four-year institution. Although NJCAA policy required two co-sponsors, which the chamber and the college had been for years, the city of Grand Junction took over for the college in 1974. The tournament itself was too well established to move it by that point even if Mesa JC was now four-year Mesa College.

Mesa did manage to earn one more trip across the street to the national baseball tournament, though not in a conventional way. In 1974, Ricks (Idaho) College declined to enter the tournament after winning the Northwest District when the school realized the schedule would require a Sunday game. So Mesa entered, won two games, and placed two players on the all-tournament team—Mike Higgins and Bob Blaser. The Mavericks eliminated the Scottsdale team that had eliminated them at the Southwest District playoffs the week before. Interestingly, Mesa had swept Ricks in a regular-season doubleheader.

As for Mesa CC, Brock started his legendary coaching career by working his magic at Mesa. After his second NJCAA championship and a six-year record of 163-80, he left the HoKams in 1971 to take the head coaching position at nearby Arizona State University. At ASU, Brock's Sun Devils earned two NCAA titles in 1977 and 1981 and finished in the top three eight other times. His total record in 23 years at ASU was 1,100-440 when he passed away in 1994, still coaching.

What Brock began, Jim Frye took over in 1972. Frye, a JUCO Hall of Fame inductee in 1997, led the HoKams to a third consecutive national championship in his first season as head coach.

The 1970s were generally a decade of stability for JUCO in Grand Junction. The NJCAA, now with a national office headed by executive director George Killian since 1969, and the host city were working smoothly together and knew that the success of one only helped the other. It was a foregone conclusion that the tournament would be in Grand Junction each successive year.

Significantly, Sam Suplizio took over the general chairman's job in 1970 after serving as tournament director since the event's arrival in 1959. He followed John McKean when business considerations caused him to leave Grand Junction. McKean had replaced D.S. Dykstra in 1967.

Continuous improvements continued at the ballpark, including a new section of permanent seats behind home plate that were first put in for the 1971 tournament thanks to volunteer work by Grand Junction Steel Fabricating. But in 1972, a symbolic change took place. The baseball and football complex, which had always gone by the name Lincoln Park Stadium, was renamed for the late Ralph F. "Red" Stocker, director of the Grand Junction Parks and Recreation Department for 44 years.

Attendance for championship games continued to grow with the park—the 1972 title tilt, for example, drew a reported 3,800 fans to newly christened Stocker Stadium, and the 1974 final brought in a reported 6,000. Profits grew too—a 1975 *Sentinel* article said that profits averaged more than $12,000 for the previous three years. The rising income allowed the committee to add seats and improvements, thus allowing more people to come, creating an interplay that provided plenty of proof that Grand Junction's tradition had nowhere to go but up.

Local fans had found favorite teams and regions to root for, civic club sponsorships had established allegiances over the years, and the ball park was understood by all to be an early summer meeting place for all ages. JUCO committee members could rest assured that the corner of 12th and North was going to be busy for many, many years—even if the Mesa Mavericks weren't on the diamond.

Women work the phones prior to the 1970 national tournament to try enticing sponsors to join the effort of supporting the event.

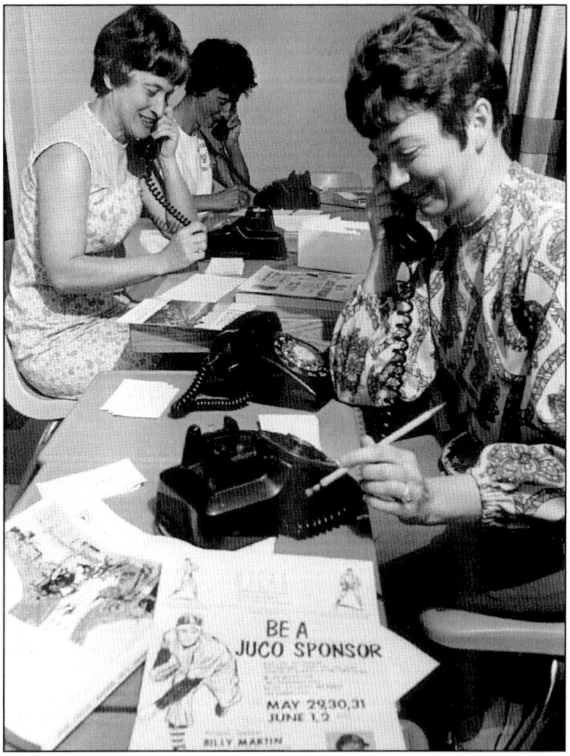


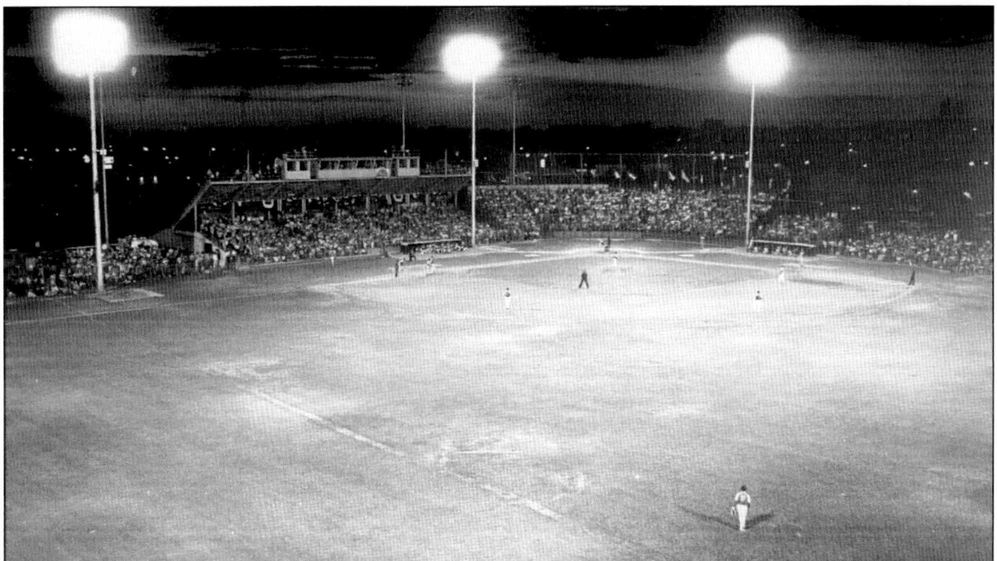

Grand Junction by night. Strong attendance at night games during tournament week was well established in Grand Junction by the 1970s. Lincoln Park Stadium, or Ralph Stocker Stadium as it was renamed in 1972, was the community-gathering place for all ages. Here, the Louisburg (NC) Junior College defense takes its place in the field with the late-evening western sky visible from this view above the centerfielder. This photo shows the progression of the park up to the late 1970s. The permanent bleachers behind home plate had been in place for several years, but the additional seats down the third-base line were still a decade away and would be done in several installments.

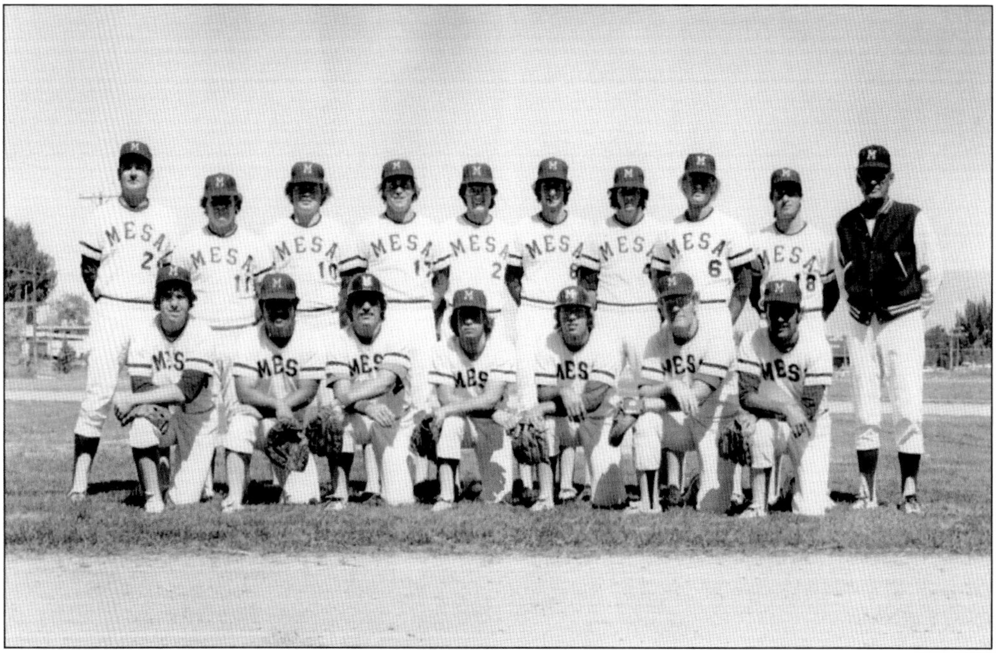

This is the 1974 Mesa JC team, the final time that the Grand Junction-based school played in its hometown tournament before becoming a four-year institution.

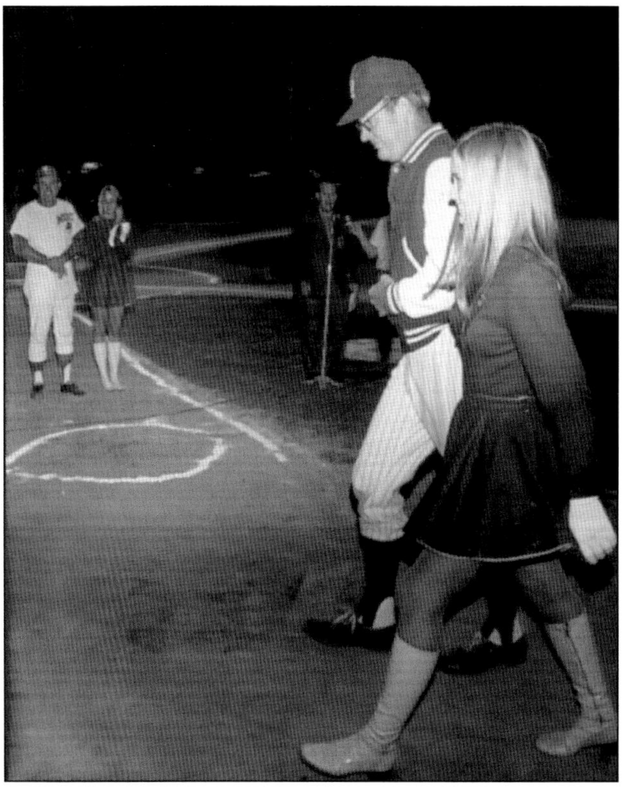

Mesa Junior College coach Bus Bergman is ushered onto the field by a cheerleader at the 1970 national tournament. Mesa Community College coach Jim Brock smiles in the background. Both men made large contributions to their respective schools' athletic success. Bergman coached the Mavericks 24 years and compiled 378 victories, won 20 conference championships, and reached the JUCO national championship game three times in 13 appearances. Brock started the HoKams' baseball program and won two national titles in just six seasons before taking the Arizona State University vacancy. Their teams met each other in the 1970 JUCO final, with Brock's squad winning the battle of the Mesas.

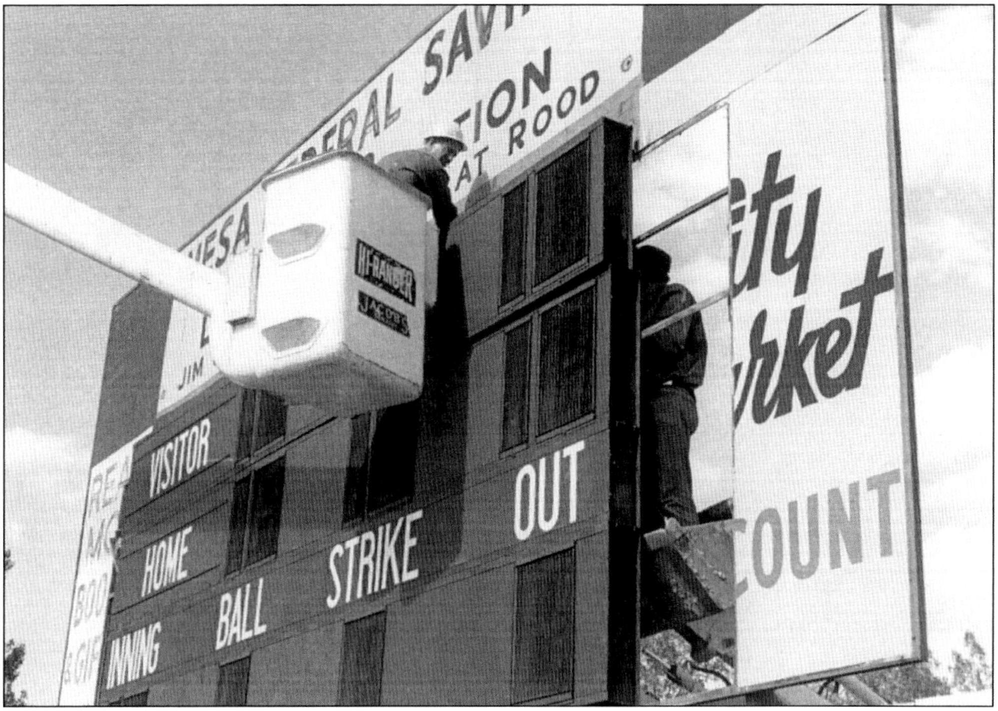

Workers get the scoreboard ready for action. The grounds crew and city parks staff tends to the field to make sure it works as well as possible and looks as professional as an amateur stadium should.

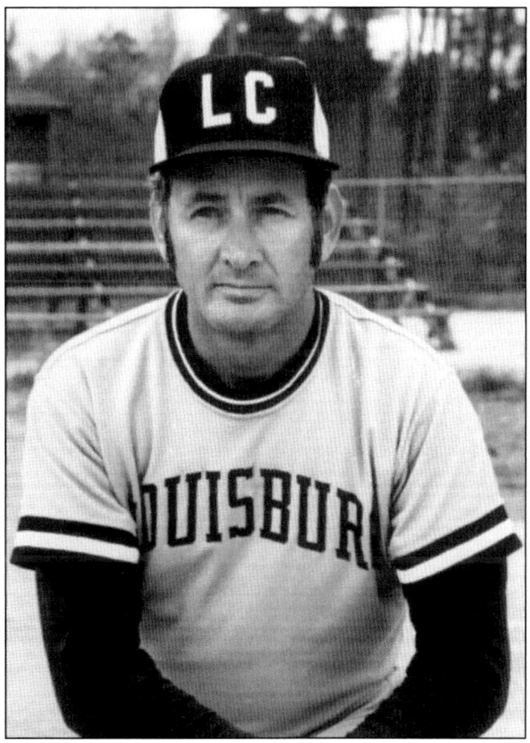


Louisburg made nine appearances at the national tournament under coach Russ Frazier, a 1987 JUCO Hall of Fame inductee: 1971, 1975, 1977, 1979, 1981, 1987, 1988, 1990, and 1992. Frazier is proof that a national championship isn't necessary to validate a prestigious coaching career. He led the Hurricanes for 40 years, starting in 1959, including nine trips to Grand Junction, 22 conference titles, and a record of 1,034-390. He groomed 12 players for the major leagues, including Otis Nixon and Chad Fonville. Frazier Field on the Louisburg campus is named for him, and his retired No. 18 jersey now hangs underneath the scoreboard in left field.

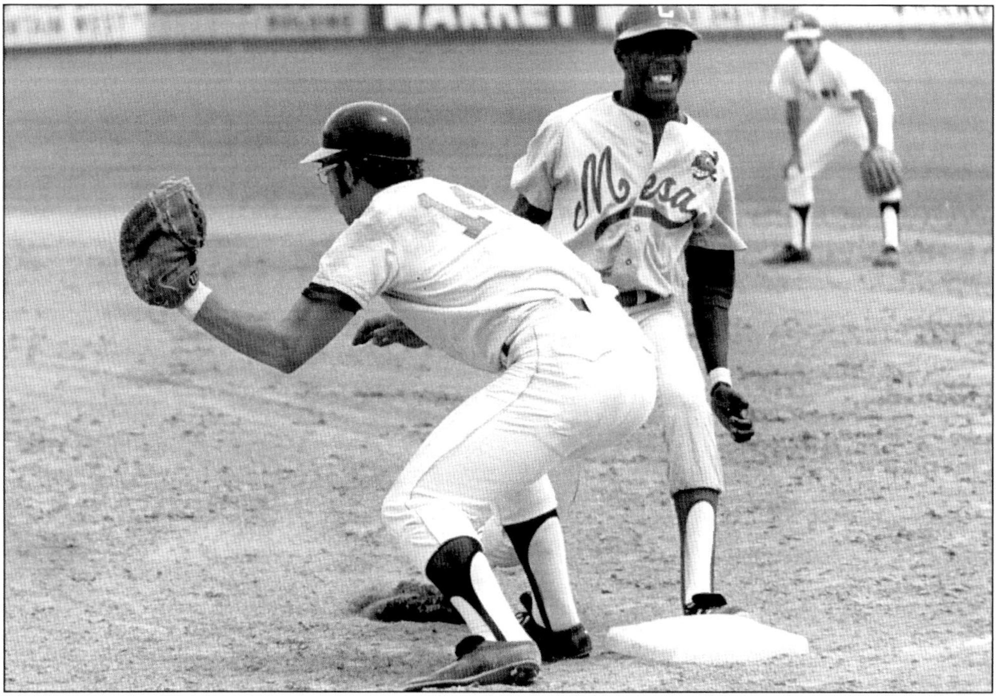


Mesa Community College was the team to beat in the early 1970s as the HoKams became the first repeat champion at the JUCO national tournament. Mesa dominated the all-tournament teams during their championship seasons of 1970, 1971, and 1972. In 1970, Jim Otten, Herb Genung, Dennis Kendrick, and Vernon Wilkins all made it. Interestingly, Larry Patton of Columbia State (TN) Community College was named Most Valuable Player. In 1971, six HoKams made all-tourney: Otten, Marty Stajduhar, Mark Reinke, Greg Snowden, Jeff Oscarson, and Wilkins. Otten earned MVP honors and Wilkins was voted Best Defensive Player. In 1972, five Mesa players made all-tourney as well, with Snowden earning the MVP award for his .435 batting average, two homers, ten RBIs, and four outfield assists. The other selections besides Snowden were Oscarson, Dave Collins, Steve Gowens, and Doug Slocum.

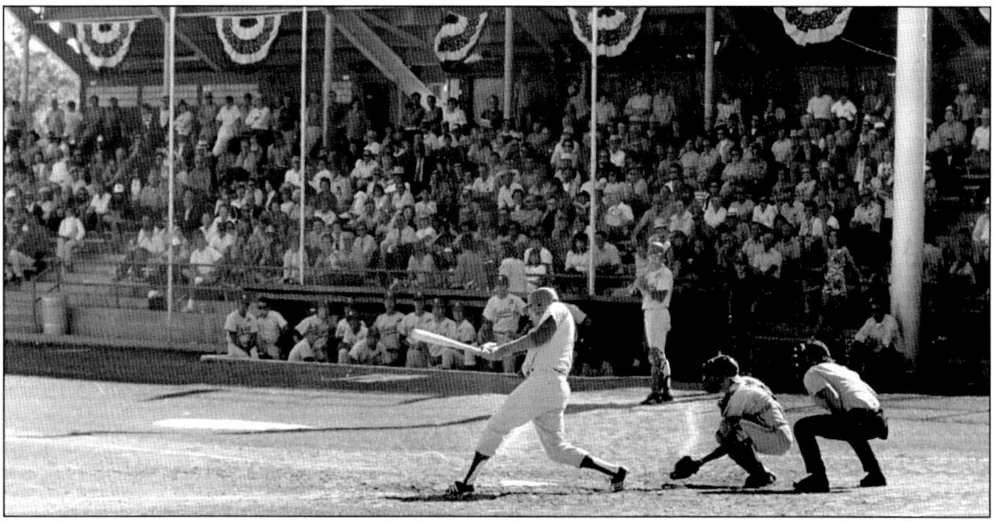

Jim Frye (right) accepts the coach of the year plaque from host coach Bus Bergman following the 1972 tournament, in which Mesa CC won its third title in a row. It was Frye's first year as head coach after Jim Brock resigned to coach Arizona State University.

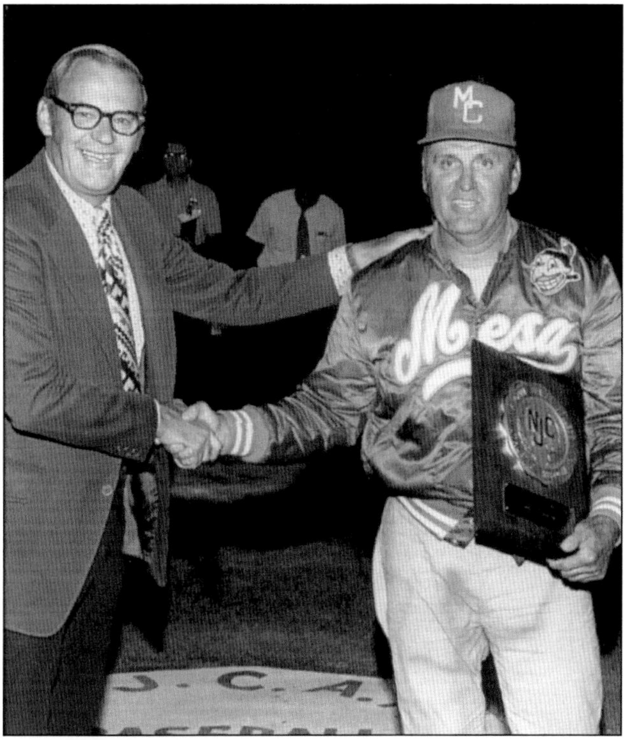

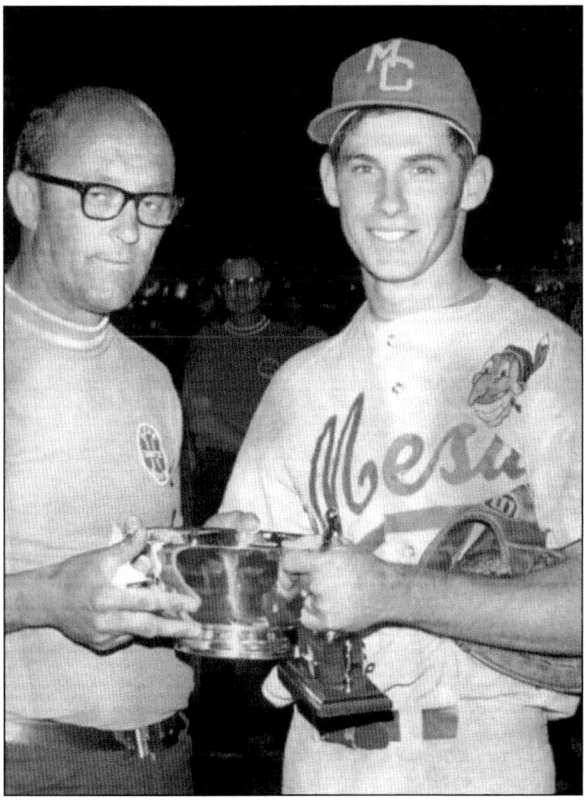

Committee member Gene Haggerty presents the MVP award to Greg Snowden after Mesa's 4-2 tournament final victory over Manatee (FL) Junior College in 1972. Pitcher Doug Slocum hurled three Mesa victories during the week. Haggerty came to Grand Junction in the early 1950s to pitch for Mesa and the semipro Eagles. For many years, he was a tournament committee member, including serving as co-chairman, and was inducted into the JUCO Hall of Fame in 1992.

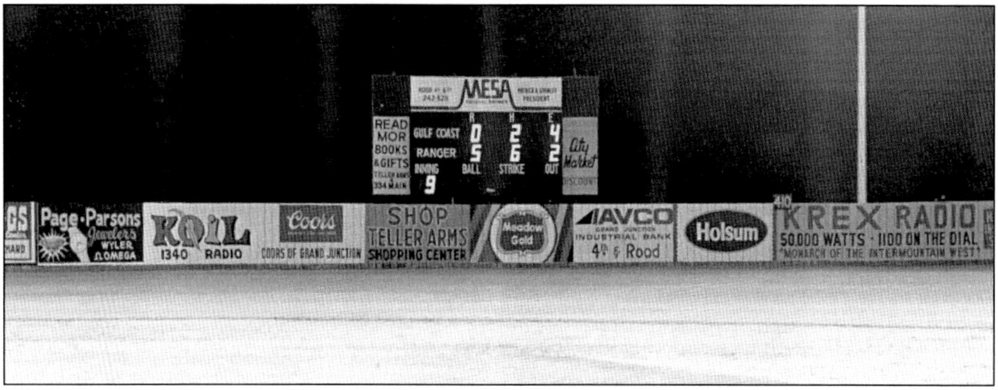


The scoreboard tells the story of the 1973 championship final, in which Ranger (TX) Junior College and star pitcher Donnie Moore blanked Gulf Coast (FL) Community College 5-0. Ranger has been one of the most efficient JUCO champions. The Rangers won two titles (1978 was the other) in four visits to Grand Junction in six years, and was only one of three non-Arizona schools to win a JUCO title in the 1970s. Moore was dominant as the '73 MVP with a tournament record four wins that still stands and a 1.20 ERA in 30 innings pitched. He beat Mesa CC in the opening round as Ranger kept the HoKams from winning a fourth consecutive crown. Moore went on to a productive 13-year big-league career in which he went 43-40, had 89 saves, and compiled a 3.67 ERA. Sadly, he is best known for the two-strike, two-out ninth-inning home run he gave up to Dave Henderson of the Boston Red Sox while pitching for the California Angels in Game 5 of the epic 1986 American League Championship Series. The Angels went from one strike away from going to the World Series to losing Game 5 in extra innings, and then Games 6 and 7 as well. Moore was said to have been haunted by the loss for years afterward. In 1989, he shot and critically wounded his wife Tonya, then shot and killed himself.

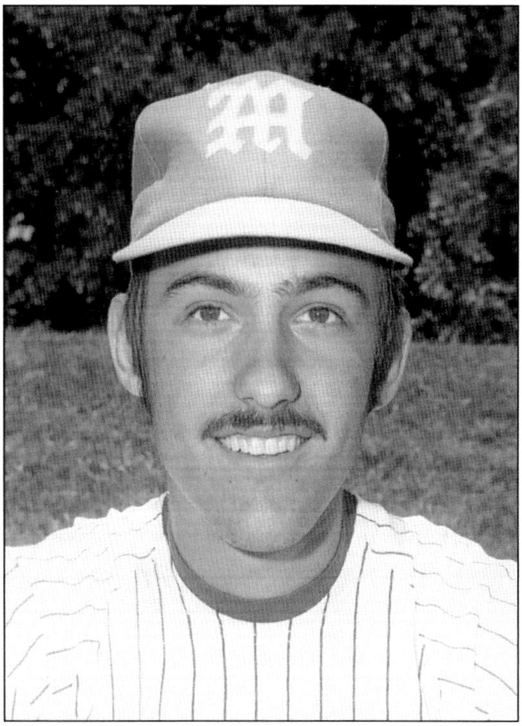

Neil Fiala's big-league career was brief—two teams (St. Louis Cardinals and Cincinnati Reds), five at-bats, one hit, one run, one RBI, all in 1981—but his junior college exploits were memorable for Meramec Community College of St. Louis. Fiala was the 1975 tournament MVP with a .529 batting average, even though the Warriors lost two straight championship games to Yavapai (AZ), which kept the team from defending its 1974 title.

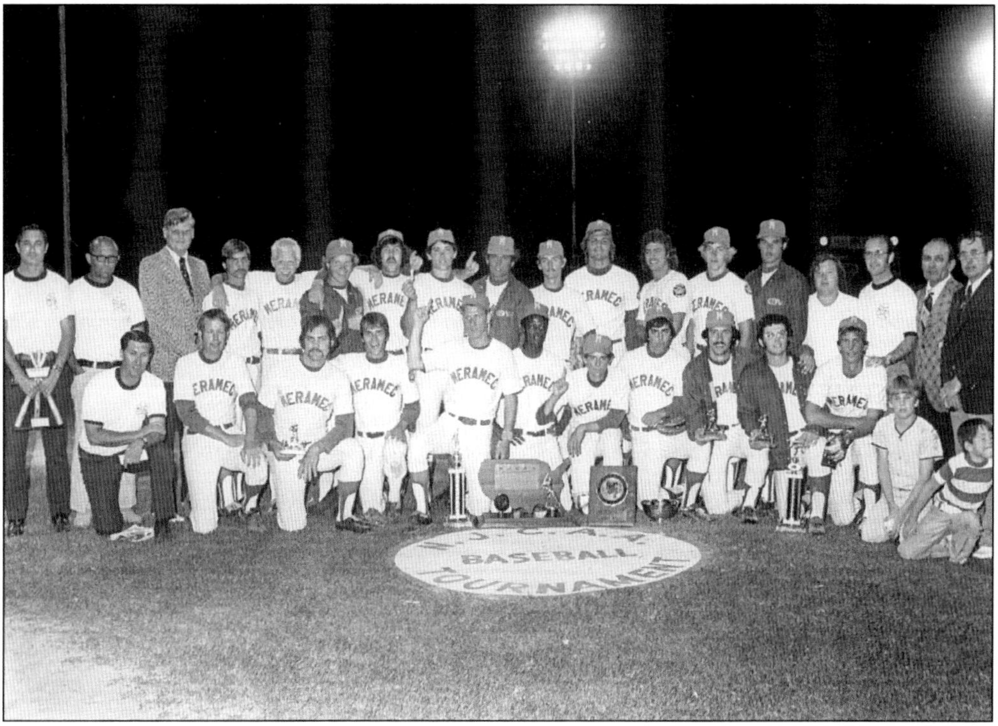


The 1974 Meramec Warriors became the first team from the Central District to ever win a JUCO baseball championship with a 6-4 victory over Miami-Dade (FL) Junior College. The suburban St. Louis school offered no scholarships and had five players get ill on the plane trip over the Rockies. Also, Mike Murphy was named Outstanding Pitcher for the tournament despite a groin injury and grounding into a triple play in the first inning of the final. MVP Steve Viefhaus (*right*) carried the team on his shoulders, although teammates Tony Barylski, Joe Muich, Tom Gallagher, and Murphy also earned all-tournament honors. Viefhaus had ten hits, a .526 batting average and was named outstanding defensive player of the week from his shortstop position. He also belted a then-tournament record of four home runs. *St. Louis Post-Dispatch* writer Rick Hummel made the trip to Grand Junction, and offered a big-city view of the western Colorado hospitality. "Of the 25,000-odd residents in this farming area, nearly one-fourth of them (6,000) showed up at the ballpark last night to watch two junior college baseball teams from more than 1,000 miles away," he wrote in the May 30, 1974 edition. "The people here have been doing this sort of thing for 16 years." And: "A check of the billboards in the outfield revealed just how intense community interest is. No fewer than 52 signs are displayed, including those of Thrifty Rent-A-Car, Vick's Kafe-Teria, and Mt. Garfield Plumbing & Heating."

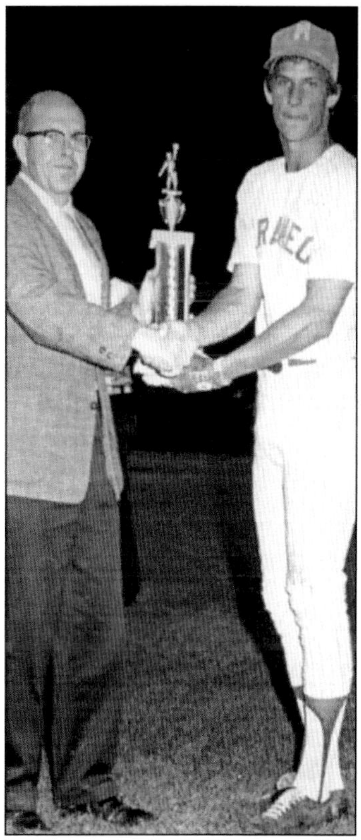

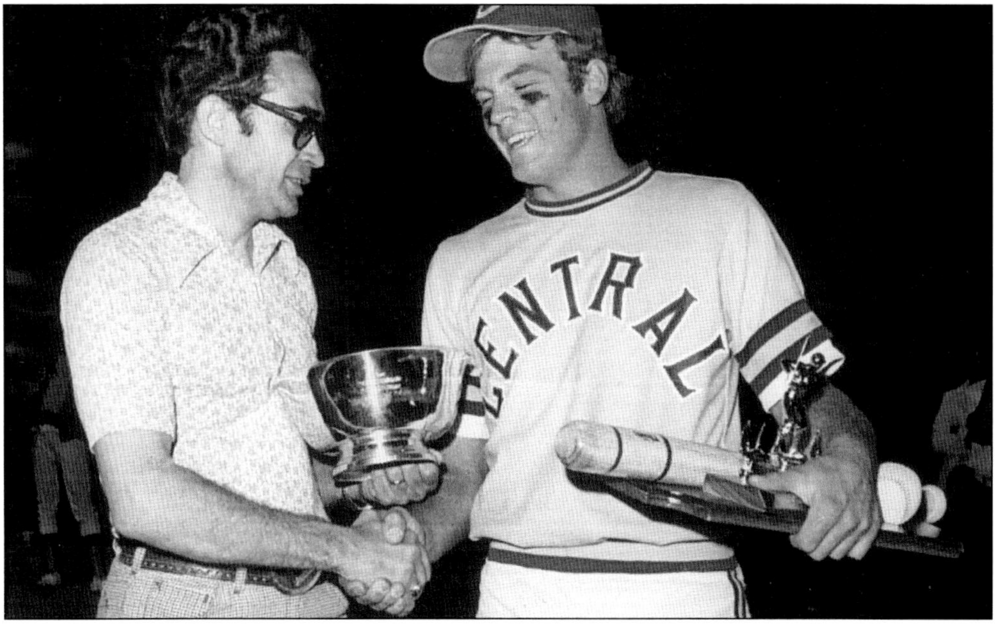

Jerry Merlino (left) of the *Grand Junction Sentinel* presents Central Arizona College's Jim Morley with the 1976 Most Valuable Player award. The daily newspaper has sponsored the MVP trophy for many years as a tribute to the late Preston Walker, the publisher in 1958 that helped find seed money for the initial tournament bid. Morley, an outfielder, batted .473 with eight RBIs during Central's championship run.

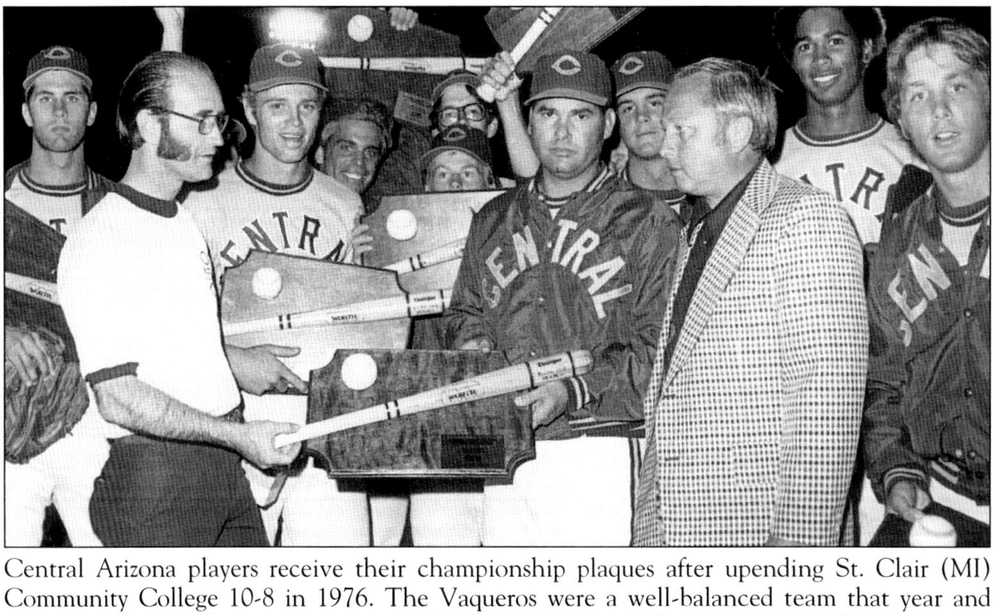

Central Arizona players receive their championship plaques after upending St. Clair (MI) Community College 10-8 in 1976. The Vaqueros were a well-balanced team that year and placed six on the all-tournament roster: MVP Jim Morley, Mike Burke, Kent Winslow, Mark Schuster (voted Best Defensive Player), Jim Manship, and Bob Most. A national tournament record 11 stolen bases was set that year by Humberto Acosta of Miami-Dade Community College Downtown (FL). Acosta had plenty of opportunities to get on base. He batted .667 to win the Big Stick Award for the tournament.

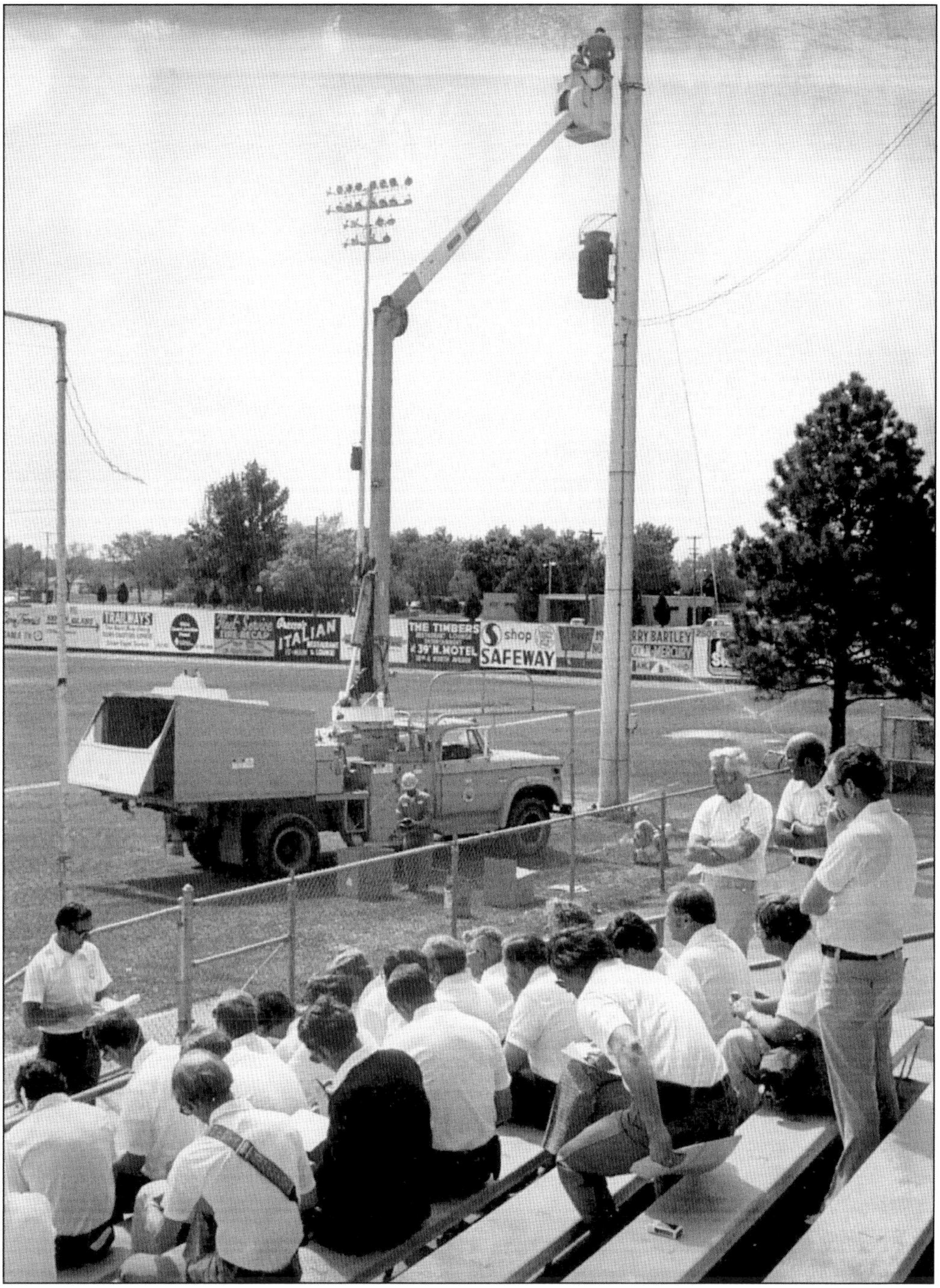


As the tournament nears, work at Lincoln Park steadily picks up. In this 1977 photo, workers check out the lights while the sprinkler runs and general chairman Sam Suplizio holds a committee meeting in the bleachers. Note the tree along the first-base line next to the bullpen. In the early years of the tournament, it actually stood in playable foul territory. The committee ultimately decided a fence needed to be added. No stories of that tree helping to dictate the outcome of a game exist, but it did give the field an interesting landmark for a few years.

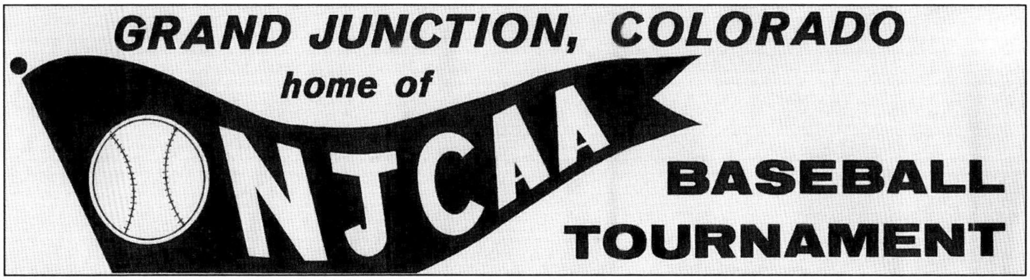


An early bumper sticker promotes the tournament. The JUCO World Series moniker didn't gain widespread use until 1979. From ribbons and pins to posters and bumper stickers, it has never been hard to find JUCO memorabilia during tournament week in Grand Junction.

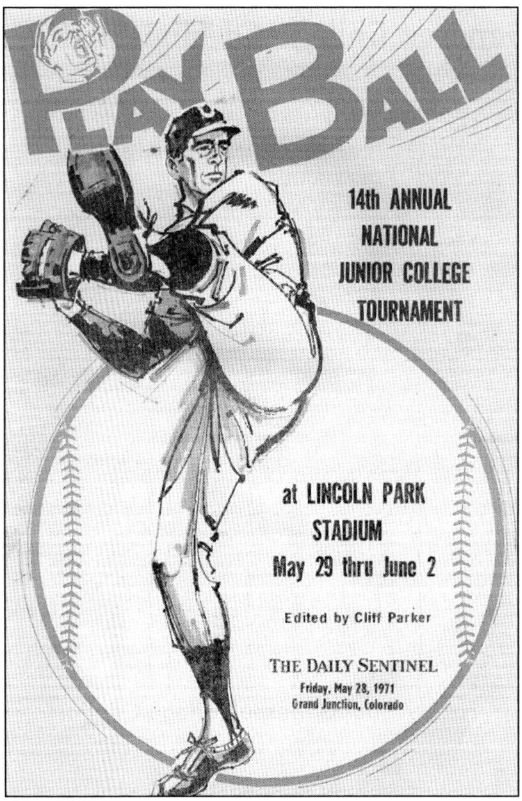


The 1971 special tournament section put out by the *Grand Junction Sentinel*.

# FOUR

# *Gator Decade 1980–1989*

Wayne Graham may now be nationally known as the coach that pushed the Rice University baseball program to an NCAA championship in 2003. Folks in Grand Junction can trace Graham's career back much farther than that. JUCO fans were aware of the coach and his San Jacinto North College squad all the way back in 1984 when the Gators placed second at the JUCO World Series in their first-ever trip to the national tournament. By the time the 1990 tournament ended, with the Houston junior college winning its fifth title in six years, Graham and the vaunted Gators had established themselves as the most dominant JUCO program in the national tournament's history. In the seven-year stretch from 1984 to 1990, San Jac grabbed five titles and two runner-up trophies.

Ask Graham now about his memories of Grand Junction, and he can run through them as though they occurred as recently as his success at Rice. There was relief pitcher Steve Camarda nursing a 6-5 lead with two outs and the tying run at first base in 1985. He struck out Pima (AZ) pinch hitter Tim Cimino on a curve ball in the dirt that Gator catcher Mike Reese blocked and threw to first base to end the game and secure San Jac's first title.

Graham remembers how the 1986 Gators that went undefeated in Grand Junction struggled most of the season, but put the pieces together behind two dominant pitchers—Camarda and Toby Nivens—to make their JUCO World Series push.

There were the 1987 Gators, led by tiny left-hander Oscar Rivas and the record-setting bat of Bill Losa, whose .688 batting average tied Kirby Puckett for a tournament record that still stands. San Jac hung on for its third straight JUCO championship with a 2-1 victory over a Seminole (OK) Junior College club that Graham calls, "The best physical personnel of any JUCO team I've ever seen."

San Jac took an easier route to its 1989 championship, blasting Northeastern Oklahoma A&M 22-4 in the title game behind a record-setting 23 hits and a .361 tournament team batting average.

Graham easily recalls the 1990 championship and a 5-0 shutout of Middle Georgia College by Robert Henkel and Jeff McCurry. San Jac also snapped Seminole's 35-game winning streak during the tournament.

Graham remembers well that his squad didn't qualify for Grand Junction in 1981, his first season at San Jac, despite a freshman by the name of Roger Clemens—a pitcher that Graham recruited because he was able to throw strikes even though, the coach says, Clemens didn't throw particularly hard out of high school.

Most of all, Graham has fond memories of the town of Grand Junction. He is grateful for long-time regional host Jim Bonella and the Optimist Club, and appreciates the city-wide hospitality.

"With every team that plays junior college baseball, it's the pot of gold at the end of the rainbow," Graham said from his Houston home. "In Colorado, you'll play in front of a packed house and great scenery. It's a great atmosphere there."

Graham is the only coach to ever lead teams to both JUCO World Series and College World Series titles. He sees Grand Junction and Omaha, Neb., the equally gracious host of the College World Series since 1950, as two distinct, wonderful tournaments, and doesn't prefer one over the other. But there is definitely something quainter about JUCO ball, and someone in Graham's position can recognize that firsthand. Items like recruiting budget, facilities, and salary are much greater at the NCAA level, but so are the demands off the field. It's only between the lines that everything remains the same.

"You never forget Grand Junction," Graham said. "Like Omaha, it's a unique experience. Certainly you get more glory at Omaha, but I'm not sure you have more fun. When you're doing it, it's pretty much the same: the tension, the determination, the gratification. The difference is at Grand Junction, you win and it's done. Here [at Rice], [the attention] never stops. It's every day."

While San Jac placed its stamp on the latter half of the decade, Middle Georgia College and JUCO Hall of Fame coach Robert Sapp won three titles in four years from 1979 to 1982. The Warriors became only the second team (after Mesa Community College) to repeat as JUCO champs.

The end of the 1980s brought two welcome additions to Stocker Stadium, both of them indicative of the upward rise of the tournament. One was symbolic, artistic, and a nod to baseball's early days; the second was practical, thoroughly modern, and signaled changing times ahead.

A permanent 600-pound, seven-foot resident arrived inside the first-base entrance to the ballpark on May 26, 1989. Mighty Casey from the Ernest Lawrence Thayer poem "Casey at the Bat" was rendered in solid bronze by sculptor Mark Lundeen. Sen. Tilman Bishop, a long-time committee member before entering politics, knew Lundeen's work and mentioned the statue to the committee. Several committee members took a trip to Avon, Colorado, and were awed at the sight of a 14-foot version of Casey. The committee decided it was worth purchasing one of the edition of 15 seven-foot Casey statues that Lundeen had done, and presenting it to the community to "remind young and old alike that Grand Junction is the hotbed of baseball." The figure has gained iconic status in the city. Images of Casey are clearly associated with the stadium and the tournament. Casey's 19th century muttonchops and button-down Mudville top are a fine embodiment for a baseball venue in a state that embraced the game in mining camps and on the western frontier that far back.

Casey arrived just in time to make a television appearance. Though the top-notch organization of the JUCO World Series had been honed for a generation prior to the 1980s, the national exposure and prestige had significantly increased by 1989. Oh sure, there was the brief article in the June 2, 1969 edition of *Sports Illustrated* and occasional regional publicity. Scouts for four-year colleges and professional teams had flocked to Lincoln Park from the beginning, and generous corporate sponsors such as Rawlings, Coca-Cola, and others had seen value in being associated in one way or another with the tournament over the years. Heck, the tournament had even been on local TV as early as 1969. Here are the rather apologetic words, usually an utterly unwelcome sight in advertising copy, that make up a half-page ad in the *Sentinel*'s 1969 tournament preview section: "Now! For the 1st time! From Lincoln Park See Baseball Live! We want you to support the NJCAA Baseball Tournament May 30 thru June 3rd by your attendance. IF you can't attend due to business reasons or other commitments, we invite you to watch it live on Comtronics Cable TV Channel 12!" Even private business didn't want to horn in on a healthy JUCO gate!

But media exposure changed dramatically in the ensuing 20 years. It became, for better and worse, far less homely. The growth of ESPN and *USA Today* during the 1980s brought others that followed their lead. More events entered a larger spotlight. The best example of this in amateur baseball was the College World Series in Omaha, which now received a great deal of television attention each year.

The JUCO World Series' first foray into broader television coverage came in 1989, when Prime Sports Network, a regional cable sports network affiliate of Prime Network, Inc., aired the tournament's final two games with Drew Goodman doing the play-by-play and Irv Brown handling color commentary. That experiment only last two years, but the subject of future TV rights is now a regular topic for the JUCO committee to consider. Grand Junction's wonderful old-time park, complete with the Casey sculpture, was entering a new era in the final decade of the 20th century.

Craig McMurtry, who signed with the Atlanta Braves after the 1980 JUCO World Series, was named the Outstanding Pitcher of the tournament when he posted a 1.14 ERA for McLennan (Texas) Community College. In the big leagues, he was 28-42 with a 4.08 ERA over eight seasons for the Braves, Texas Rangers, and Houston Astros.

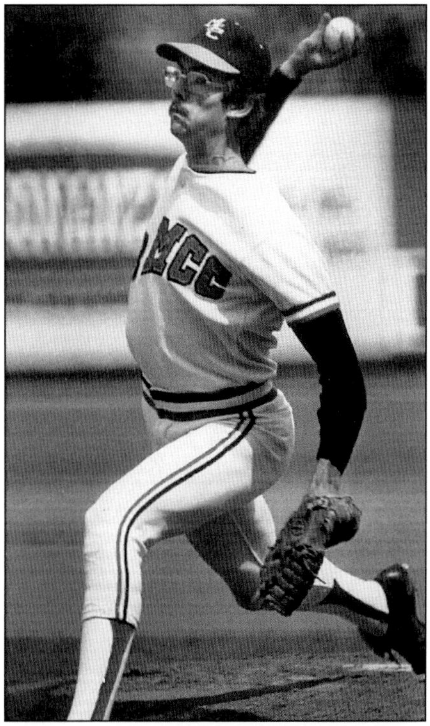

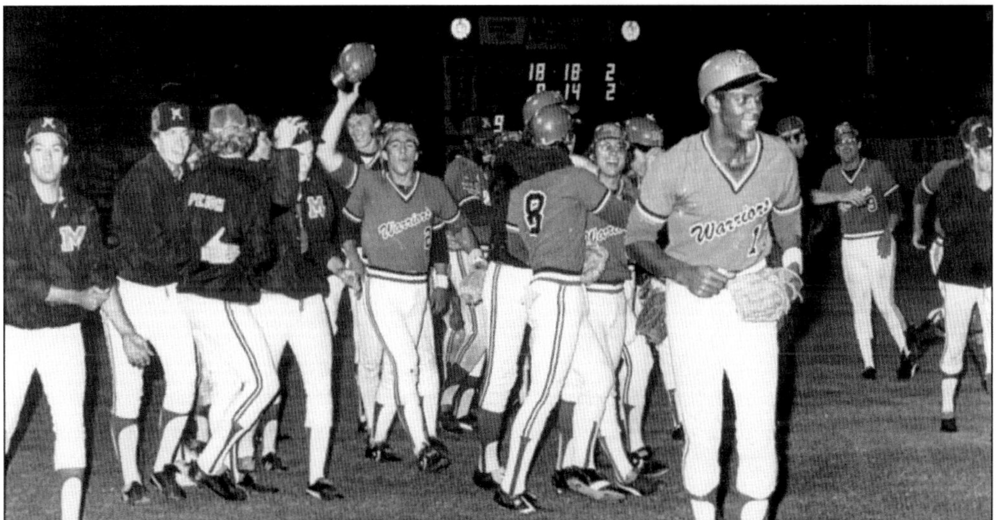

Middle Georgia celebrates its 1980 championship with the scoreboard behind the players telling the story. The Warriors defeated Cleveland (TN) State 18-8 in the final. MVP Greg Geren of the runner-up squad knocked in a tournament record 18 RBIs that still stands. Ernie Riles headlined five Warriors on the all-tournament team, and he was named Best Defensive Player in the tournament before going on to a productive nine-year big-league career. The Warriors won three titles in four years (1979, 1980, and 1982) and appeared poised for a decade of domination. "Grand Junction was always the goal we strived for," coach Robert Sapp said. "For my players, it was a once in a lifetime experience. Even the players that have made it to the Major Leagues still talk about Grand Junction when I see them."

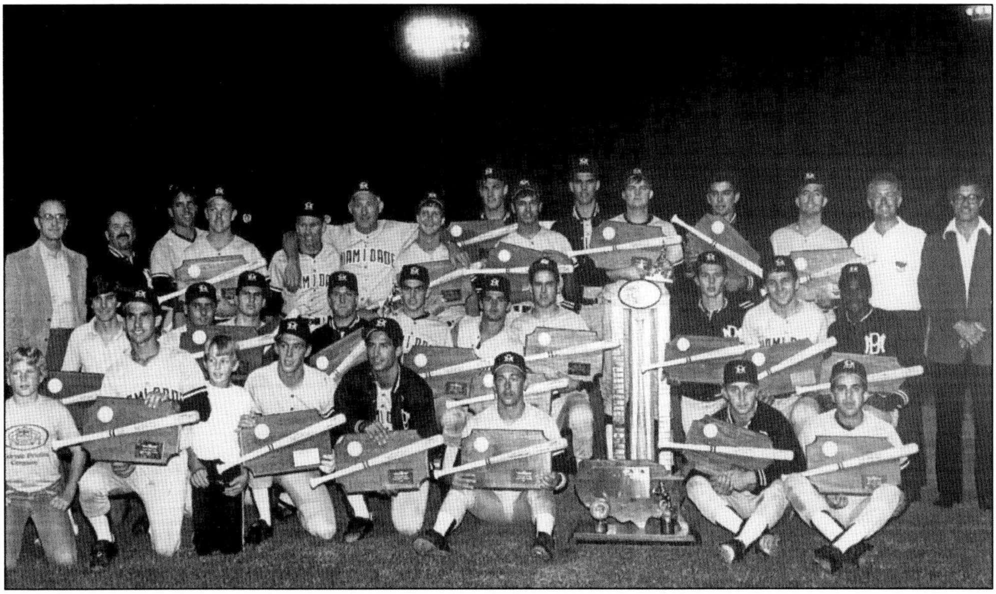

Miami-Dade South (FL) took home the 1981 title in only the school's second JUCO World Series appearance with a then-tournament team record of 66 runs scored in five games and a .388 batting average. Five players earned spots on the all-tourney team: Ron Kelly, Gary Miller-Jones, Ralph Codinach, Nelson Santovenia, and Best Defensive Player honoree Alberto Lorenzo. MVP honors that year, however, went to runner-up Seminole (OK) JC's Curtis Morgan, who had 15 RBIs, 14 hits, and 3 homers.

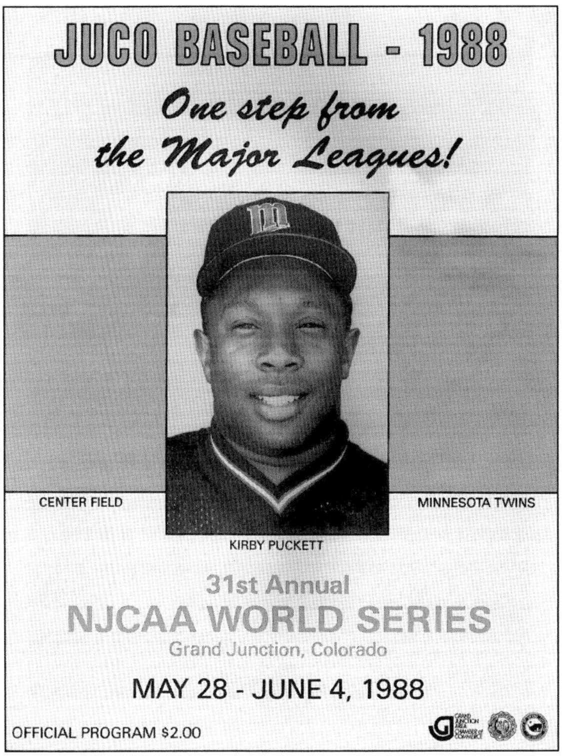


Showcasing his Baseball Hall of Fame skills at an early age, Kirby Puckett set a tournament record in 1982 with a .688 batting average for Triton (IL) College. Puckett is easily the JUCO World Series alumnus with the greatest major league career. "It was a great experience," Puckett said in the 1988 JUCO program. "They did an outstanding job in setting up the tournament. They really took care of the players. I remember it being a beautiful area and a fine baseball field. It was so nice to be treated that way while playing for a junior college." Puckett was the third player selected in the 1982 draft shortly after the national tournament had ended, and by 1984 he was named to the American League all-rookie team as a member of the Minnesota Twins. He went on to lead the team to two World Series titles and a career .318 average before glaucoma forced him out of the game in 1996 after 12 seasons.

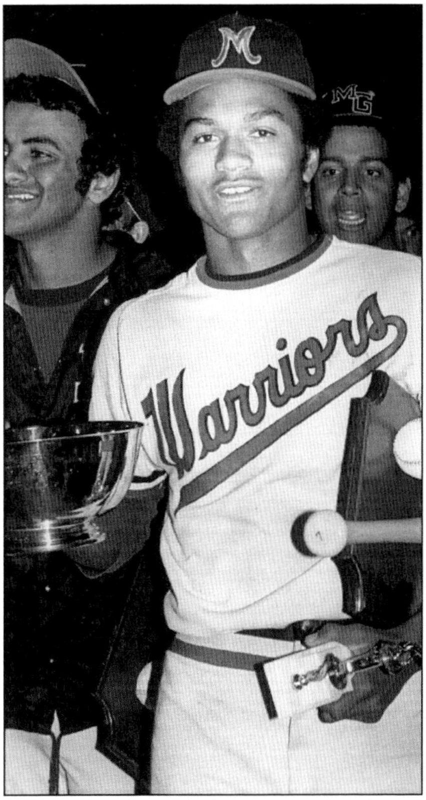

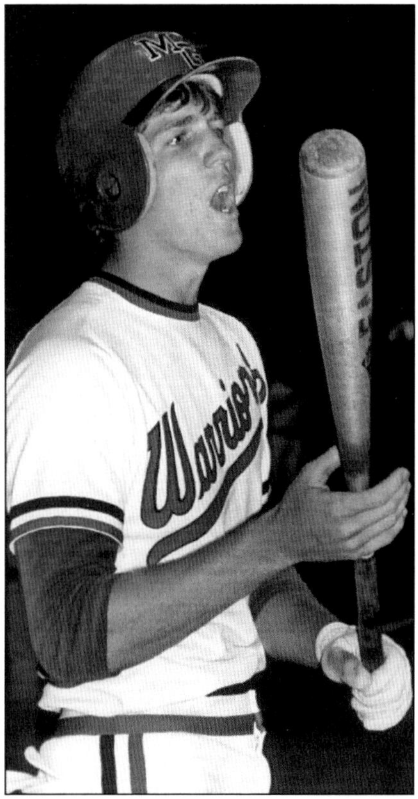


Kal Daniels (*left*) had plenty of hardware to bring home at the 1982 JUCO World Series. Middle Georgia defeated Seminole JC 11-7 in the final that year aided by the future major leaguer's two-run homer and three RBIs. Daniels went .476 for the tournament and shared MVP honors with teammate Scott Skripko (*right*). Skripko batted .448. The 1982 JUCO World Series had a distinct big-league flavor. No fewer than nine future major leaguers participated that year: Keith Miller, Steve Peters, and Jose Tolentino (Seminole); Daniels and Alex Diaz (Middle Georgia); Kirby Puckett and Lance Johnson (Triton); Mike Devereaux (Mesa CC), and David Johnson (Community College of Baltimore).

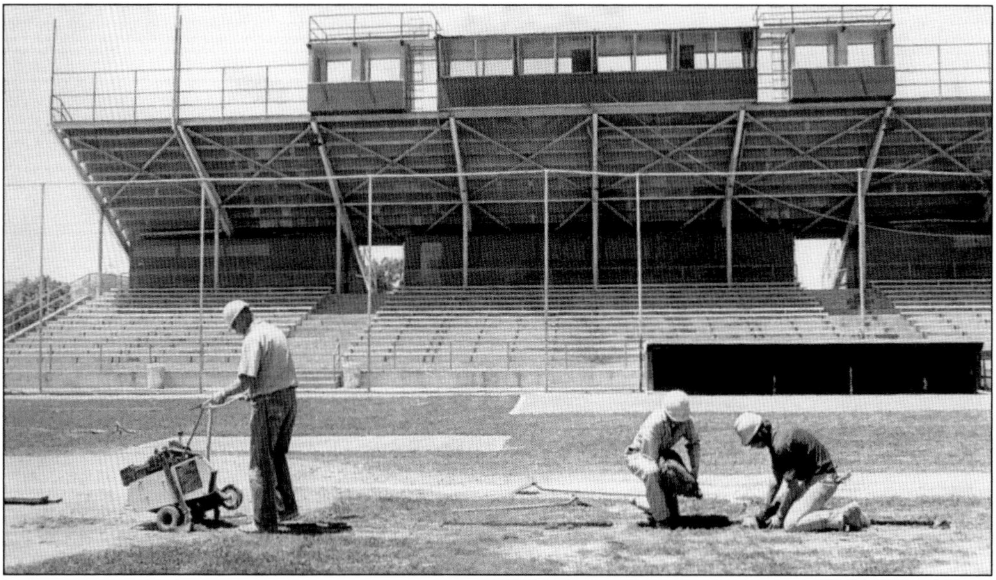

Floyd Neighbors (left), LeRoy Ellis (middle) and Ron Felt work on keeping the Stocker Stadium turf in prime playing condition. Neighbors toiled in the background for many years as the park's groundskeeper.

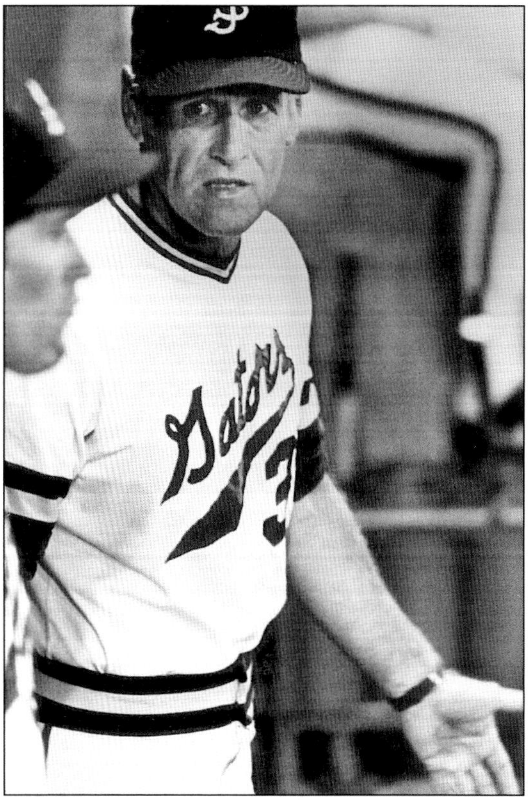


San Jacinto-North (TX) coach Wayne Graham looks frustrated talking to assistant coach Paul Miller during the Gators' 9-7 loss to Southern Idaho in the 1984 JUCO championship game. Graham's time would come, however. After this runner-up finish in the team's first-ever trip to Grand Junction, the Gators reeled off three consecutive national titles.

Shell Scott led Southern Idaho to the 1984 JUCO championship in the school's sixth appearance in Grand Junction. Scott went 3-for-4 with this homer (*right*), double, and triple in the Eagles' 9-7 title-game victory over San Jacinto-North. Southern Idaho earned the win on Jeff Schow's dramatic two-run homer in the top of the ninth, which broke a 7-all tie. Scott had 17 hits during the week, a JUCO World Series record that still stands. Earlier in the tournament, Scott slides home ahead of Quinsigamond (MA) catcher Paul Gedman (*below*) during Southern Idaho's 10-8 first-round victory.

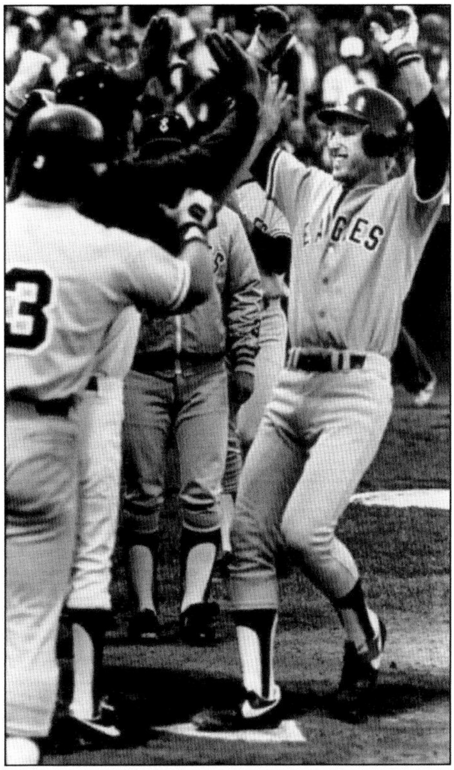


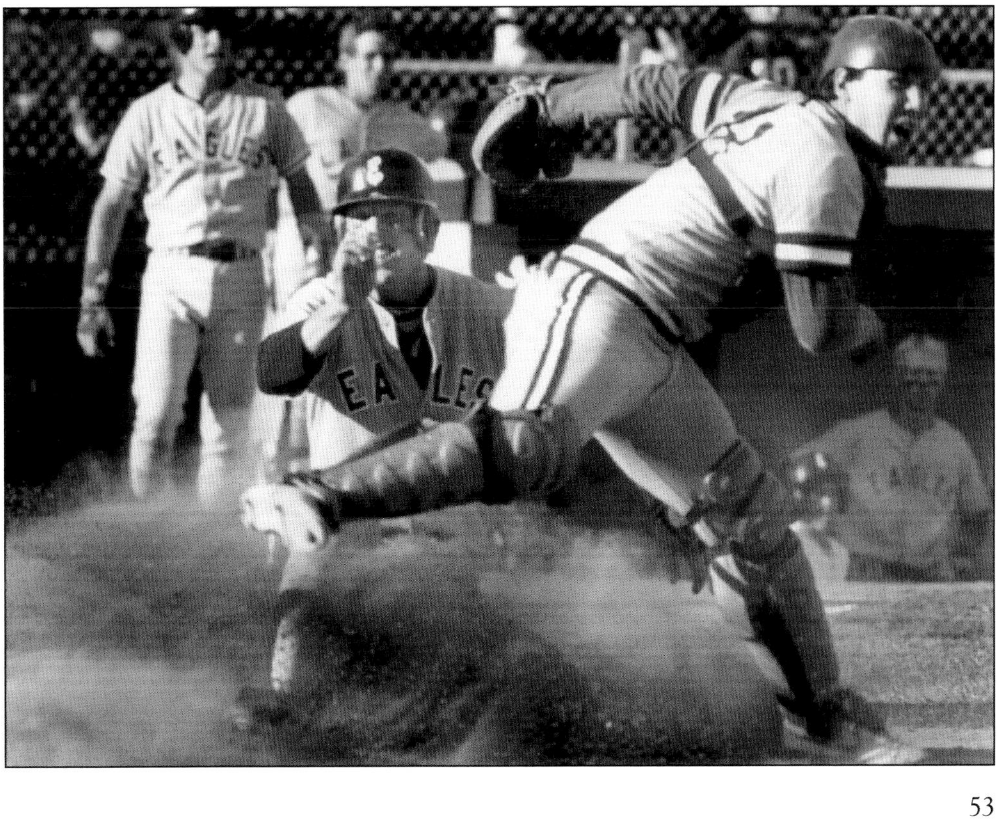

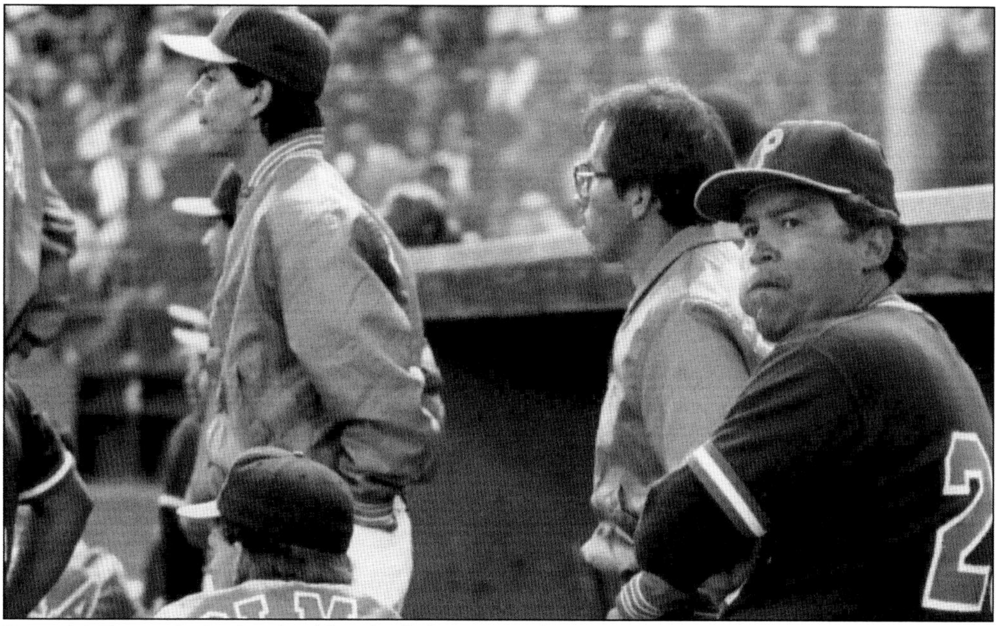

Pima (AZ) coach Richard Alday (right) surveys the situation during the 1985 tournament. Pima reached the championship game and needed to beat San Jacinto-North twice for the title. The Aztecs managed a 9-4 win to force a second game, but lost 6-5 with the tying run on base in the final. Gil Heredia made all-tournament for Pima and went on to a 10-year big-league pitching career. Alday, who began the Pima program in 1973 and took teams to Grand Junction in 1981, 1983, and 1985, eventually took the head coaching job at the University of New Mexico and is starting his 15th season in Albuquerque in 2004.

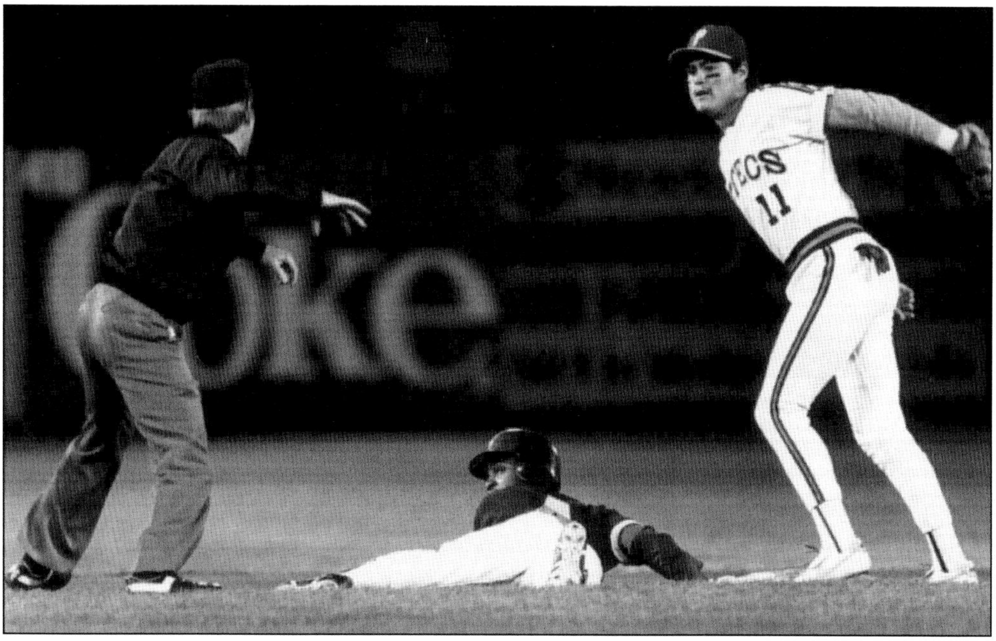


Pima all-tournament shortstop John Alva tags out 1985 tournament MVP Randy Randle of San Jacinto-North on this play, but the Gators won the tourney. Bill Martin is the umpire.

County College of Morris (NJ) 1985 all-tournament outfielder George Bargfrede receives congratulations after he hit the first pitch of the game for a home run.

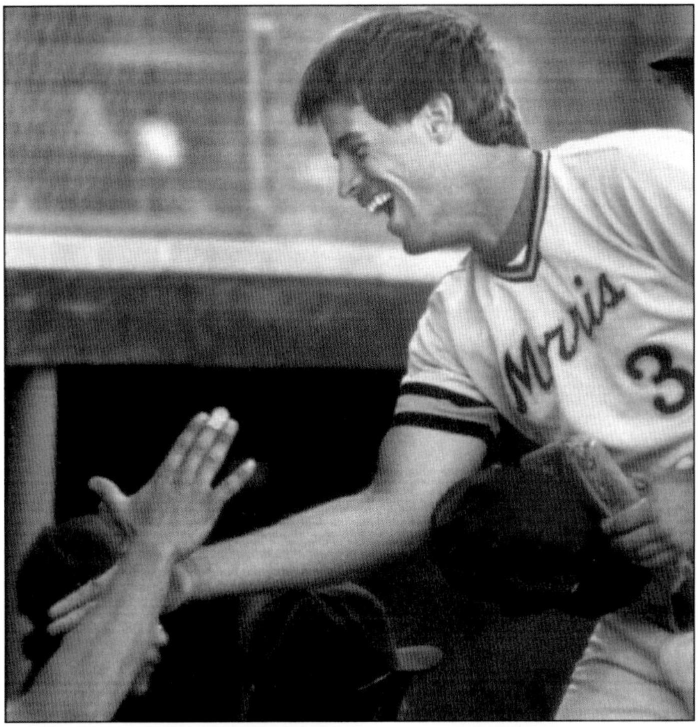


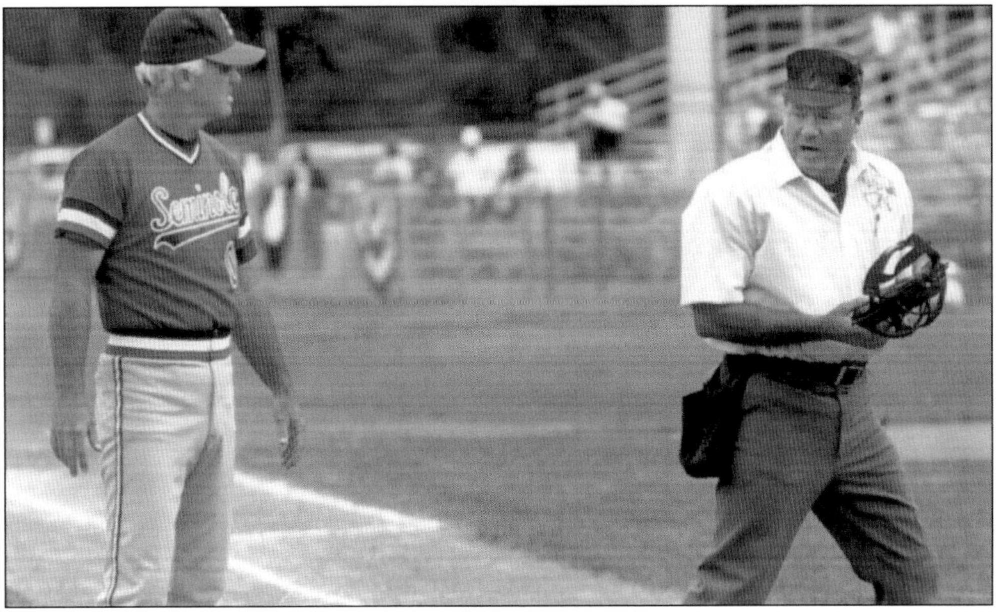

Lloyd Simmons (left) and Seminole (OK) Junior College perhaps deserve the title of best JUCO program never to have won a national championship. Known as "Zero" for the ever-present No. 0 on his Trojans jersey, he took 13 teams to the JUCO World Series, finishing runner-up four times and in third place twice. Simmons garnered a junior college record 1,600 victories during his 27-year Seminole stint, plus 16 regional titles, and 13 district championships. Seminole produced 41 NJCAA All-Americans while more than 130 of Simmons' players signed professional baseball contracts.

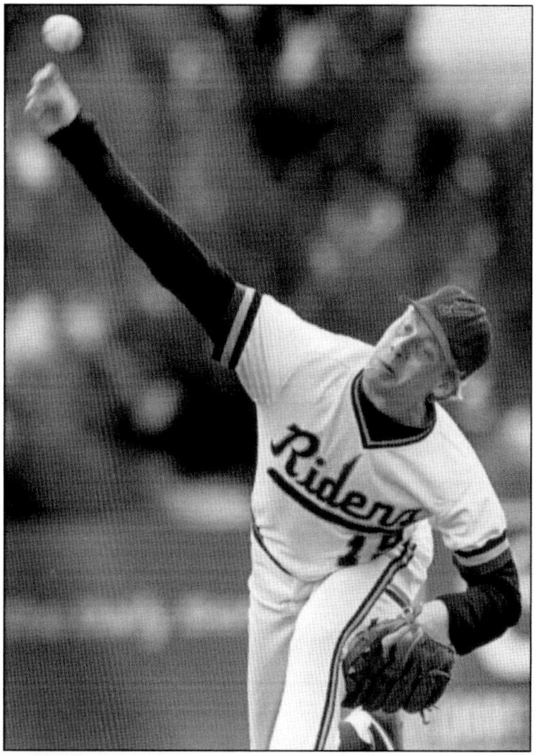


Curt Schilling throws for Yavapai (AZ) College during the 1986 JUCO World Series. Although Schilling started an 11-9 loss to eventual champion San Jacinto-North during the tournament, he has gone on to a fantastic big-league career, including two 20-win seasons through the 2003 season and a World Series championship with the Arizona Diamondbacks in 2001. San Jac coach Wayne Graham says that Schilling threw hard in 1986, "but throwing hard isn't good enough at Grand Junction." As the consummate professional, Schilling has learned to do much more than throw hard to last more than 16 seasons and earn more than 150 victories as a major-league pitcher. Adds Graham: "If he threw all the stuff he can throw now, we wouldn't have beaten him."

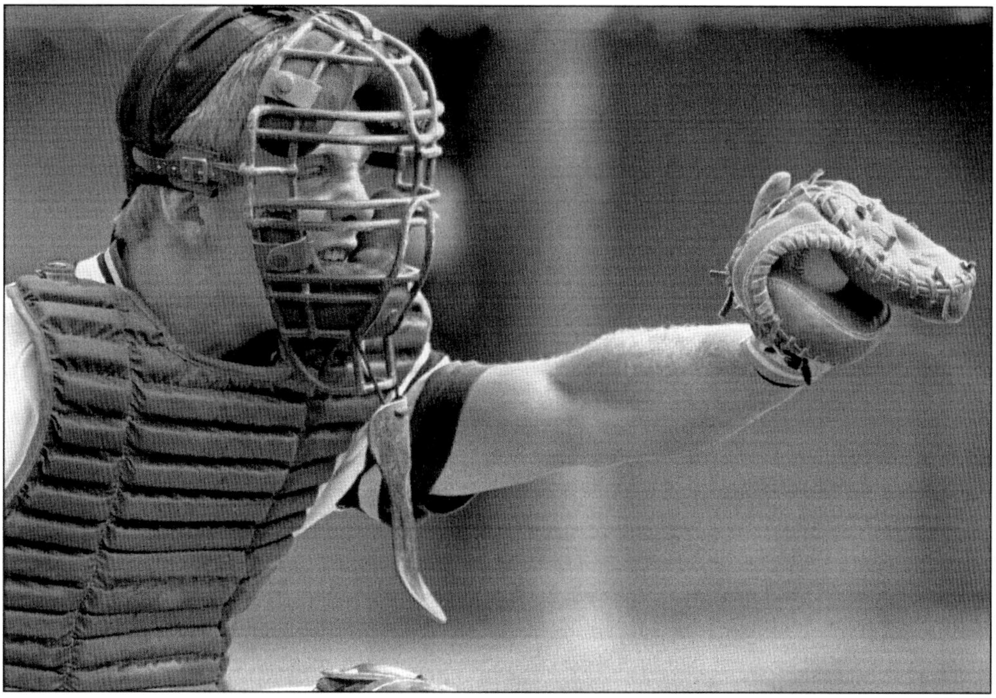

Although Yavapai placed third at the 1986 JUCO World Series, catcher Brian Deak was named Most Valuable Player. Besides handling Schilling and the other Rough Rider pitchers, Deak batted .444 with 4 home runs and 10 RBIs.

Michael Miller of Meramec (MO) Community College beats the throw home against Jon Prather of San Jacinto-North at the 1986 JUCO World Series. San Jac won the game 12-10.

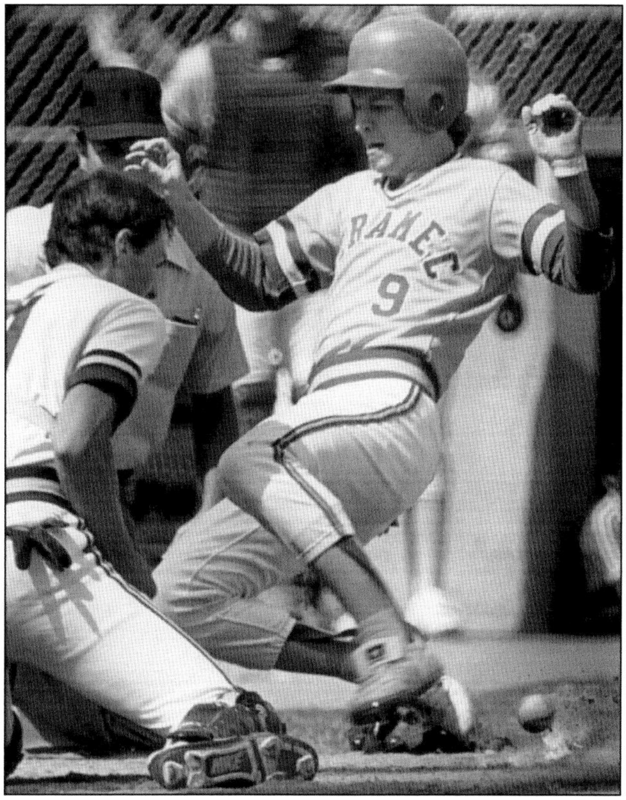

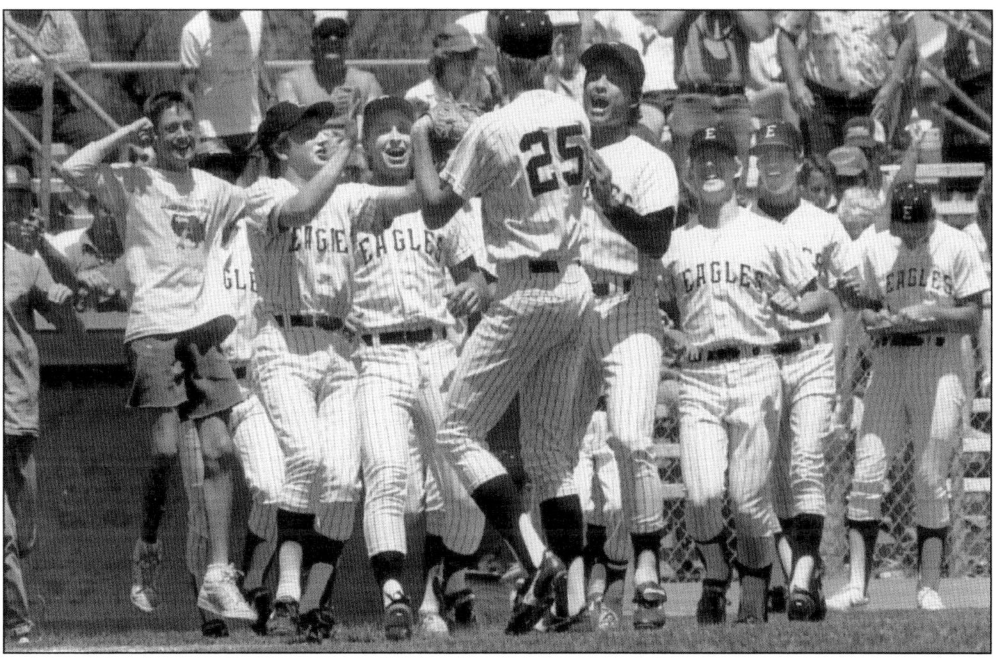

The College of Southern Idaho hangs on to eliminate Meramec 7-6 behind the relief pitching of David Carter (25) in 1986.

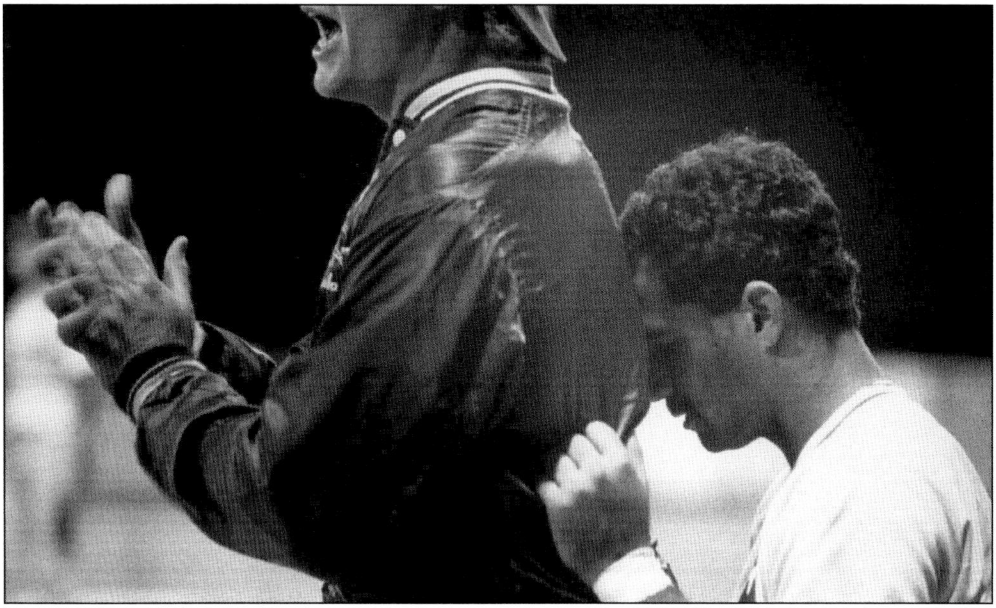

Laz Balsera of Brevard (FL) tugs on his teammate's jacket in the dugout during a tense moment at the 1986 tournament. It was the Melbourne-based school's first of four JUCO appearances.

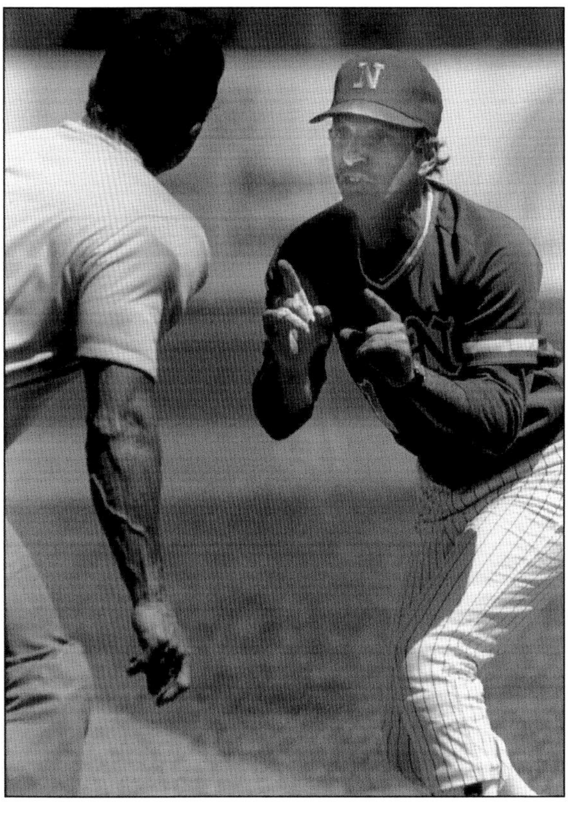


Nassau (NY) Community College assistant coach Bob St. Angelo disputes the call after Nassau base runner Mike Morales was ruled out on the play. The Garden City-based school made four tournament appearances in five years in the late 1960s (1965, 1966, 1967, and 1969), including the 1966 championship, but this photo from 1986 was their next subsequent Grand Junction qualification.

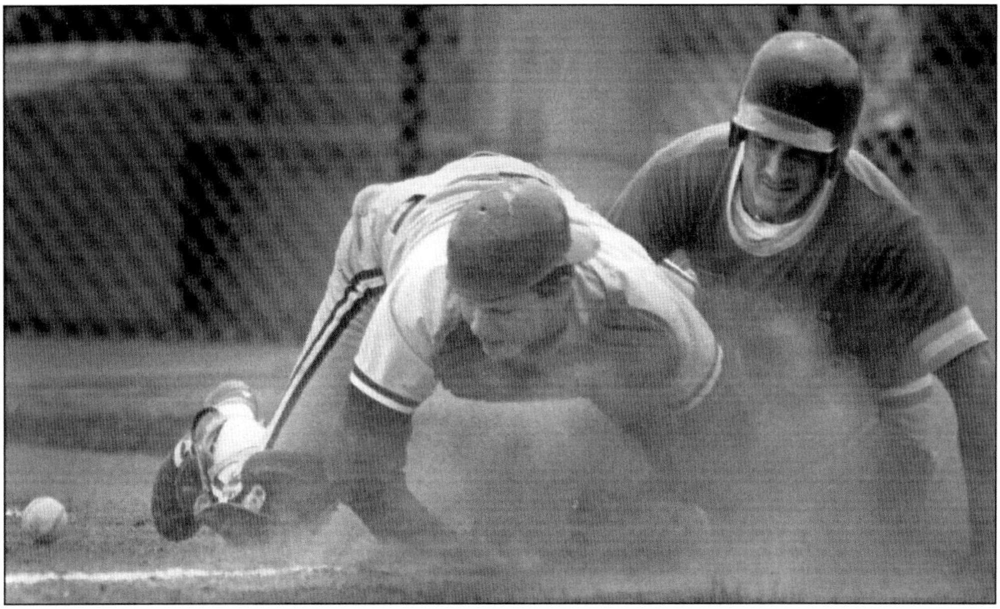

Catcher Todd Walsack of Brookdale (NJ) Community College keeps busy during the Jersey Blues' 1986 JUCO World Series game against Brevard (FL). All-tourney performer Rob Stiegele is safe on this third-inning play (*above*), but Walsack got his man, Bradley Harvell, later in the fifth inning (*right*). Brevard managed to reach the championship game before losing 11-4 to San Jacinto-North.

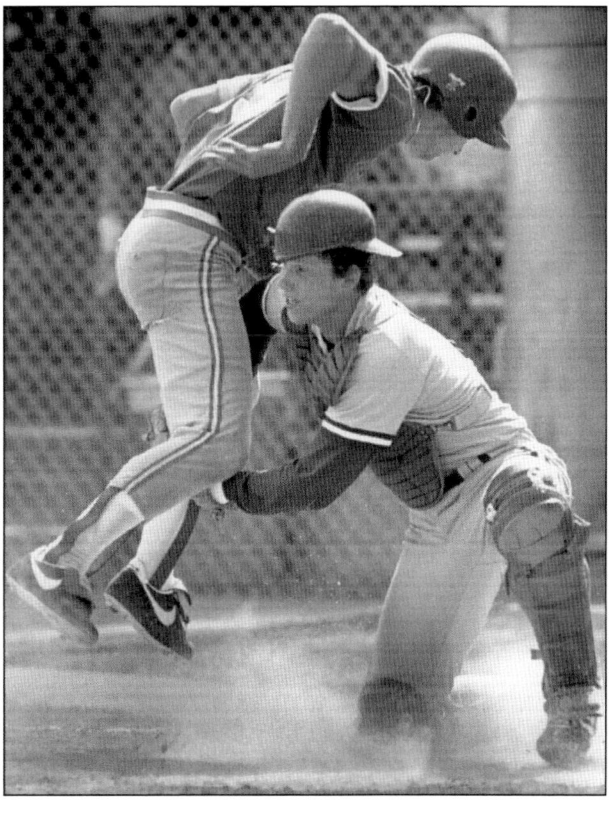

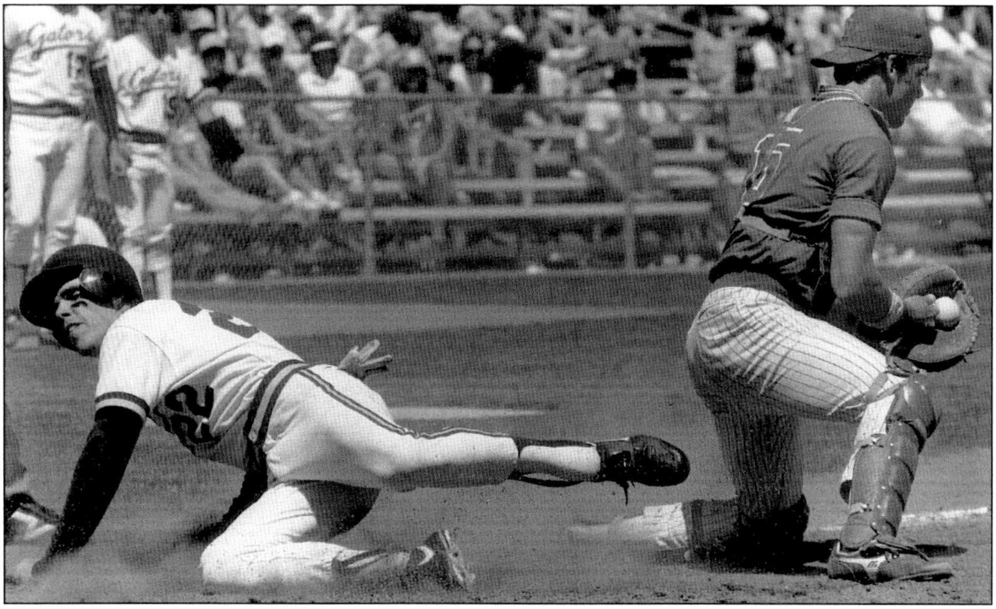

San Jacinto-North's Thomas McGee is safe at home against Nassau (NY) catcher Rich Ironside with San Jac's fourth run of an 18-3 romp in a 1986 game. Both players earned all-tournament status.

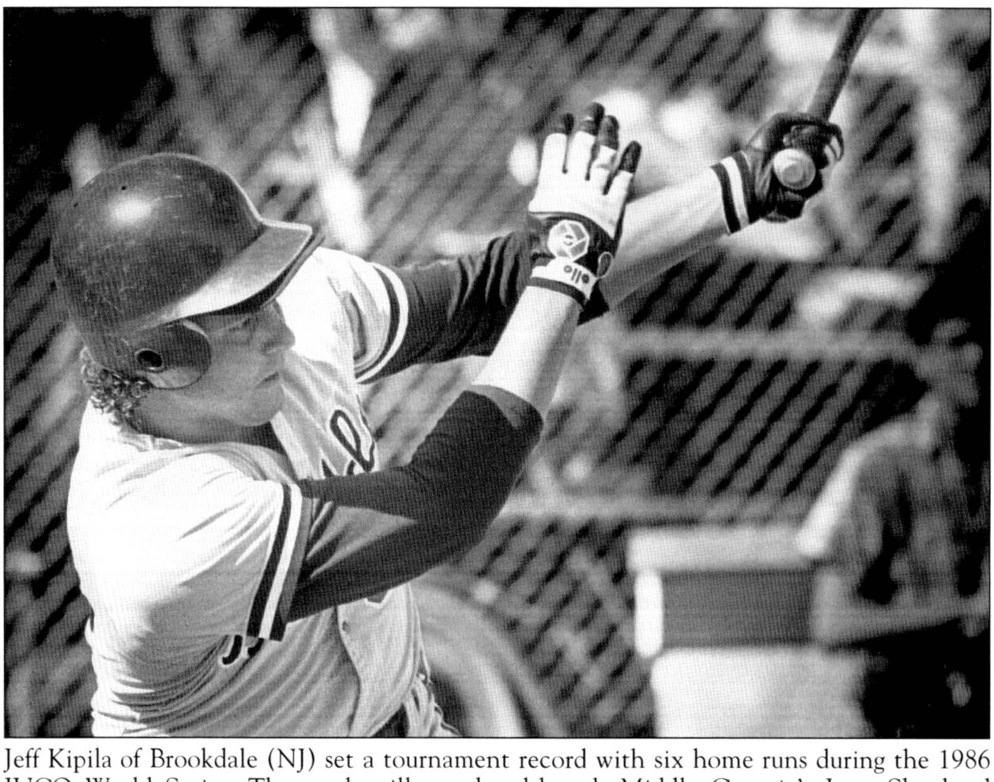

Jeff Kipila of Brookdale (NJ) set a tournament record with six home runs during the 1986 JUCO World Series. The mark still stands, although Middle Georgia's Jerry Shepherd equaled the feat in 1990.

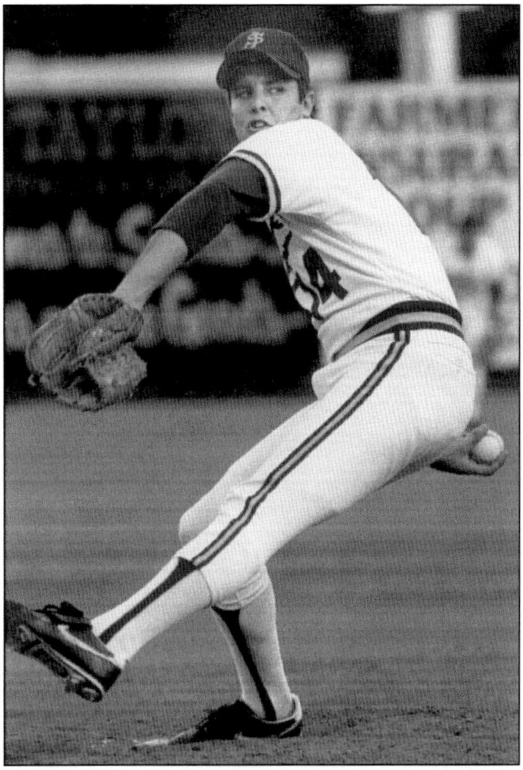

All-tournament selection Toby Nivens throws a pitch during his 11-4 complete-game victory over Brevard (FL) in the 1986 championship (*right*). It was San Jacinto-North's second consecutive title (*below*).

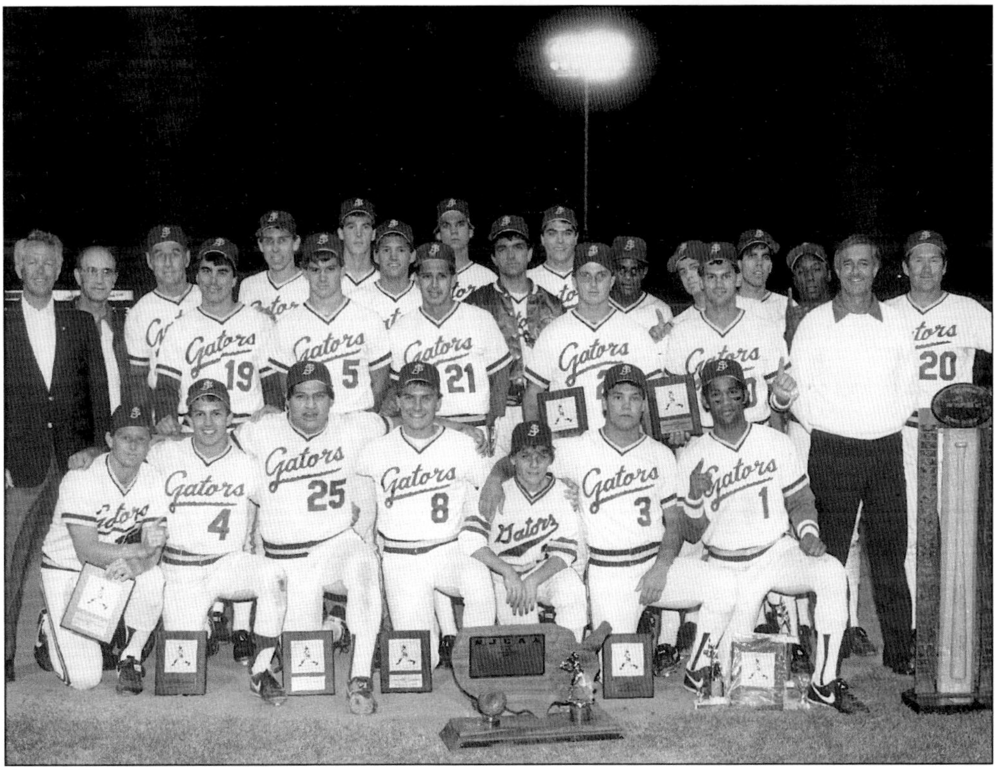

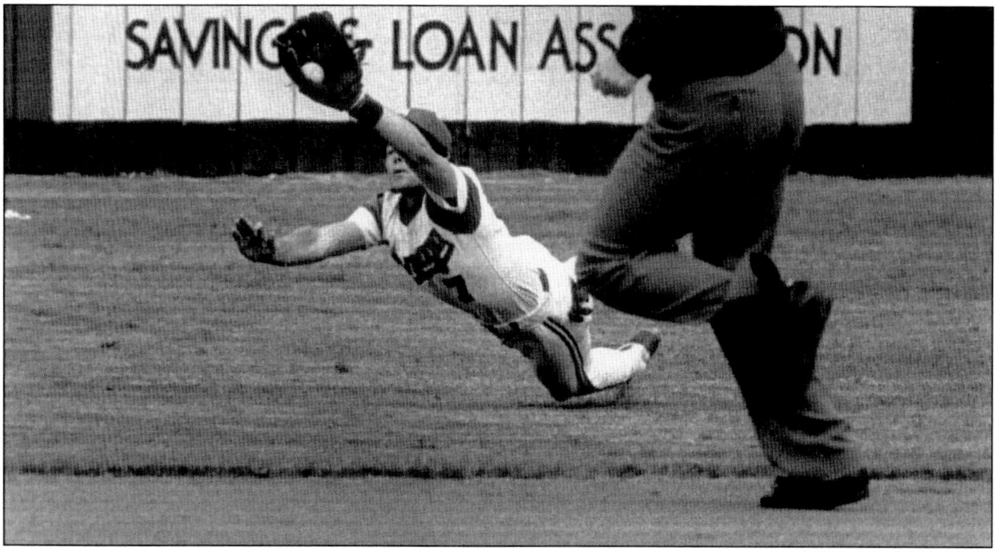


Ed Donohue of Onondaga (NY) Community College makes a stellar catch in the outfield during the 1987 JUCO World Series.

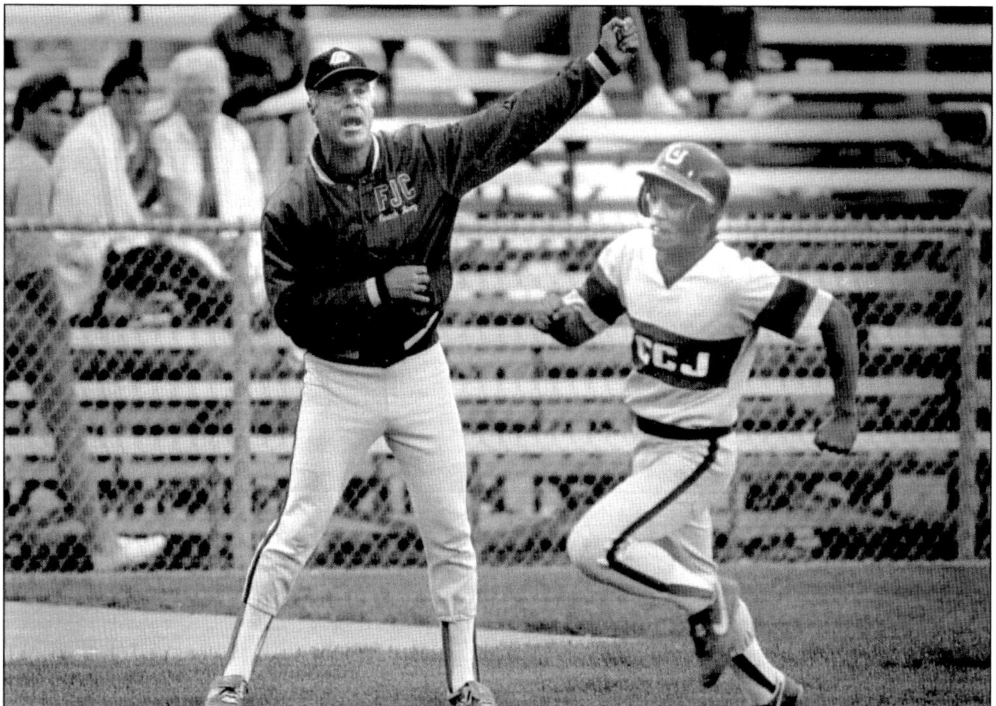


Florida Community College of Jacksonville coach and JUCO Hall of Famer Howard Roey waves Winston Relaford around third base during the 1987 JUCO World Series. Roey's FCCJ squad returned to Grand Junction in 2000.

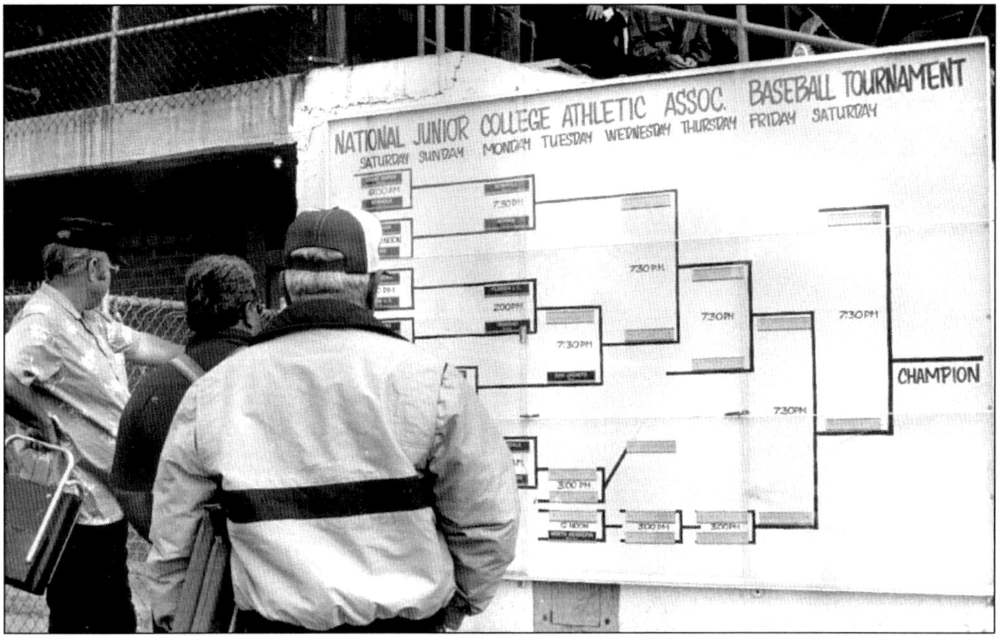


Fans check out the tournament bracket during the 1987 national tournament. The large board with up-to-date results has been on the south end of the first-base bleachers for many years near the entrance to the stadium and the concession stand.

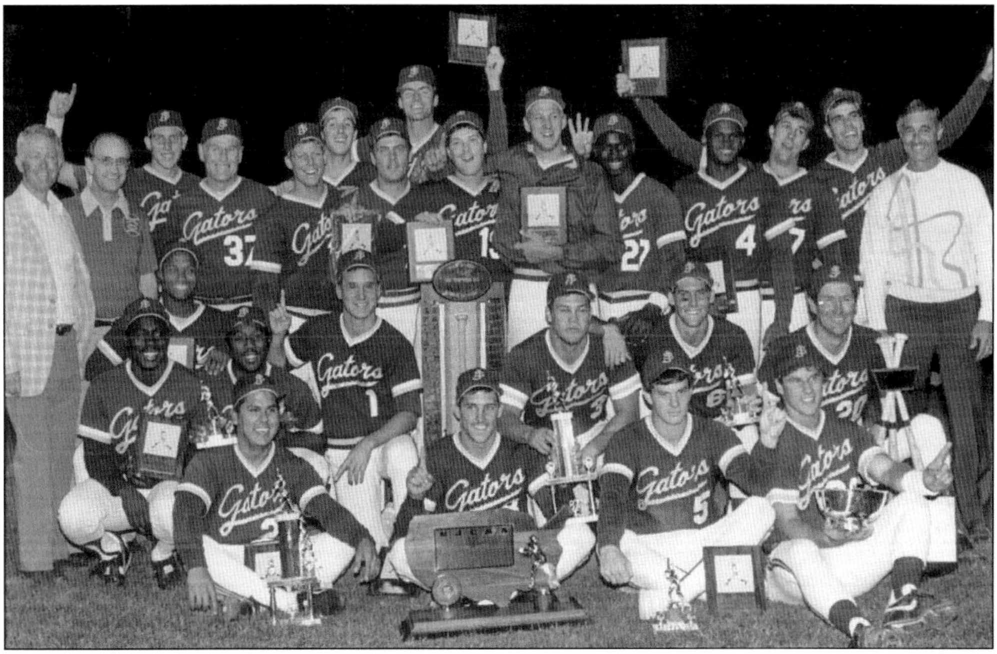

San Jacinto-North players raise their fingers with the No. 1 sign—and in one case in the back row, the No. 3 sign—after becoming just the second JUCO team ever to win three consecutive national titles. This was in 1987, the middle of the most spectacular dynasty in junior college baseball history. Although the Gators would finish second in 1988, they went on to nab the 1989 and 1990 titles as well.

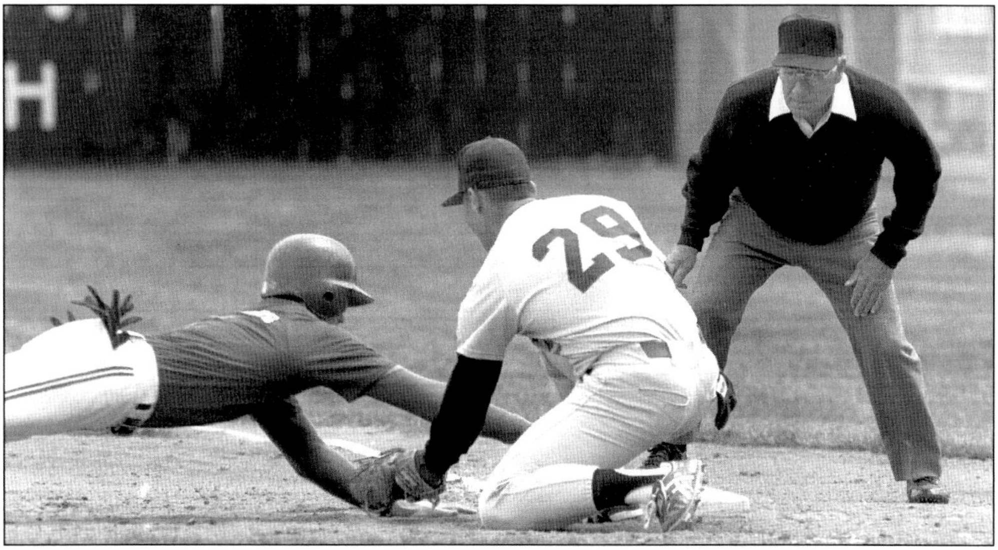


Umpire John Toppi keeps a close eye on a pickoff play during the 1988 JUCO World Series. Toppi was inducted into the JUCO Hall of Fame in 2003, the first umpire ever so honored. The gruff-voiced but ever personable Rhode Island native known as "Top" has been involved with the tournament for 28 years, the last 13 as supervisor of umpires.

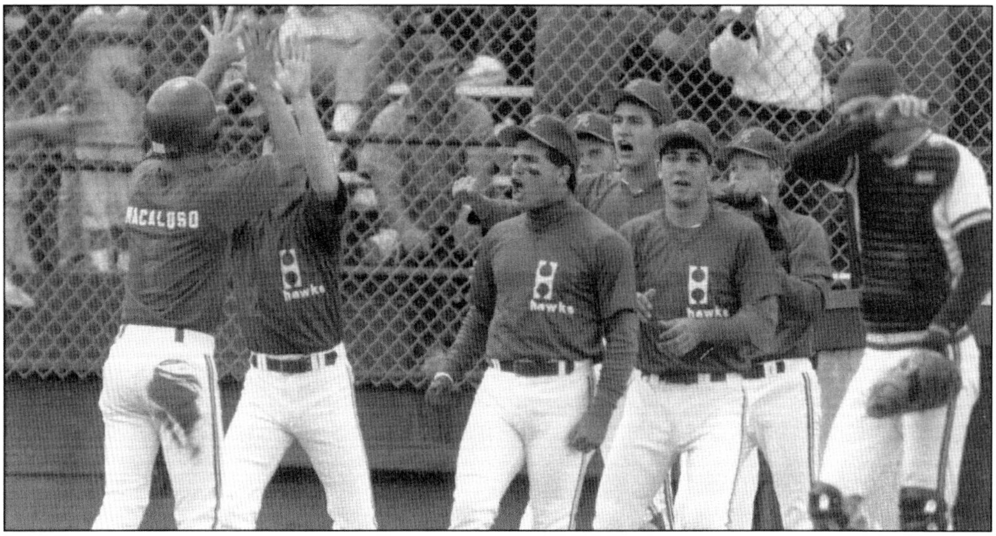


Hillsborough (FL) Community College celebrates with David Macaluso (left) as he scores a first-inning run against San Jacinto-North in the 1988 JUCO World Series. The Hawks stunned the three-time defending champions from Texas by taking an 11-4 victory in the final in their only national tournament appearance. Matt Hines, who had arm problems during the season, earned the decisive victory on the mound. Hillsborough stumbled with a 13-9 loss to the College of Southern Idaho, which was bolstered by 7,000 fans cheering for CSI's four local products (Sam Atkins and Bill Moeller from Grand Junction, and Jeff Warren and Chris Hanks from nearby Carbondale). But when San Jac squeezed by CSI 8-7, the title tilt featured the reigning champs and the Florida upstarts. For the second time in three years, the MVP came from the third-place team. Hanks took the honor in 1988 with a .471 batting average, 4 homers, 13 RBIs, and 13 runs.

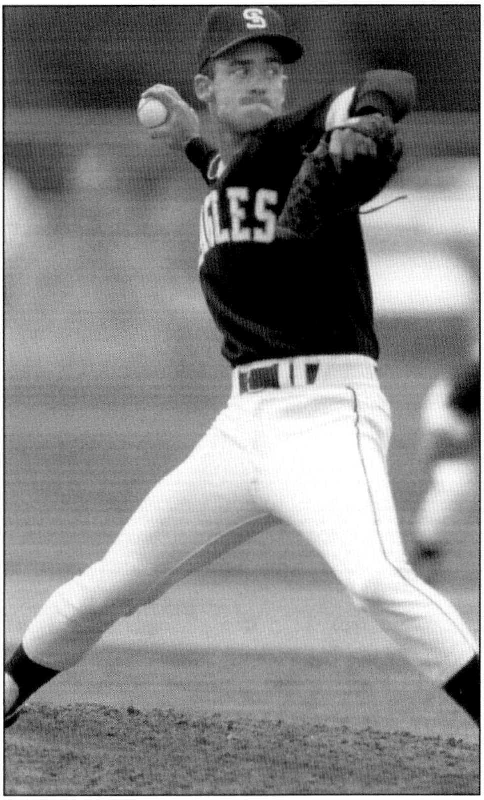 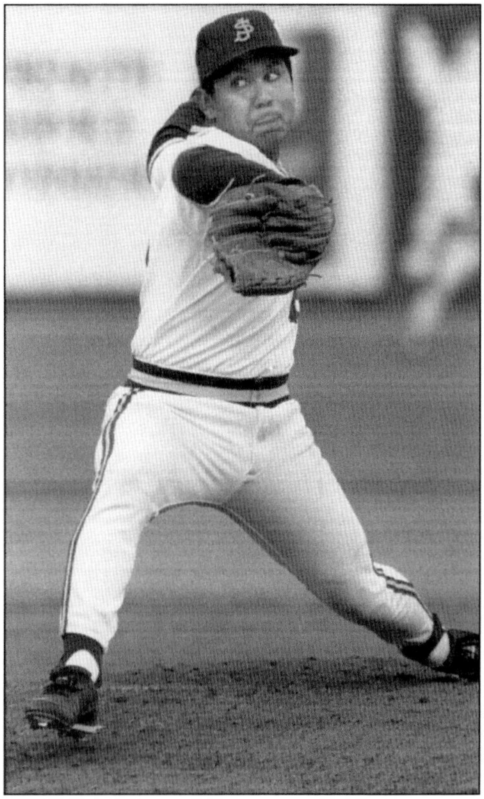

Righty Bill Moeller of the College of Southern Idaho (*left*) was the Most Valuable Pitcher at the 1988 JUCO World Series, and lefty Oscar Rivas of San Jac (*right*) was Most Valuable Pitcher at the 1987 tournament. Moeller, a Fruita-Monument High School product, had two wins and a save, but Rivas got the win in the Gators' critical 8-7 semifinal victory over CSI in 1988. A local radio announcer gave Rivas the name "Little Fernando" during his freshman season, when he pitched coolly out of three high-pressure situations during the Gators' 1987 championship victory over Seminole. The crowning moment was when he coaxed a game-ending ground out with the bases loaded and San Jac clinging to a 2-1 lead.

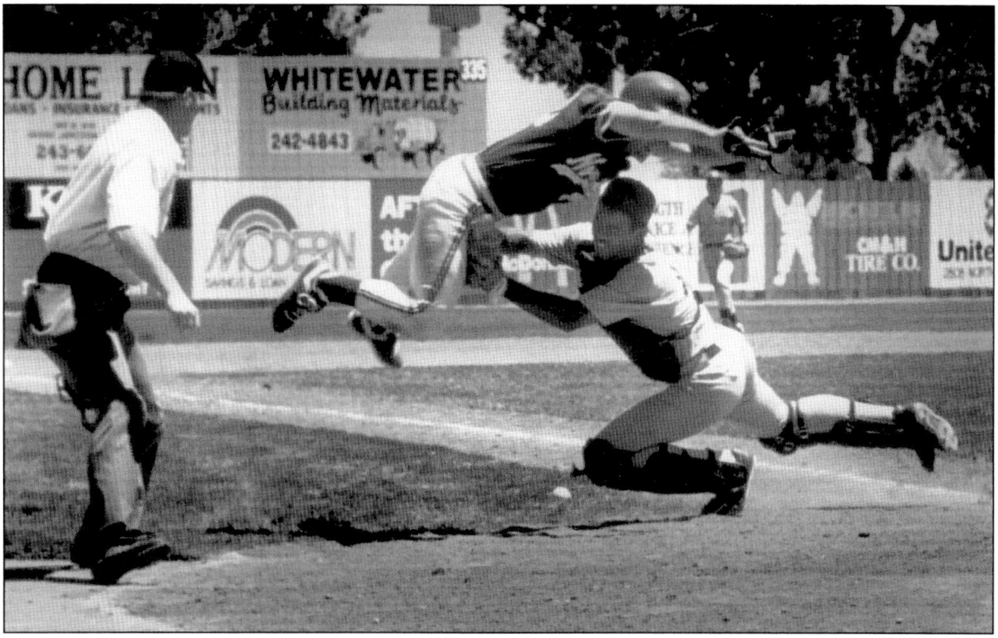


Brad Dolejsi of Northeastern Oklahoma A&M is out at home even though Hinds (MS) catcher Terre Woods doesn't hang on to the ball. Dolejsi missed the plate and then was tagged out. This was during NEO's 14-6 opening-game victory in 1989. This is a good photo to show what the *Grand Junction Sentinel* dubbed the "mini-monster," the second tier of the leftfield wall that was added that season to make home runs more challenging.

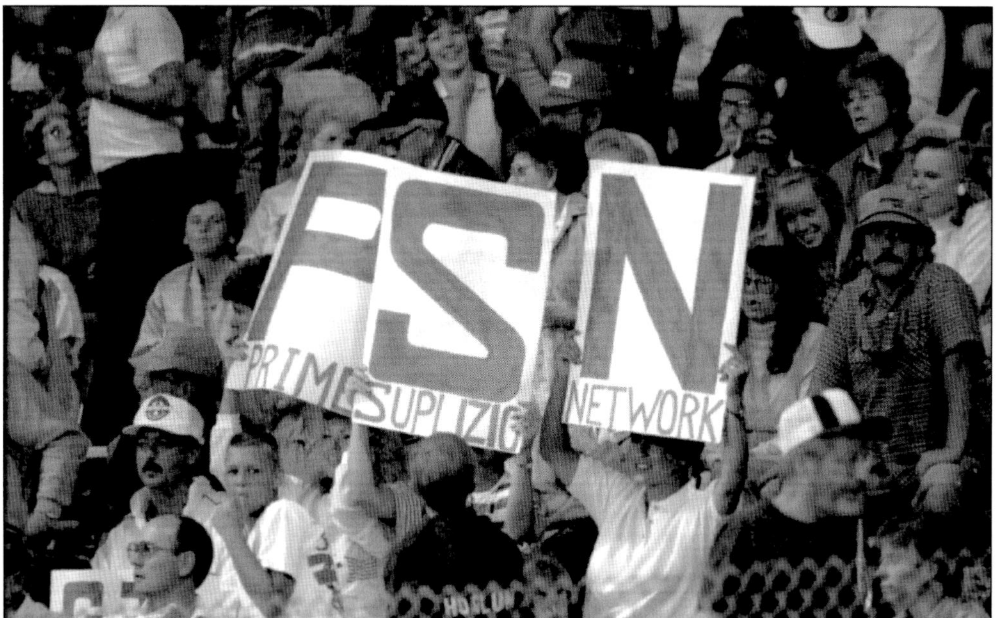


Grand Junction baseball fans show a Prime Sports Network audience what they think PSN really stands for during the 1989 championship game that the network televised. PSN returned in 1990, and although television hasn't returned since it is brought up for discussion from time to time.

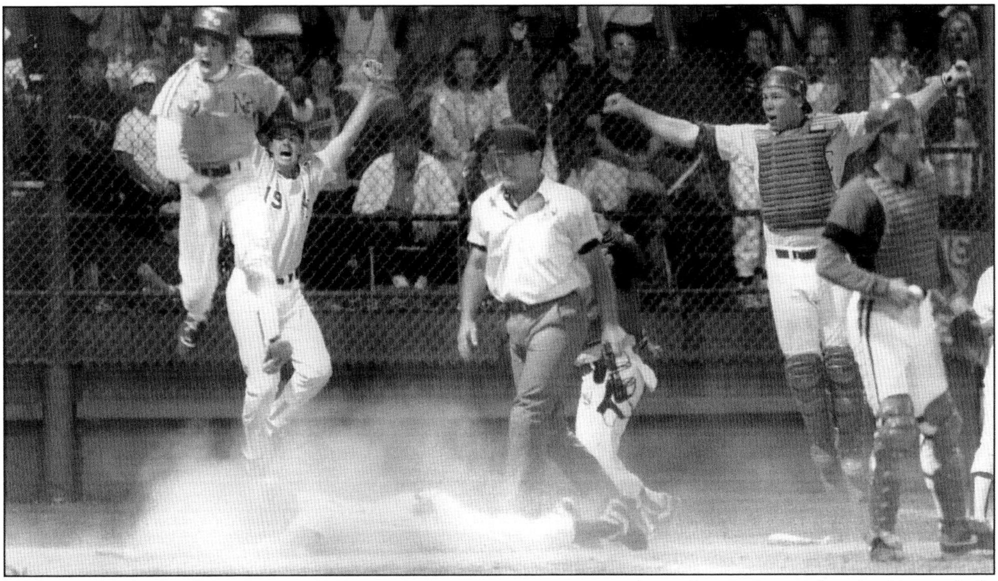

The Northeastern Oklahoma A&M bench erupts as Monte Gibson brings up a cloud of dust while scoring the winning run in the 1989 semifinals. George Day's double off the left-centerfield wall brought Gibson speeding home with a 3-2 victory over Cochise (AZ) and a date with San Jacinto-North the next night for the championship. "I was going to run through the fence if I had to," Gibson told the *Grand Junction Sentinel*. "Once I thought it was a gap shot, I just put my head down and gave it all I had." NEO's quest for a title abruptly ended the following night, however, as San Jac had a record-setting 22-4 outburst to regain the JUCO crown.

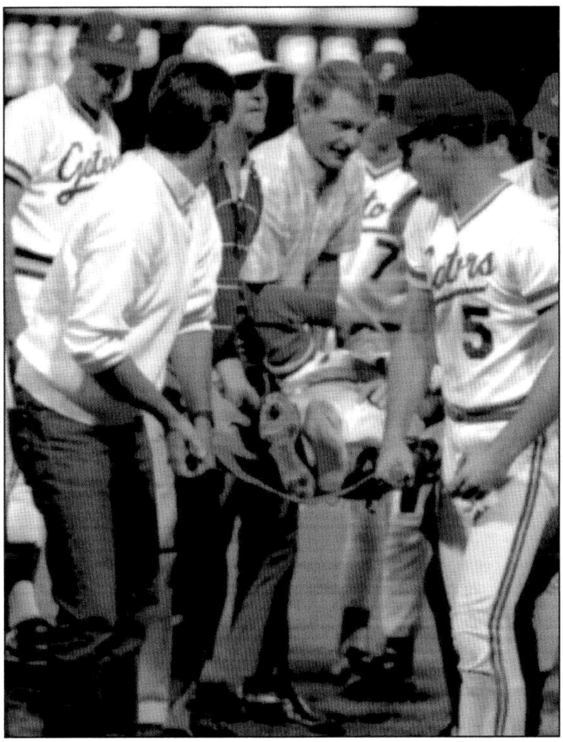

San Jac's David Evans earned his third victory of the 1989 tournament during the final-game rout of NEO and was the MVP of the tournament, but he wasn't around to see the end of the game. He got drilled in the leg by a line drive in the seventh inning with the Gators leading 18-1 and was taken off the field on a stretcher. After a brief examination, he hobbled back to the dugout to watch the end of the game with his teammates.

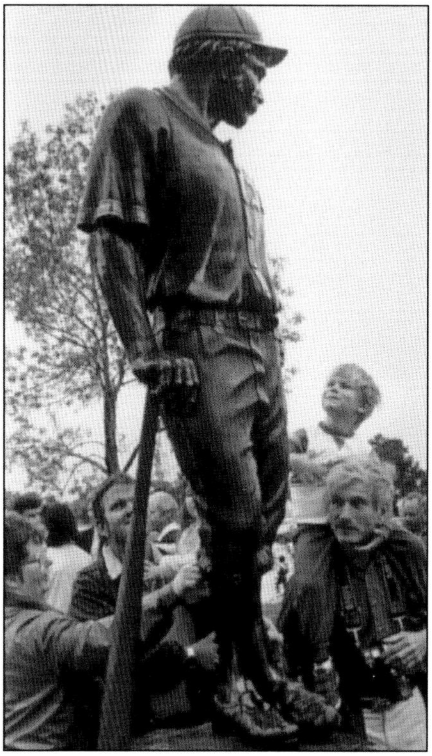

Seven-foot-tall "Casey" greets fans shortly after his arrival in Grand Junction. The sculpture by Colorado artist Mark Lundeen was placed near the right-field entrance to the park in time for the 1989 JUCO World Series.

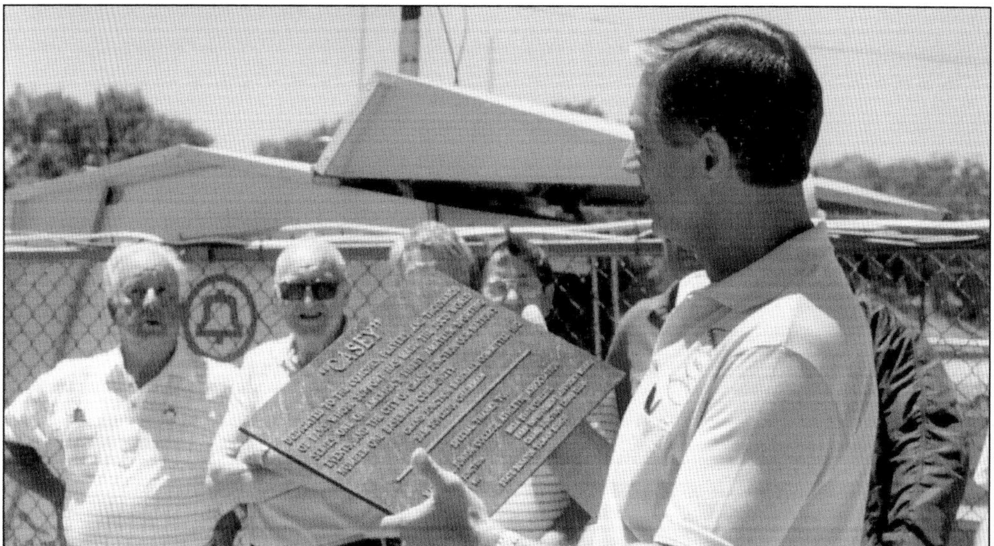


Tournament chairman Sam Suplizio shows the plaque for the new "Casey" statue during its dedication. It reads, in part:

*"Casey"*

*Dedicated to the coaches, players, and thousands of fans whose support has made the JUCO World Series one of America's finest amateur sporting events, and the city of Grand Junction, our nation's number one baseball community.*

# Five

# The Modern Era 1990–Present

The JUCO World Series in Grand Junction is nearing the half-century mark, but instead of showing signs of age or apathy, the event now is stronger than ever and, although it is dangerous to speculate too much about the future, it seems poised to stay that way long past its golden anniversary. But it would be wrong to assume it had to evolve with such strength. The people that strive to maintain the tournament each year spent most of the 1990s recognizing that the JUCO World Series was in a transition period. Like the leaders that staged the first national baseball tournament in Grand Junction back in 1959, the leaders in the 1990s made sound decisions to keep the event steered on the right course. Not surprisingly, some of those key figures were integral to both eras.

Baseball is often praised for its timelessness. A person could be dropped into the bleachers across several generations, it has been said, and he or she would feel familiar with this wonderful game and the actions that surround it. Three strikes is still an out. A pitcher pays when he walks the leadoff batter in an inning. A home run still brings fans to their feet, but a well-placed hit behind the runner still deserves a tip of the cap. On the field itself, as the flow of a baseball game unfolds, perhaps these examples are ageless and comforting. But to think that the only changes over the years are aluminum bats and uniform styles is just not true. While Grand Junction has been impressive in keeping ticket prices from getting too high ($20 for a week-long 19-game pass—$15 for students—is nothing to complain about), in the 21st century, much at Lincoln Park is no longer old school.

The arrival of television by Prime Sports Network in 1989 and 1990 was short-lived, but the issue still is raised from time to time. The JUCO World Series is now officially the Alpine Bank JUCO World Series after the local corporate sponsor. Lincoln Park Stadium is now Sam Suplizio Field, and instead of bare spots down the foul lines, chicken wire backstops, splintered bleachers built for a few hundred, and bandbox dugouts, the venue rivals high-level minor league ballparks and squeezes in more than 100,000 fans during tournament week. The overall operation is more polished, as some committee names remain the same, others move smoothly into replacement roles, and still other names look familiar (Bergman, Tolman) but are inhabited by sons (Walter, "Tex") of pioneering fathers ("Bus", Jay). Returning visiting coaches have become so familiar with the Grand Junction officials that they seem almost as though they are local residents. Even George Killian, the only executive director the NJCAA office has ever had, has indicated he will retire in Summer 2004. Successful teams aren't merely a handful from Texas, Arizona, and Florida. Instead, talent can be found in all regions of the country, and the junior college ranks themselves have swelled to where there are now 129 schools competing in NJCAA Division II baseball and 83 schools competing in Division III, along with the 184 in Division I that vie for a spot in Grand Junction. With that sort of competition, it's hard to imagine another dominant Mesa (AZ) or San Jacinto-North (TX) emerging.

The JUCO organizing committee and the city of Grand Junction saw all of these developments occur during the 1990s, and responded like a community that knew how significant its possession is. Take television, for example. TV brings welcome exposure, dollars, and opportunities for growth, but it also can bring competition to the long-time host, possible loss of control of the event, or misguided attempts at deciding what the tournament's future should be. Jamie

Hamilton had been groomed for the tournament chairman's position for years by Grand Junction icon Sam Suplizio. (Hamilton even took over as acting director in 1992 when Suplizio got called into first-base coaching duty by the California Angels when a bus accident injured several coaches.) Hamilton officially took over the job for the 2003 tournament. He told the *Grand Junction Sentinel* that he has discussed the possibility of TV with Fox Sports Net, which bought out Prime Sports. "I'm talking about it not for the money but for the exposure," he said. "If that's the case, then I think we'd take a look at it as long as it doesn't take away from the integrity of the tournament."

Back in 1989 and 1990, the arrival of TV gave the event exposure that allowed larger cities to eye opportunity. Killian and Suplizio responded adamantly that the JUCO World Series was not for sale, and they weathered some alleged competition from Orlando, Florida; Columbus, Ohio; and others in 1990. "No, emphatically no," Killian told the *Sentinel* when asked about the rumors of Grand Junction being in danger of losing the tournament. "There is no interest on the part of the NJCAA to leave Grand Junction, period. We've been in Grand Junction so long and we get great fan support. Why would we want to go? Most of the talk is a lot of hot air." Added Suplizio: "Last year, the JUCO grossed $120,000, and made a profit of $50,000. The JUCO turns better profits than other national tournaments around the country." As if to punctuate those statements, tournament attendance surpassed the 100,000 mark in 1990.

Another major change in 1990 was the renaming of the stadium to honor Sam Suplizio, a man that had been in charge of the tournament for 20 years and, in a sense, had prepared the committee for the transition period that was already underway. The baseball field, originally known as Lincoln Park Stadium, took long-time parks and recreation director "Red" Stocker's name in 1972 in memorial. The football field next door retained Stocker's name after the 1990 dedication of Sam Suplizio Field, making two distinctly named venues that taken together were part of Lincoln Park. The Moyer Pool and water slide opened in 1989 just beyond right field, and a nine-hole golf course and picnic and playground areas also constitute the midtown park.

If ever there was evidence that JUCO was progressing with the times, it was in 1999. Alpine Bank became the event's official corporate sponsor, following a recent trend in sporting events nationwide. Also by 1999, Major League Baseball was contributing $50,000 to travel costs for qualifying teams. The money JUCO brings in has come a long way since the 100-dollars-and-change profits and a several-thousand-dollar travel allotment from the bigs. But the volunteer-run event also hands out money through scholarships to local high school students, and contributions to local middle school and Little League programs. JUCO also puts money back into many facilities, from Suplizio Field, to the Stocker Stadium football field and track next door, to the stunning $1 million Canyon View Field located north of town by Interstate 70 that is used by local teams.

Hamilton was drafted by the California Angels and even got a single off Fernando Valenzuela in his first professional at-bat (followed by three strikeouts). He reached Class AAA before his playing career ended, and then he coached in the Milwaukee Brewers system. He had been a star infielder at Mesa College in the mid-1970s as it was transitioning from a junior college to a four-year school. Now, Hamilton is Suplizio's heir and as a committee member since 1986, he has experienced JUCO's transition to the corporate era in the new century. He doesn't see any need to make drastic changes. Other than a possible pursuit of TV, he wants to keep things moving along smoothly and make sure the new generation of the committee stays excited about what they have inherited. He talked to the *Sentinel* about how his children have enjoyed the JUCO experience. "It's neat, these last 17 years, to watch them grow up (with the tournament) and to have more people in this community be able to experience that as they watch their children grow up," he said. "That's what I have as far as a burning desire."

A community of people with that sentiment is perhaps the best proof that the Alpine Bank JUCO World Series—JUCO, if you prefer—will have a home on the Western Slope of the Colorado Rockies for another half century.

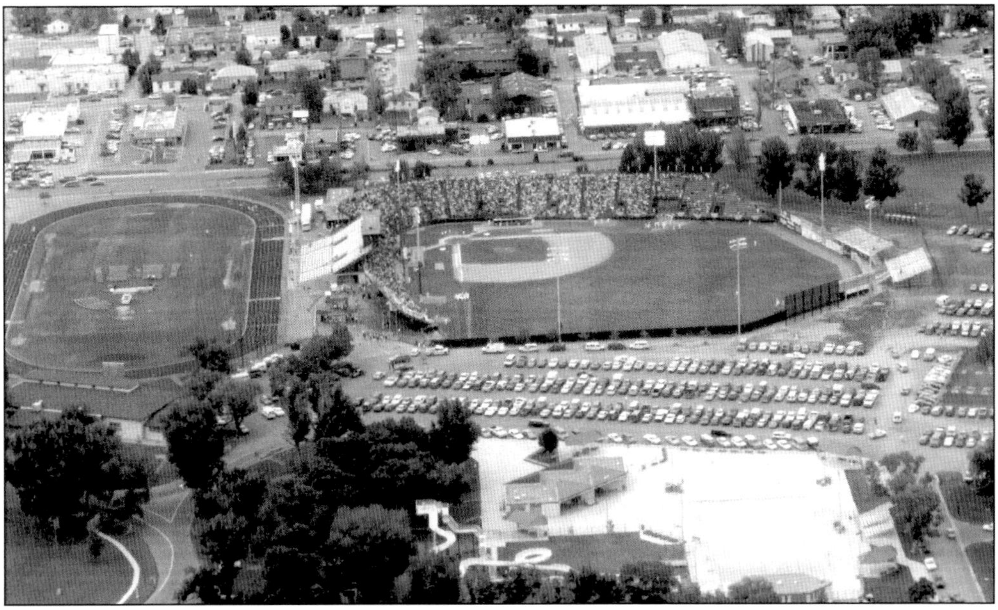

By the 1990s, Lincoln Park featured a baseball stadium now christened Sam Suplizio Field and bleachers that extended from foul line to foul line (and even beyond left field). Lincoln Park also had a new swimming pool and water slide, and more than ever, was an integral part of the Grand Junction community.

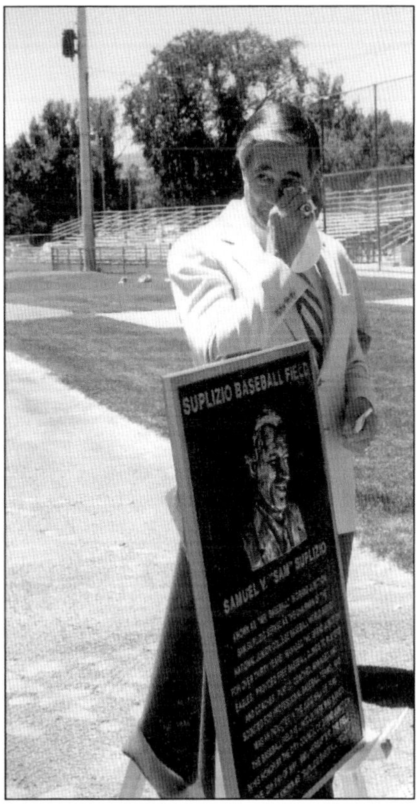


Tournament chairman Sam Suplizio gets teary-eyed as the plaque showing the renaming of the field in his honor is unveiled in 1990. Known as "Mr. Baseball" in the state of Colorado, Suplizio's mark on the JUCO World Series is unmistakable. Many in town call the tournament "Sam's baby." Suplizio is not a Colorado native; he's from DuBois, Pa. But he joined the Grand Junction Eagles in the summer of 1952 when he was still a two-sport athlete at the University of New Mexico. He became a New York Yankee farmhand, and Casey Stengel had in mind that Suplizio might become a defensive stalwart in center field that would allow him to either move his injury-prone star Mickey Mantle to right field or replace him in the late innings. Days before the September call-ups in 1956, when Suplizio was to join the sport's most hallowed franchise, he shattered his arm on a routine slide in Birmingham, Alabama, that effectively ended his pro career. He had married a local girl and had moved back to town to work at Home Loan Investment Company around the time that Jay Tolman and D.S. Dykstra were putting together a plan to host the national junior college baseball tournament. Since, he has become the city's baseball icon and prominent civic leader.

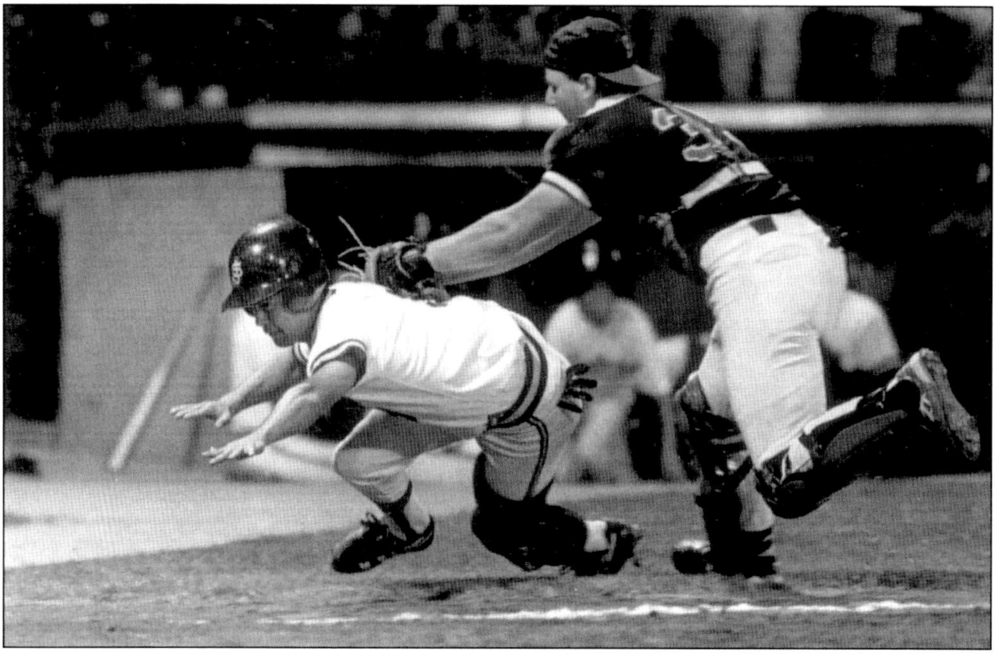

Seminole (OK) catcher Kelly Stinnett tags out a San Jacinto-North (TX) runner during the 1990 JUCO World Series. Stinnett has turned into a durable big-league catcher over the past decade, and headlines a list of Seminole stars that have made it to the majors. That list includes All-Star reliever Eric Gagne, Keith Miller, Steve Peters, Jose Tolentino, Doug Lindsey, Ryan Franklin, Joe Nelson, and Stinnett's 1990 teammate, Shane Halter.

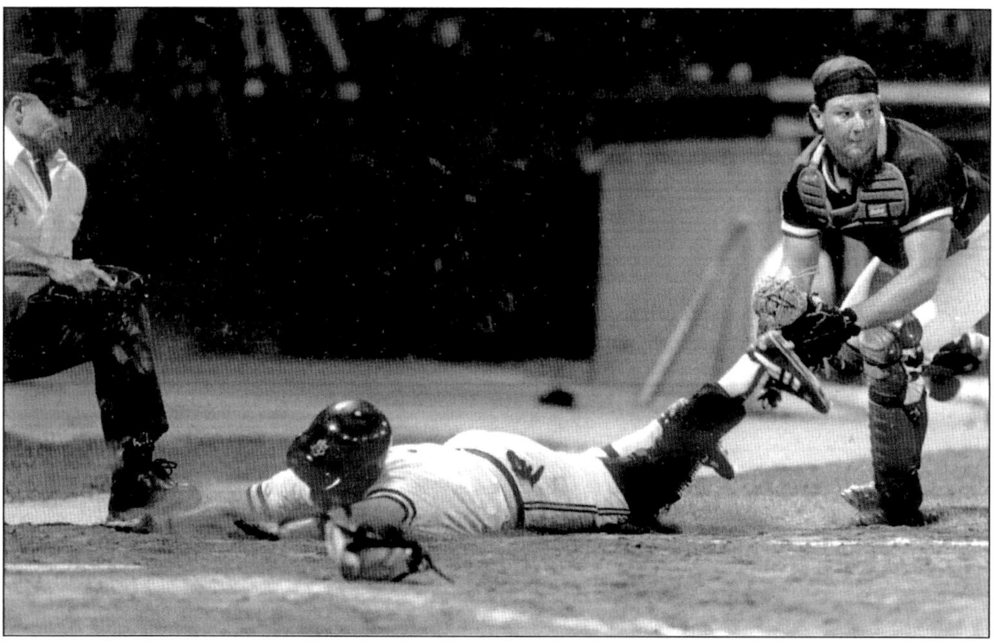

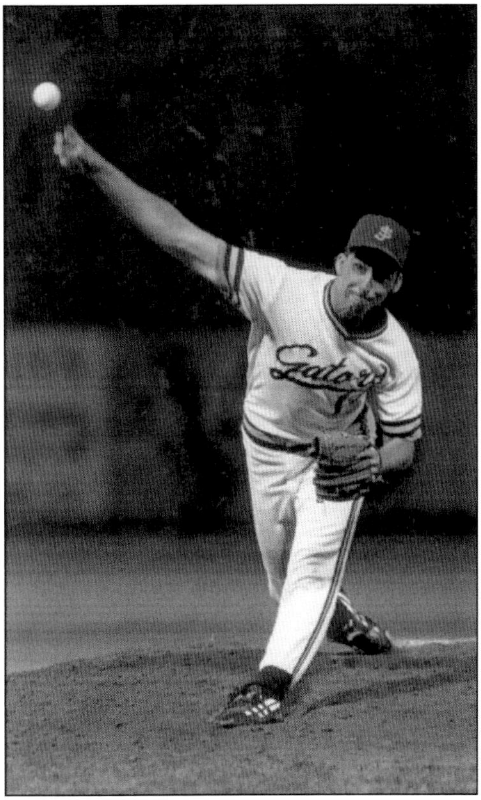

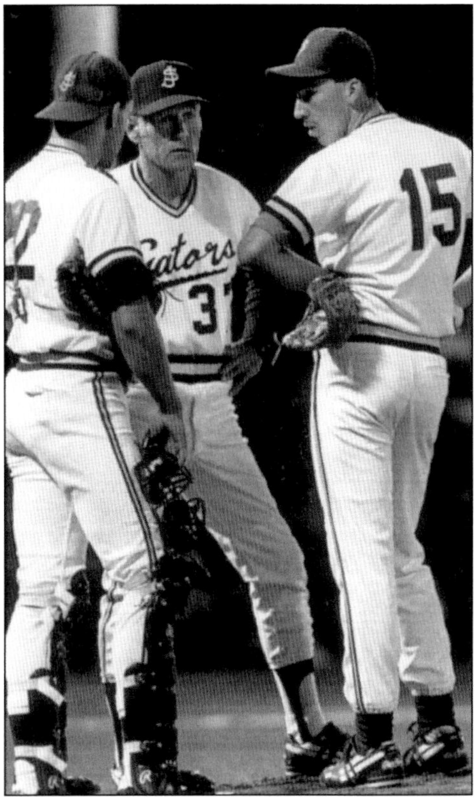


San Jac coach Wayne Graham (*center of right photo*) meets with pitcher Robert Henkel (*left photo*) and catcher Joe Sommer during the 1990 tournament. Henkel was named Most Valuable Pitcher in the tournament, in part for his 7-2 victory over Seminole that snapped the Trojans' 35-game winning streak.

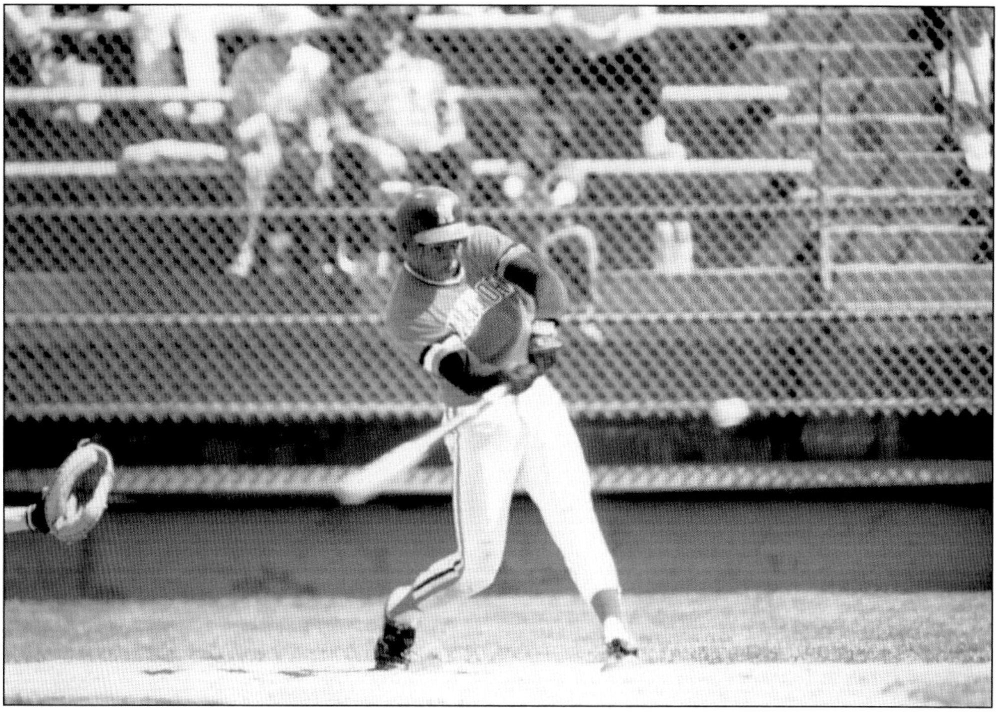

Middle Georgia all-tournament player Garey Ingram swings (*top*) and slides (against San Jac's Shan Gilder) during the 1990 JUCO World Series. Ingram played three seasons with the Los Angeles Dodgers after his collegiate career ended.

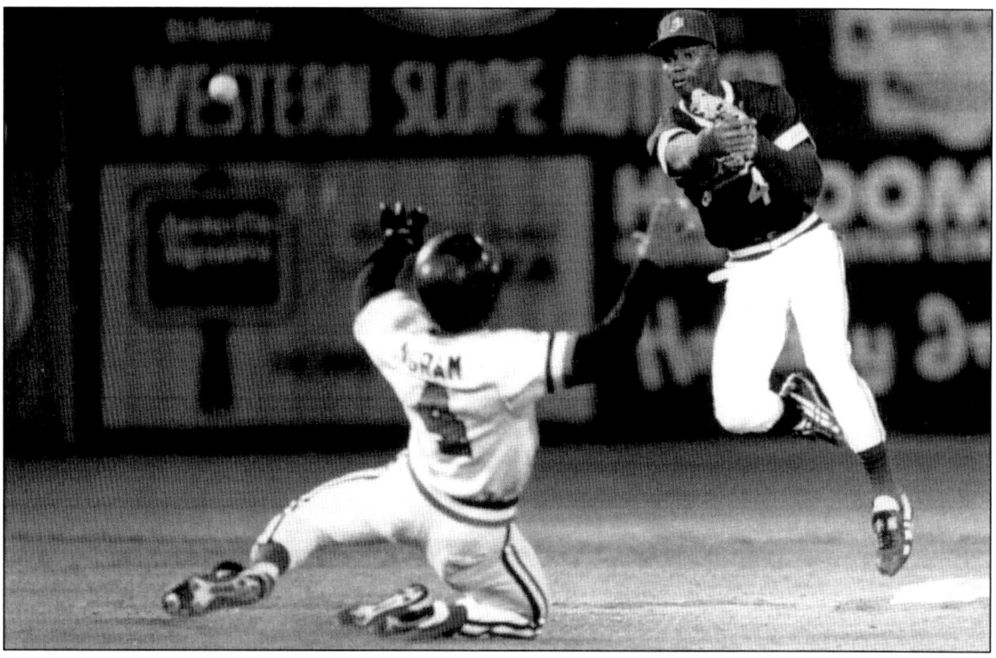

Jerry Shepherd of Middle Georgia (right) accepts the Big Stick Award from tournament co-director Walter Bergman after the 1990 JUCO World Series concludes. Shepherd batted .524 during the week. Bergman, the son of Mesa (CO) Junior College coaching great Bus Bergman, is one of several sons that have carried on the tradition started by his father of serving on the local JUCO organizing committee.

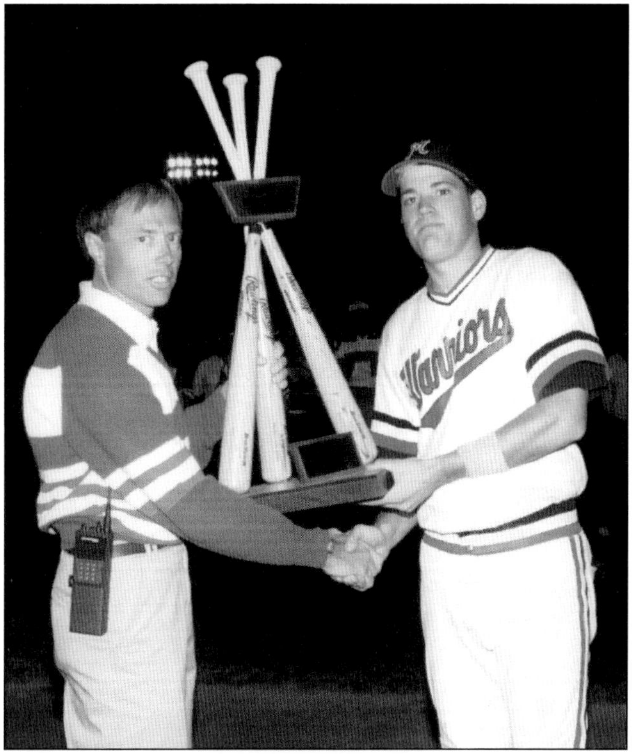

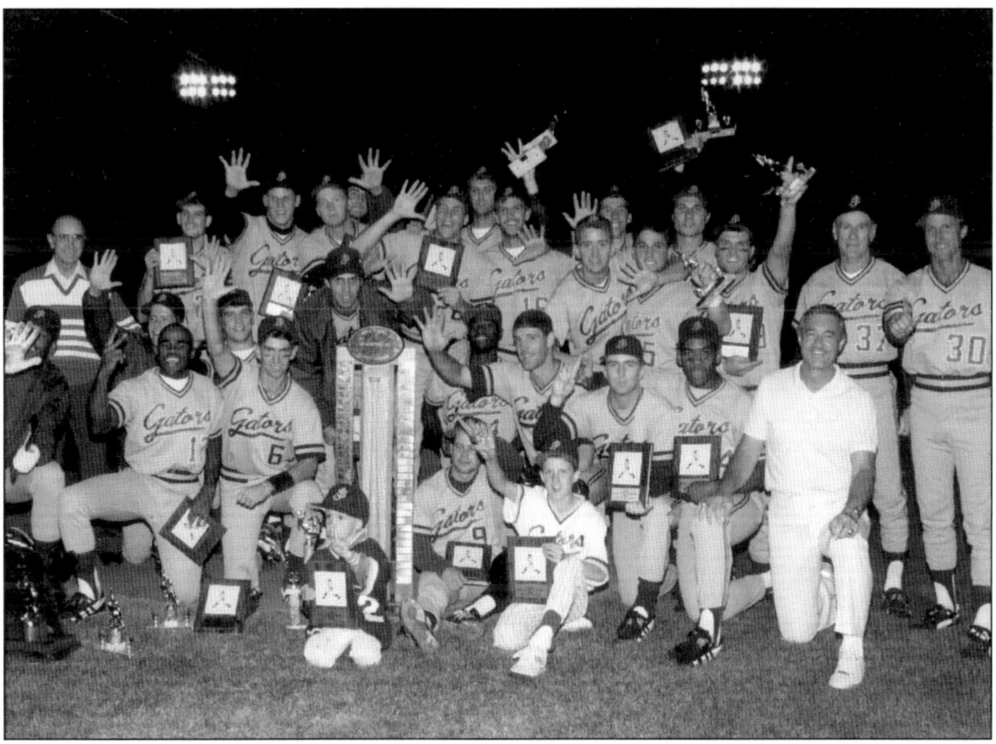

High fives! San Jacinto-North celebrates title No. 5 after beating Middle Georgia in 1990.

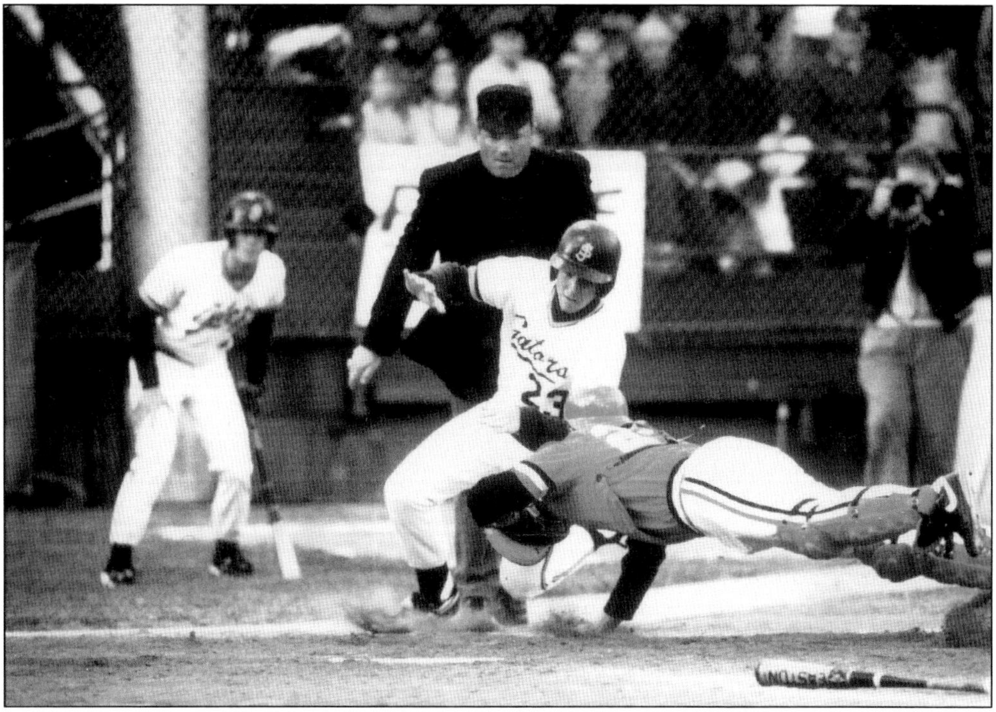

Middle Georgia catcher Greg Almond makes the tag against San Jac runner Braxton Hickman in the 1990 tournament (*above, below,* and *opposite, top*). The two powers played three times in that year's JUCO World Series. San Jac had to beat MGC twice after losing 10-7 to the Warriors earlier in the tournament. The Texans did just that, and in the process took their fifth title in six years.

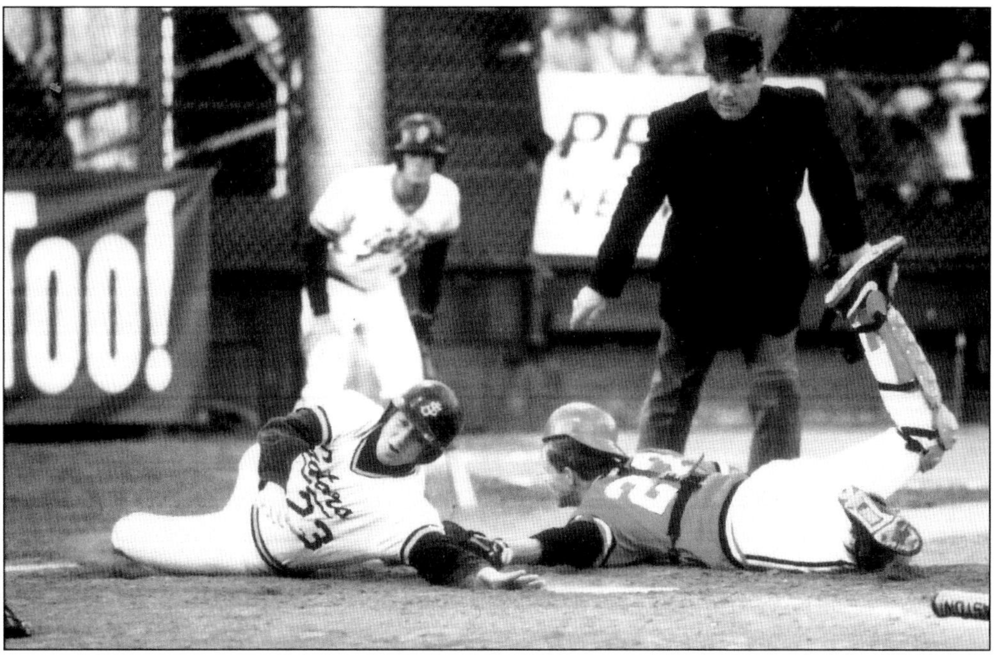

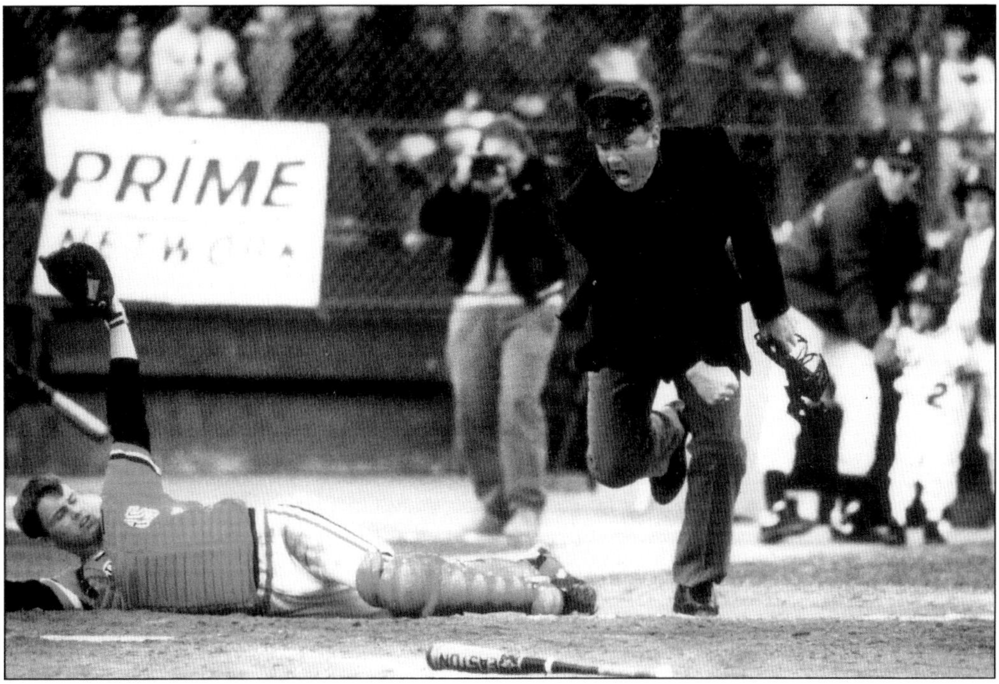


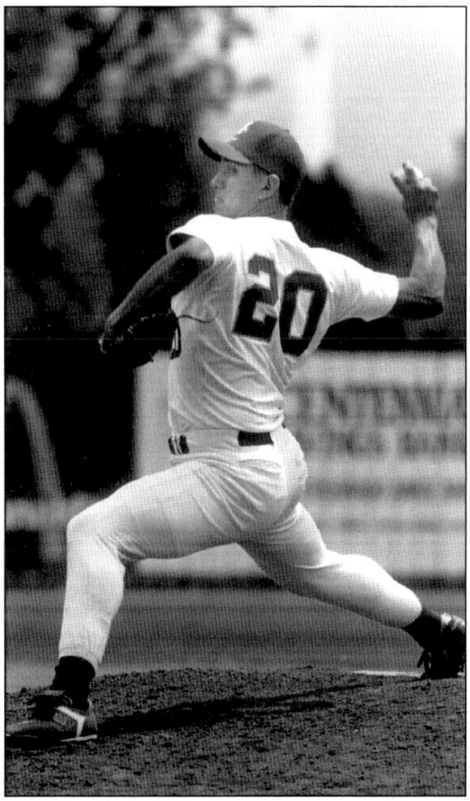

Albie Lopez aims for home plate while pitching for Mesa (AZ) Community College in 1990. The future big leaguer helped the Thunderbirds place third in only their third JUCO World Series appearance since 1973.

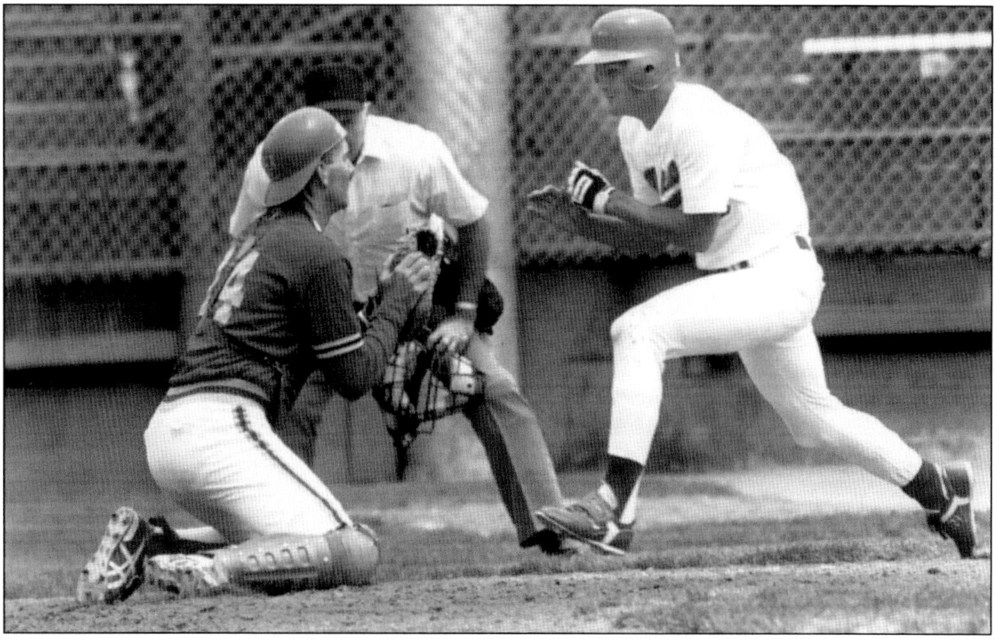

Mesa CC baserunner Shawn Gift wins this battle against Normandale (MN) catcher Jim Schutz at the 1990 JUCO World Series. Normandale qualified for the tournament five times from 1979 to 1990.

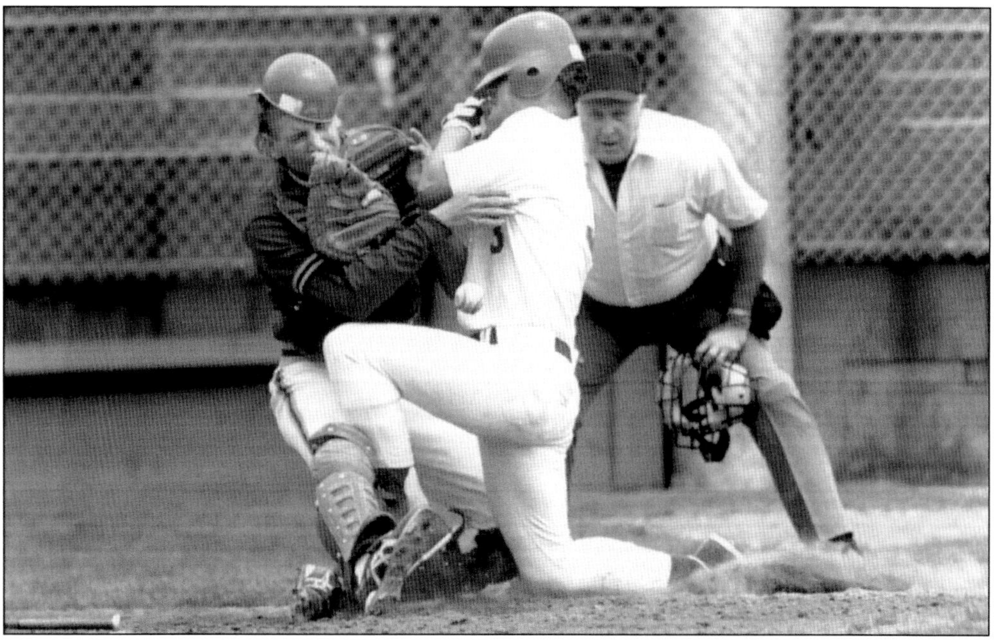

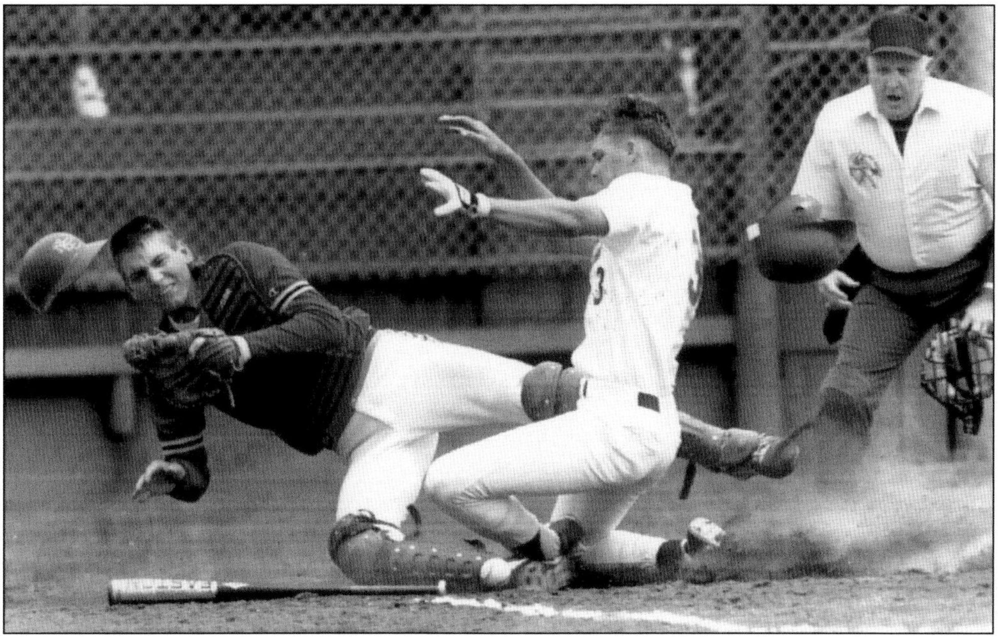

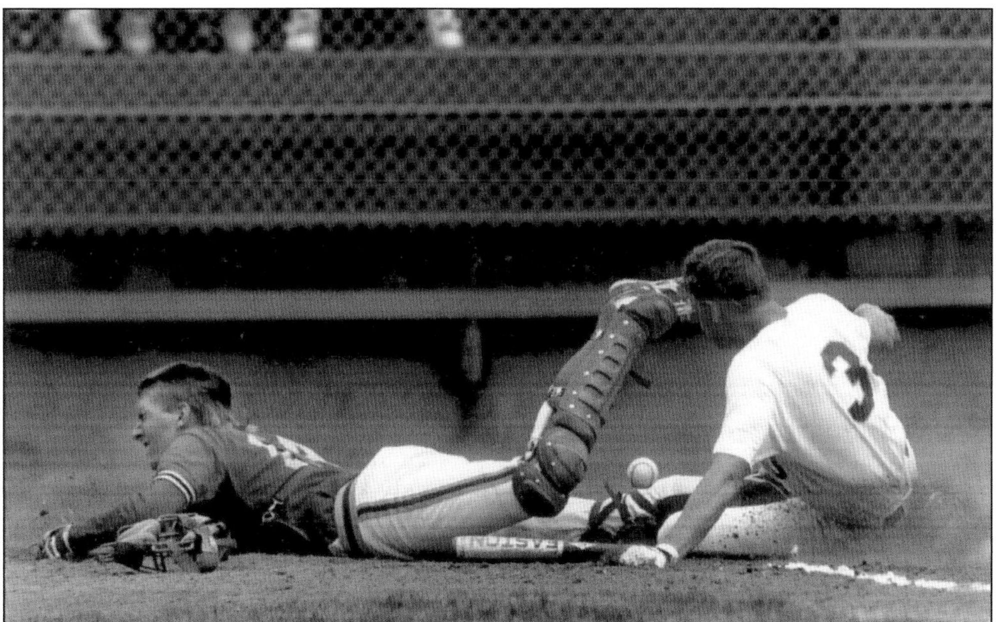

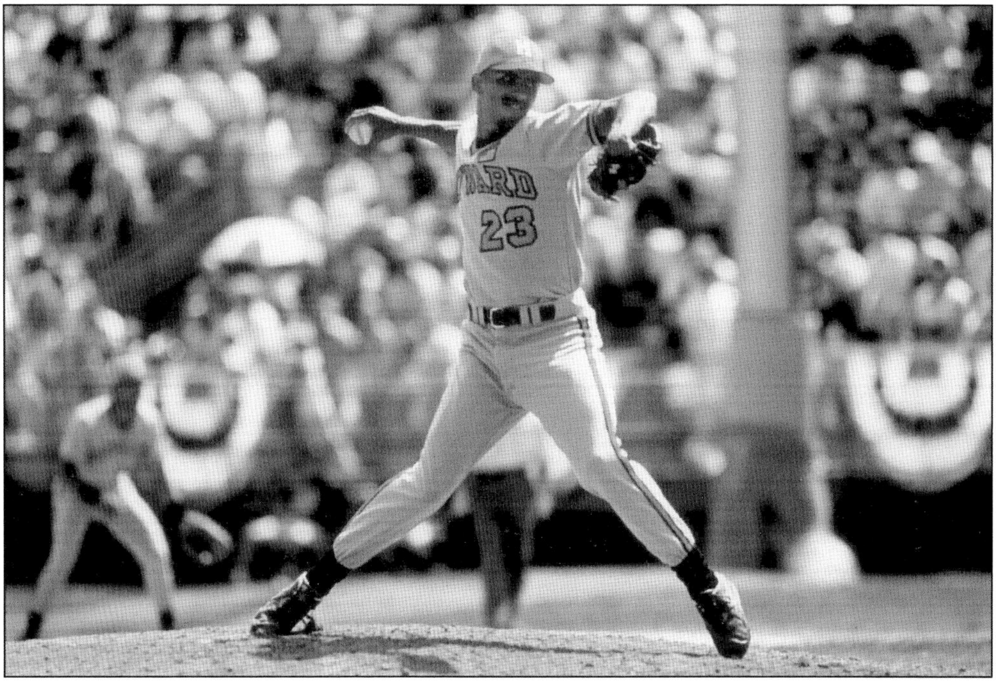


Right-hander Frank Rodriguez (*top*) and left-hander Jesse Armendariz (*bottom*) were the 1-2 punch of 1991 national champion Howard (TX) College. Both were all-tournament pitchers for the Hawks and Rodriguez was named Most Valuable Pitcher when he tied a 19-year-old JUCO World Series record held by Mesa CC's Doug Slocum with 33 tournament strikeouts. Rodriguez earned 29 wins in a seven-year big-league career.

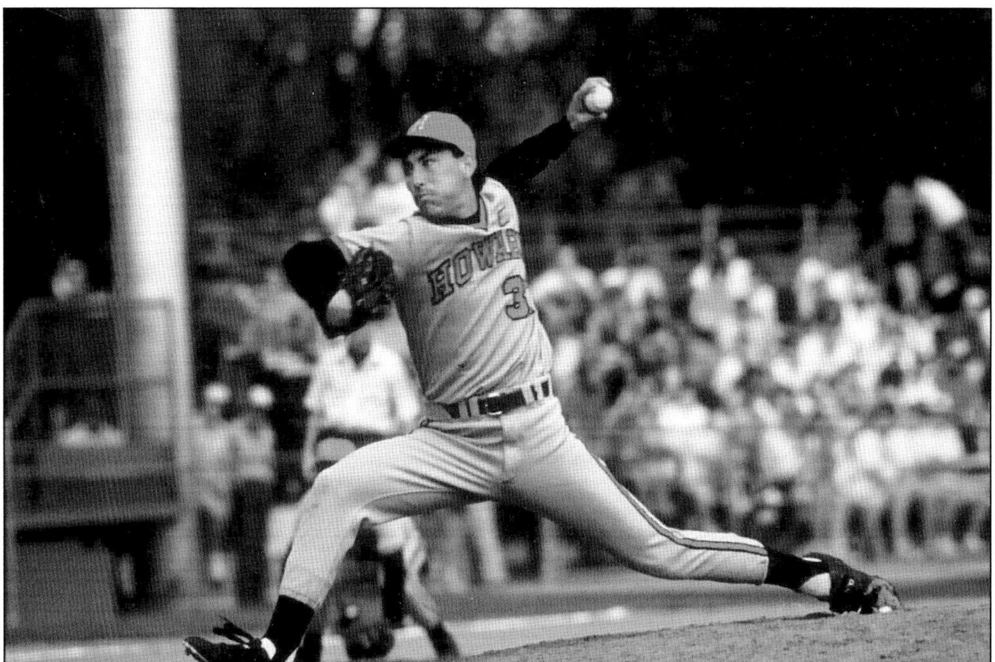

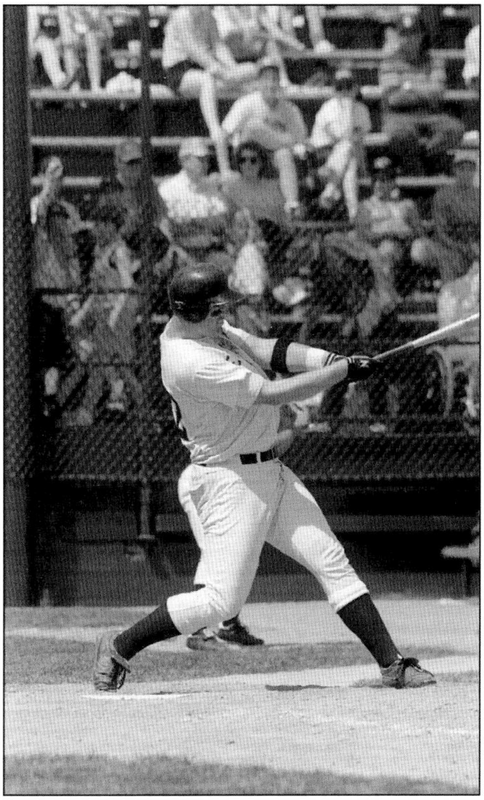 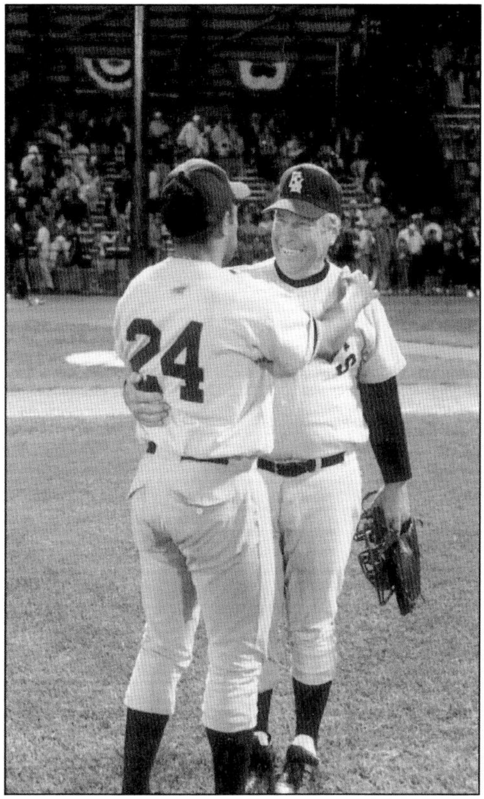

Essex Community College became the first team from Maryland to win the JUCO World Series when the Knights defeated Pima (AZ) 14-1 in the 1992 final. Essex was the first team from the east coast to take home the crown since Nassau (NY) in 1966. Essex was led by the slugging of catcher Mike Peters (*left*), who hit .360, had 11 RBIs, and hit three home runs in his first three plate appearances of the tournament. Coach George Henderson (*right*) led Essex to the championship season by compiling a scrappy squad that had fun; the Knights were the first championship team to ever win the sportsmanship award. Another highlight of the tournament was Pima third baseman "King" George Arias, who set a tournament record with three grand slams.

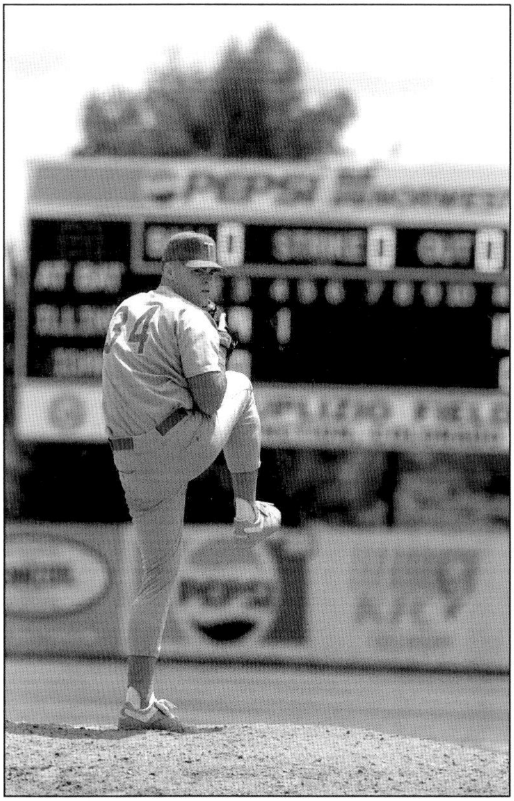

Triton (IL) pitcher Jason Ruskey looks toward home plate in the 1993 national tournament. Ruskey was a fan favorite because he had lived for seven years in Grand Junction when his father was assistant city manager in the baseball hotbed. The young Ruskey had even been a JUCO batboy. He won three games during the week and was named Most Valuable Pitcher for the tournament, but was chased after six innings in a 6-3 loss to Yavapai (AZ) in the final.

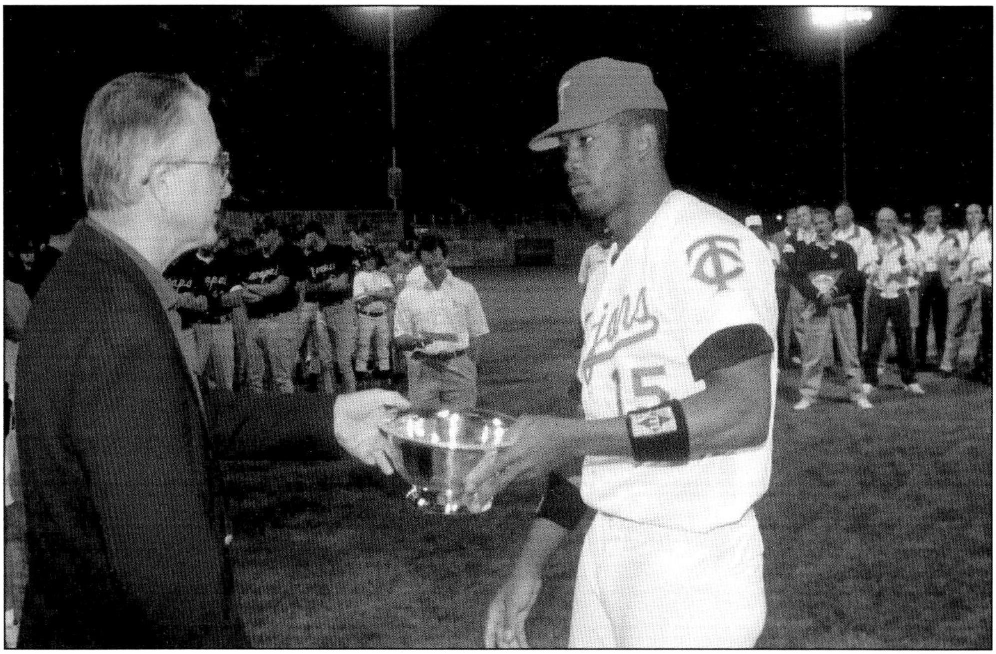

Most Valuable Player Kevin Pitts of Triton (IL) won the Best Defensive Player award for his glove work at first base, and hit .461 with five homers, 11 RBIs, and 12 hits, but Yavapai proved too much for the Trojans.

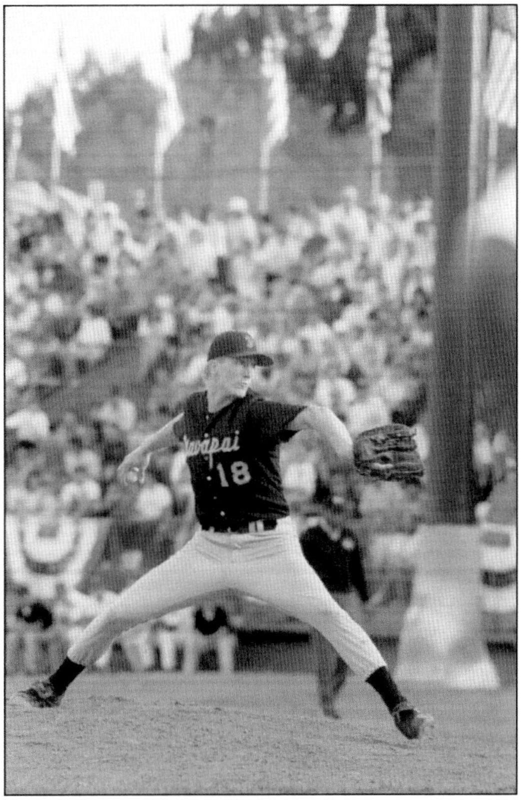

The 1993 national champion Yavapai Roughriders placed just three players on the all-tournament team: outfielder Gus Kennedy, catcher Travis McClendon, and pitcher Bob Lowry.

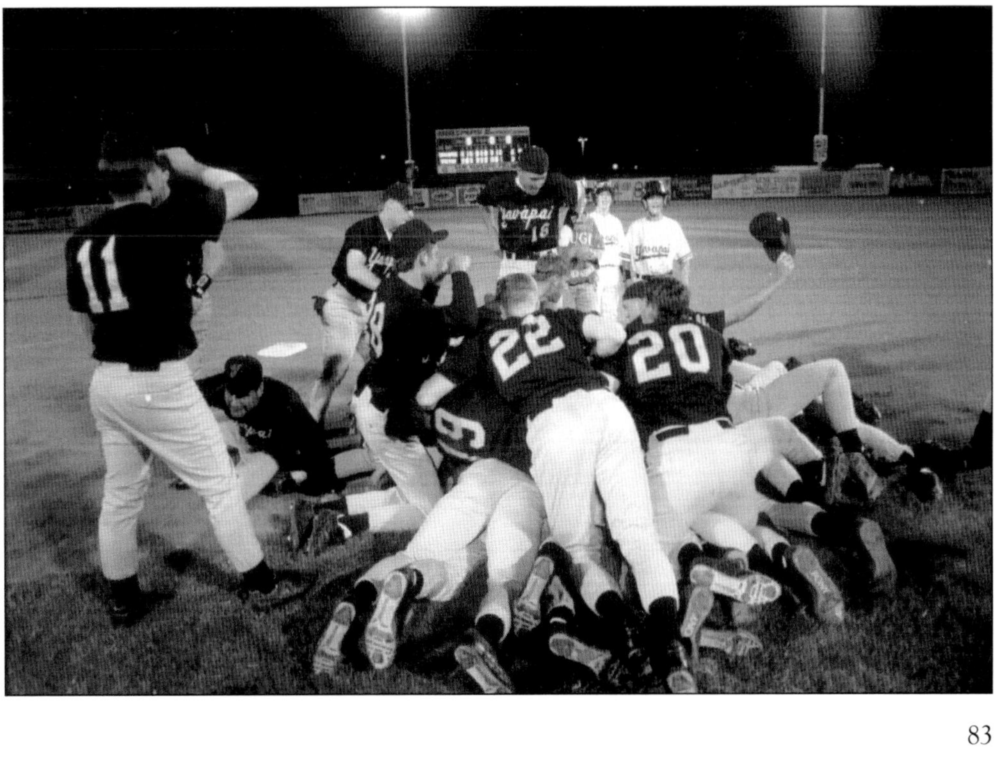

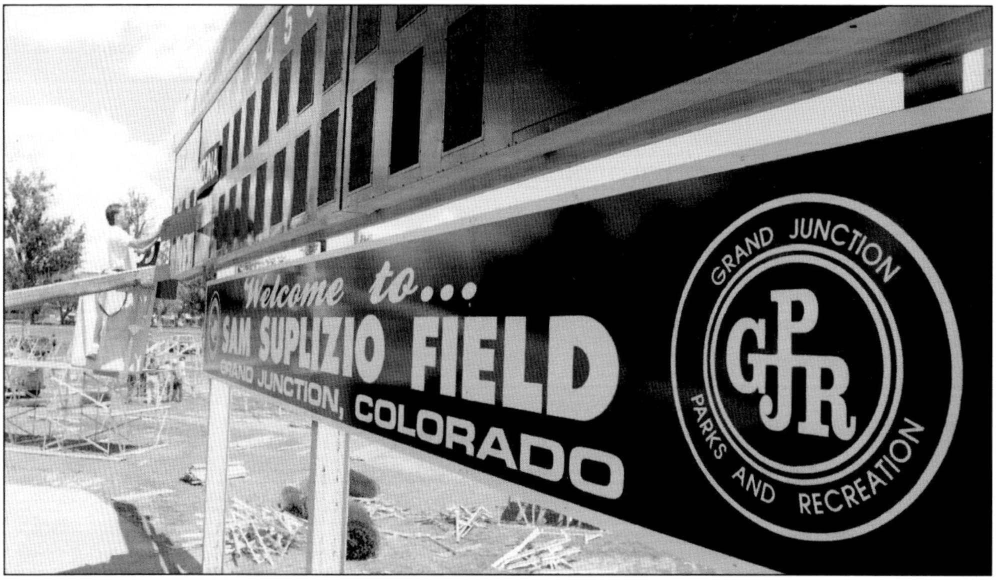

A new computerized scoreboard went up for the 1993 JUCO World Series. Note in the background that other workers are setting up the new permanent metal bleachers that were added beyond the left-field fence that year. The extra seating, as well as a solid performance by former Grand Junction resident Jason Ruskey of Triton, helped the tournament set a new attendance record of 119,380 for the 19-game event.

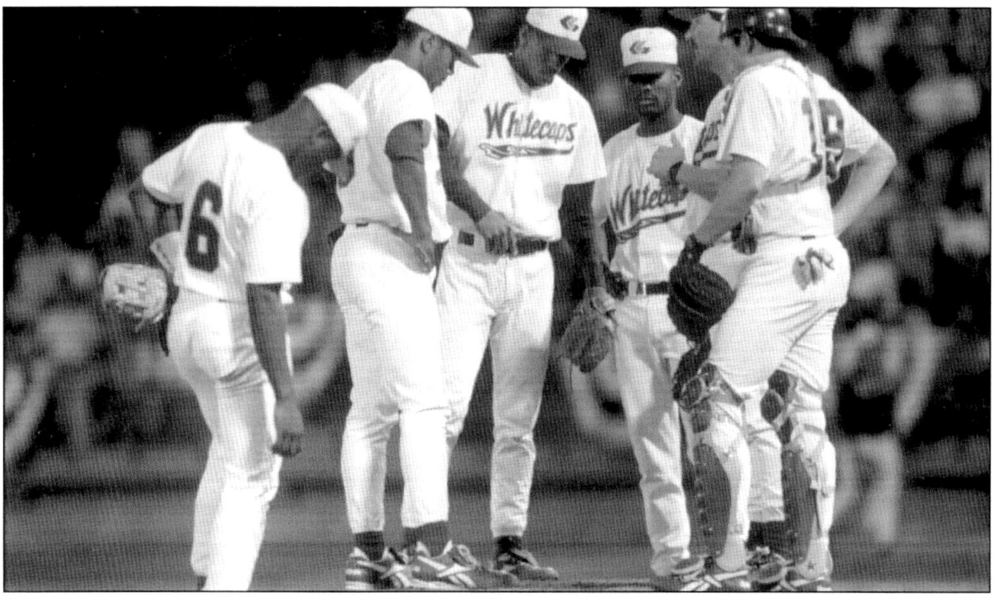

Galveston (TX) College players and coach Dick Smith talk over the situation at the mound during their 1994 championship run. The Whitecaps, whose baseball program only began in the early 1990s, managed to fight off Triton's ninth-inning rally and hang on for a 10-9 championship game victory. The Whitecaps pounded out 98 hits to break the old mark of 89 set by Panola (TX) in 1979. Pitcher/outfielder Jose Rosado earned the Most Valuable Player award by pitching out of a bases-loaded jam in the ninth inning of the finale and batting .500 for the tournament. Rosado won 37 big-league games in five seasons with the Kansas City Royals.

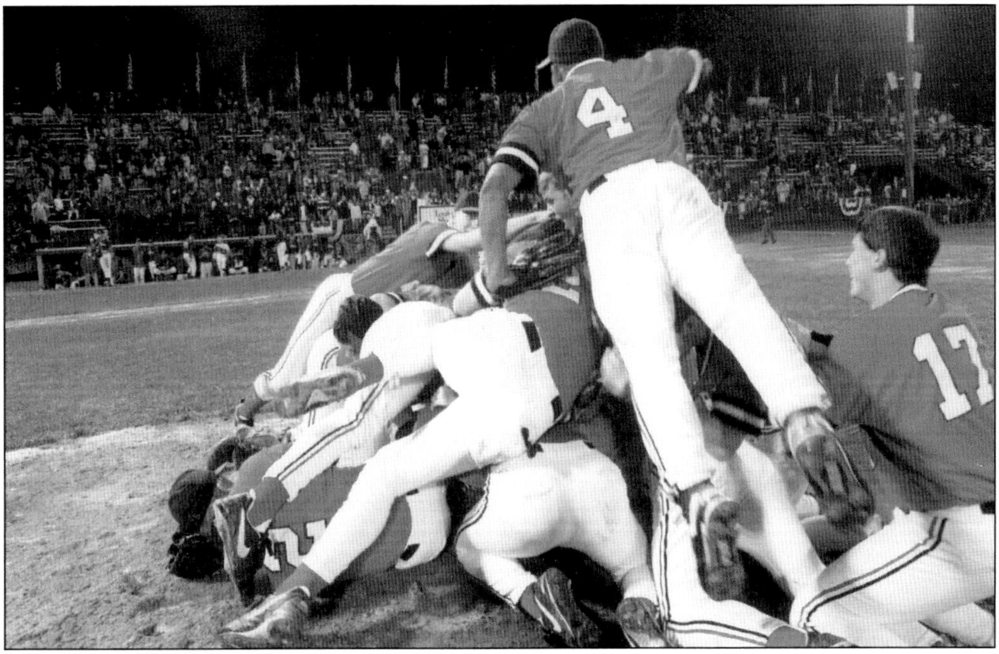

In 1995, a year that veteran coach Robert Sapp was inducted into the JUCO Hall of Fame to start the tournament, Middle Georgia College knew how to celebrate in style. Although the Warriors lost their opener 6-5 Allegany (MD) on the heels of the pre-tournament banquet, they recovered to take their first title since 1982. Brian Davis earned Most Valuable Player honors with a .481 batting average, seven RBIs, a complete-game victory, and two championship-game homers against Indian River (FL). A new attendance record was set of 120,320 fans.

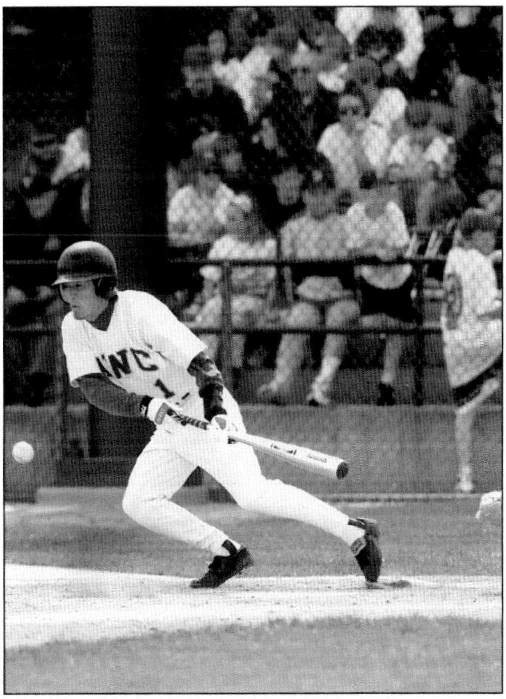

Arizona Western's Ryo Higuchi lays down a bunt during the 1996 JUCO World Series. The Fukuoka, Japan, native was one of three Japanese players joining a roster made up primarily of Arizona players that year for the Yuma-based school. The Matadors placed third in their only Grand Junction appearance.

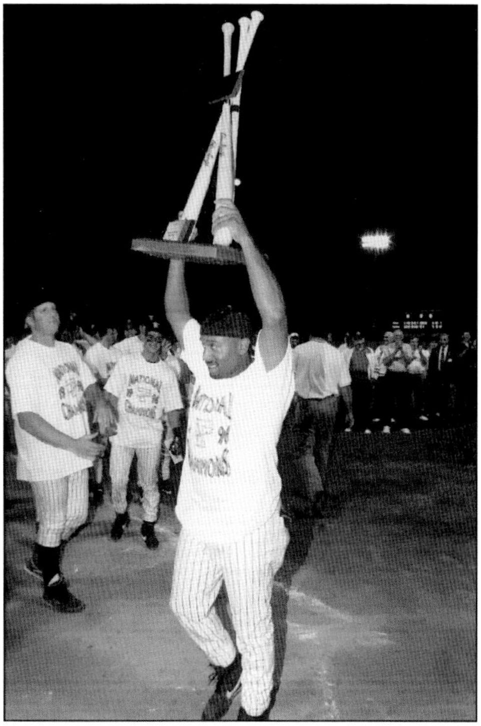

Robert Vaz lifts the Big Stick Award after Northeast Texas Community College earned the 1996 JUCO title in the Eagles' only time to qualify for the tournament. Northeast Texas nipped Meridian (MS) 4-3 in the title game. Vaz took home a lot of hardware all by himself. The outfielder won the sportsmanship award and MVP award in addition to the Big Stick Award.

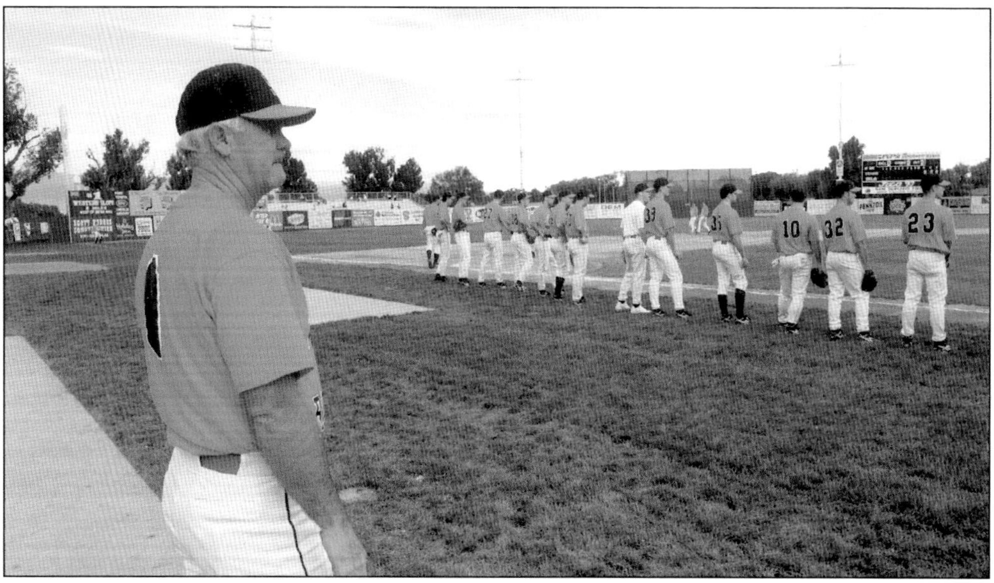


Seminole (OK) coaching legend Lloyd Simmons surveys his squad prior to a 1997 JUCO World Series game against San Jacinto-North (TX). The school had a name change prior to this tournament, becoming Seminole State College, but the presence of Simmons was a constant. The Trojans met San Jac three times in the 1997 national tournament, winning two of them (including a 17-4 semifinal drubbing), but upstart Cowley County (KS) defeated Seminole 4-2 in the final—the second consecutive year that a first-time JUCO participant won the tournament. This was Simmons' 11th JUCO qualifying team. He would manage two more trips to Grand Junction, the latest in 2000, before retiring.

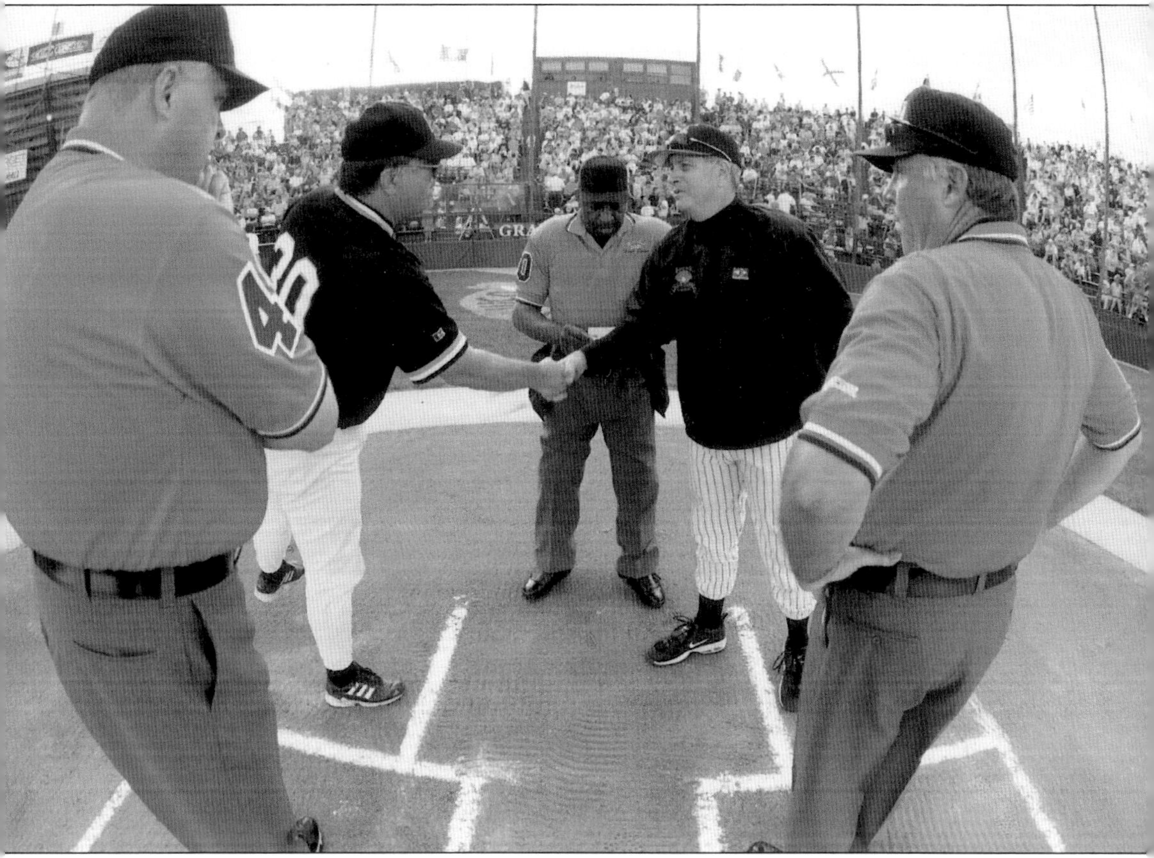

As the umpires look on, Cowley County coach Dave Burroughs (left) shakes hands with Wallace State (AL) coach Randy Putman prior to Cowley's 12-8 elimination-game victory over the Lions in 1997. The Arkansas City, Kansas-based school surprised veteran observers of the tournament with not one, but two titles, in 1997 and 1998, becoming only the fifth repeat champion at the JUCO World Series. The first championship in 1997 was keyed by Most Valuable Player and future major-leaguer Travis Hafner's three-run homer in a 4-2 victory in the final over Seminole. The second championship in 1998 required Cowley to outslug San Jacinto 15-11 in a game that saw five lead changes. Josh McMillen won the MVP with a .941 slugging percentage, while teammate Aaron Robbins took home the Big Stick Award with a .556 batting average and 10 RBIs. The victories were especially sweet for Burroughs, a former Kansas City Royals draft choice who has toiled at Cowley since 1988. "Last year we came in and nobody knew nothin' about us," the Ketchum, Oklahoma, native said immediately after the second title. "This year people pointed at us all year long. This was tough. I'm emotionally spent right now. I'm not a crying person, but I was over there crying a minute ago."

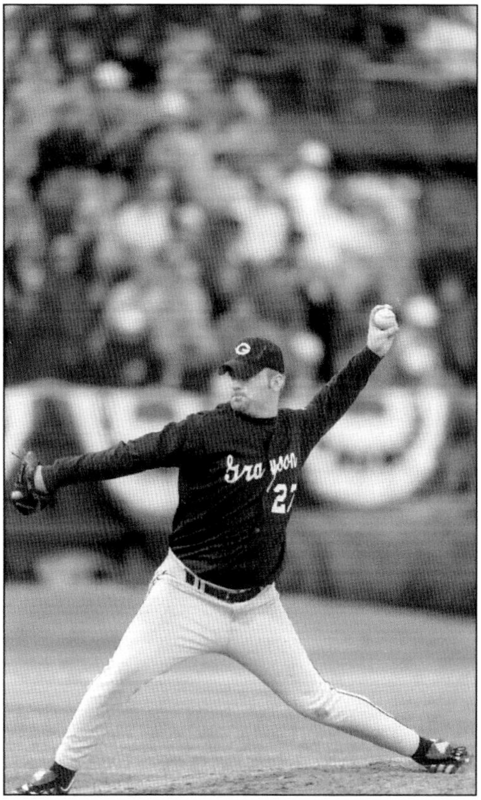

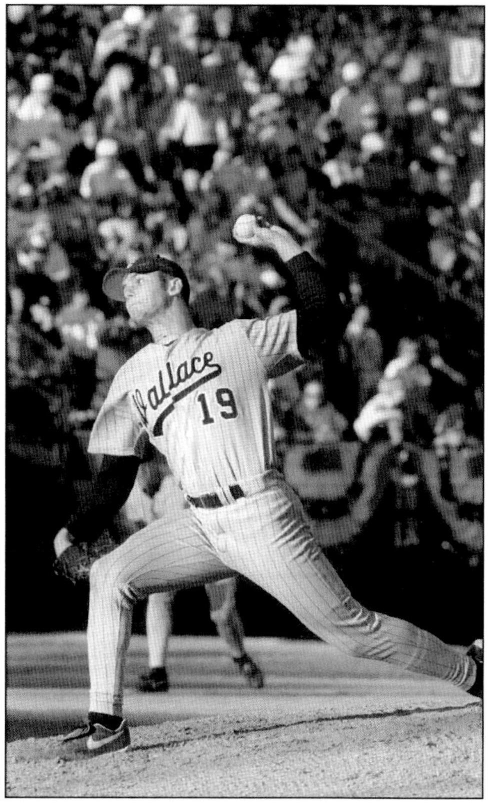


Matt Gawer of Grayson County (TX) College (*left*) and Mark Carter of Wallace (AL) State Community College were key figures for their respective teams at the 1999 JUCO World Series. Gawer defeated San Jacinto-North twice, including 12-7 in the championship game, and earned Most Valuable Player honors. Carter was an all-tournament pick for the Lions. The oddity of two Texas teams making it to the championship game occurred because of redistricting that took place prior to the 1998 national tournament. Texas junior colleges were split into two different districts rather than vying for a single spot for the state. It was an interesting match-up for another reason as well. While San Jac is JUCO's most storied program, the Denison-based Grayson just reinstated baseball in 1997 for the first time since 1977.

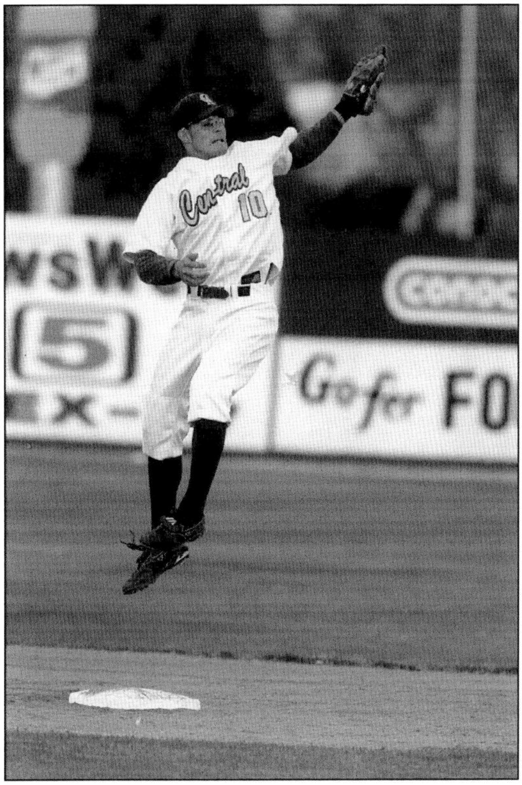

Central Arizona shortstop Joe Reyes leaps to make a play at second base during the 1999 JUCO World Series. Reyes and his half-brother Justin Davis both qualified for the tournament that year, albeit for different teams. Davis played for the national champion Grayson County squad. Both players are from Farmington, N.M., home of the Connie Mack World Series since 1965, and both had played for the host team there prior to entering college.

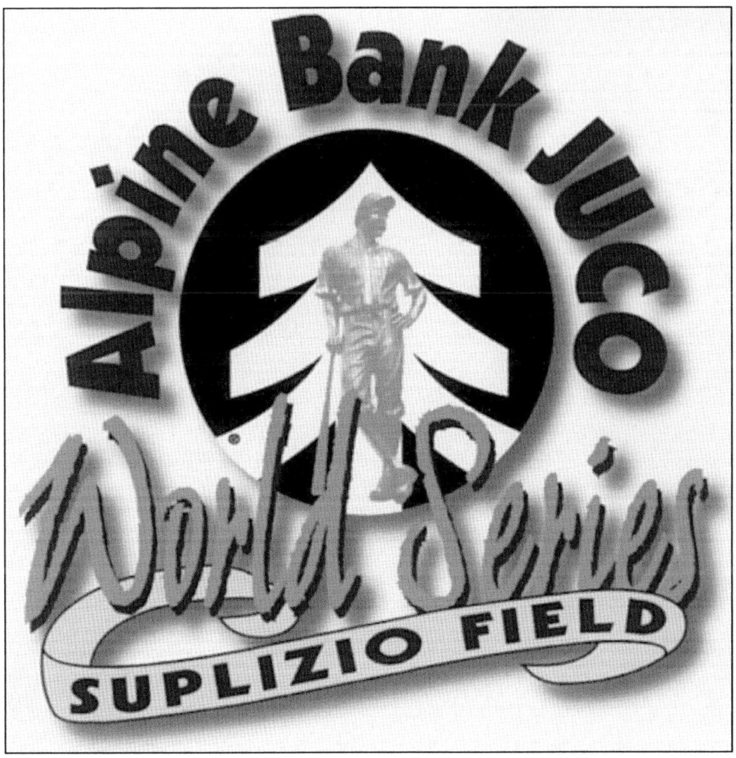


Alpine Bank became corporate sponsor of the JUCO World Series in 1999, ushering in a new era for the tournament. Alpine Bank is a 10-story building in downtown Grand Junction, by far the highest in the city. From the southwest-facing sixth-floor JUCO committee office, a person can peer west toward the picturesque Colorado National Monument. Sam Suplizio Field is just a few blocks to the northeast.

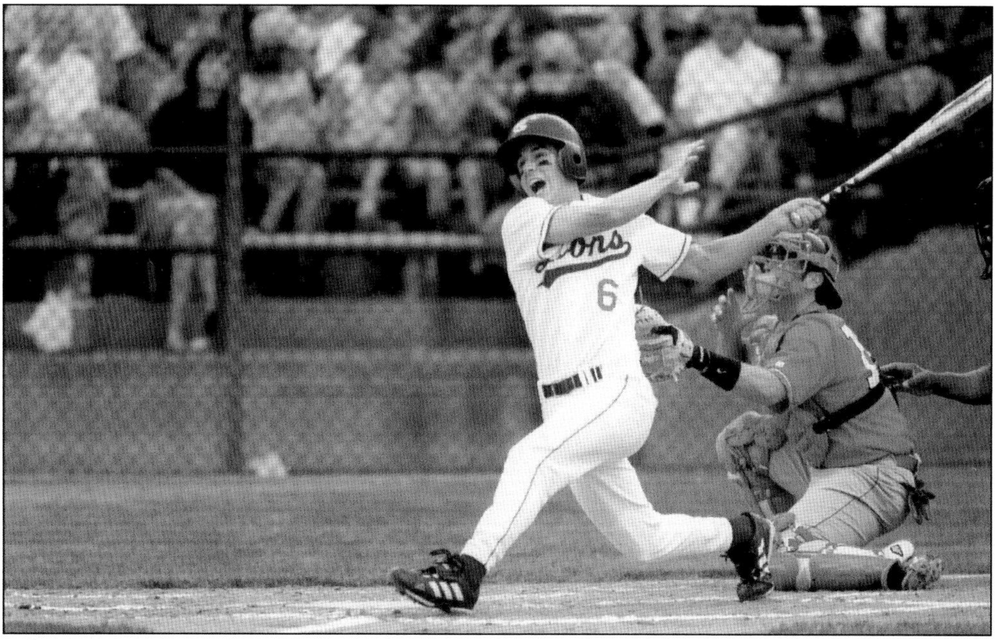

All-tournament performer Craig Stansbury hits the ball deep during North Central Texas' 2001 championship run. Blake Justice was the Lions' key performer. The 5-foot-8, 150-pounder hit .368 for the week and helped North Central Texas turn eight double plays on his way to the MVP award.

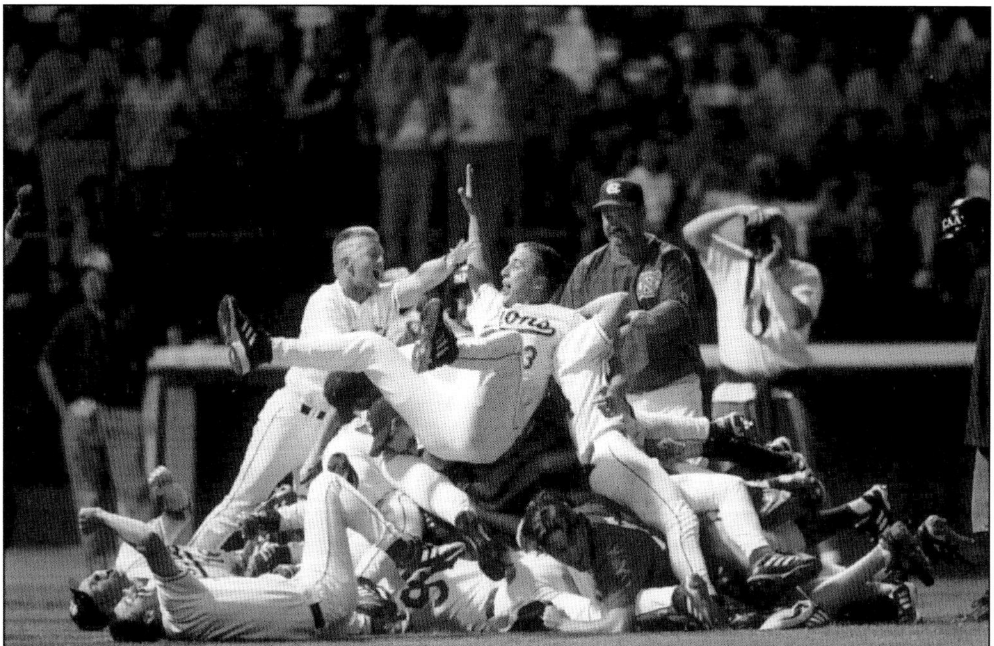

North Central Texas celebrates its national championship in 2001. The Gainesville-based school became the ninth distinct Texas junior college to win a JUCO title, and overall the Lone Star State has won 16 of the 46 championships. That's four ahead of runner-up Arizona's 12 total titles.

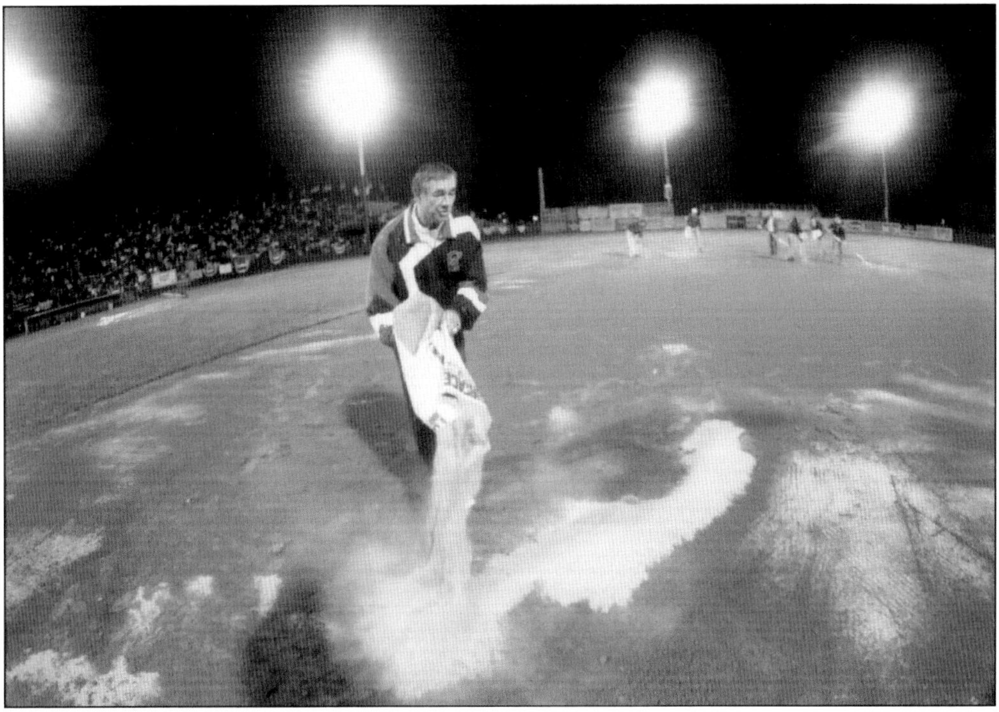

Sam Suplizio, shown here trying to dry out the infield during the 1995 tournament (*top*), was always a hands-on chairman, but he handed his leadership position to Jamie Hamilton (*bottom, right*) prior to the 2003 JUCO World Series. Hamilton now is in charge of making sure the 46-year-old tournament moves smoothly into its second half century.

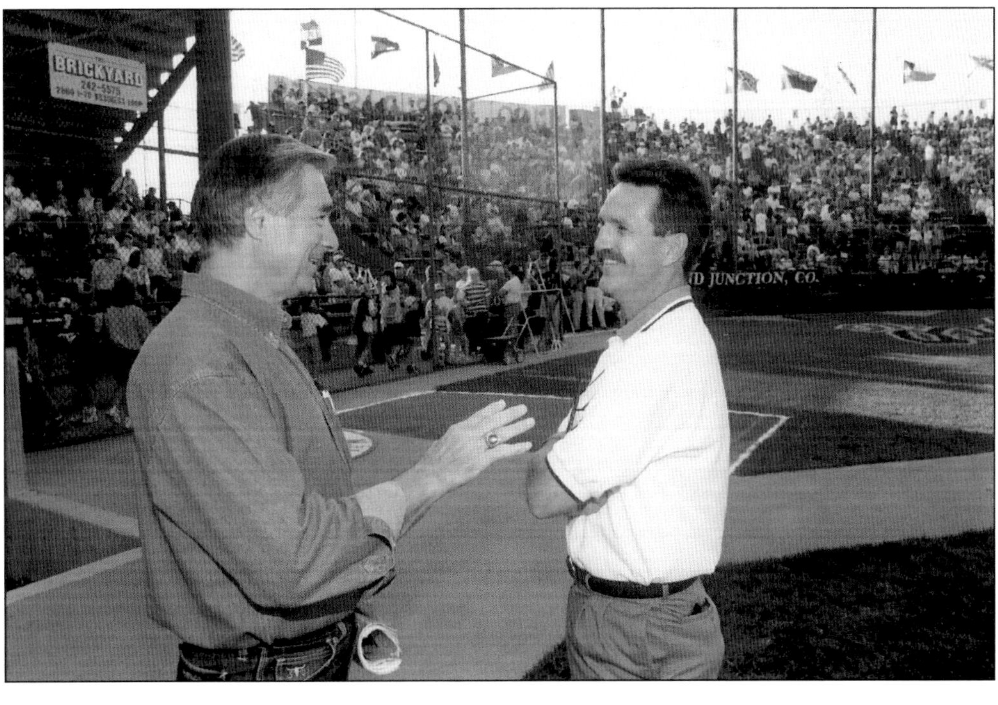

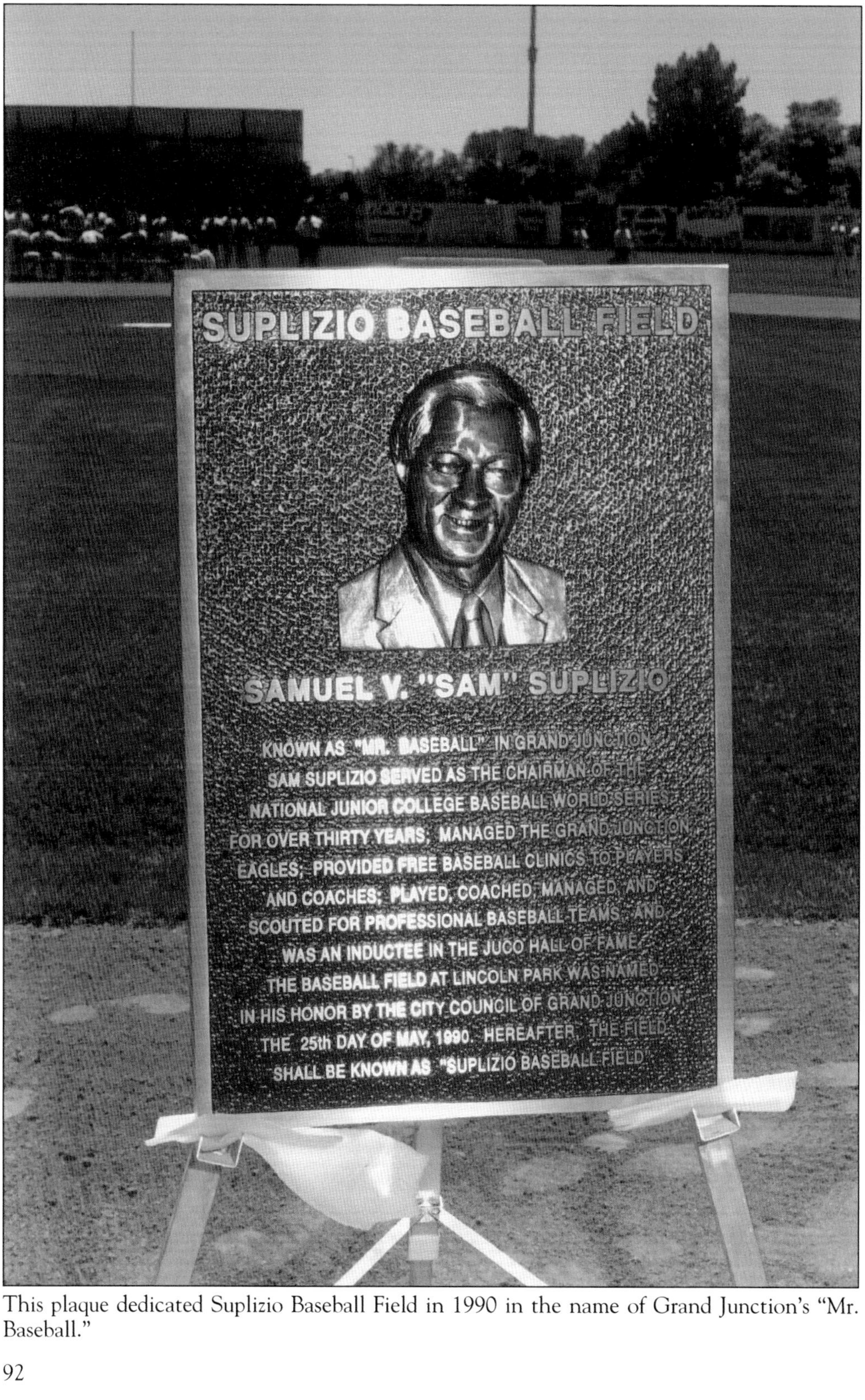


This plaque dedicated Suplizio Baseball Field in 1990 in the name of Grand Junction's "Mr. Baseball."

# Six

# *Prestigious Guests*

Lefty Gomez visited the national tournament numerous times over the years. Four times he was the banquet speaker; other years he came as a representative of Wilson Sporting Goods. Considering his introduction to Grand Junction, the city was lucky the former New York Yankees pitching star had a sense of humor and thick skin rather than a large ego.

As tournament chairman emeritus Sam Suplizio, the key contact for virtually all of the all-star list of major leaguers over the years, tells it, Gomez was to throw out the ceremonial first pitch during his first trip to Grand Junction. Suplizio gave him the ball and told him to wait for the public address announcer to call his name. The announcer inadvertently forgot to do so, the home team took the field, and the game began. During the third inning, Gomez found Suplizio and, pointing to the baseball, asked, "What am I supposed to do with this, eat it? I don't mind not starting a baseball game, but the only one who ever kept me from starting was (Yankee manager) Joe McCarthy, not Sam Suplizio."

The next year, Gomez returned to the tournament and again was asked to throw out the first pitch. Gomez obliged, but he had a trick up his sleeve. Suplizio gave him the baseball, a Rawlings model donated by the sporting goods company. When Gomez got out to the mound, he yelled out: "Who do I work for?" The Wilson-employed Gomez proceeded to take out a pen, scribble out Rawlings, and write in Wilson in its place. Then he threw the ceremonial pitch. The story made it as a blurb in next day's newspaper, and his publicity coup—not to mention revenge—was complete.

Gomez was a significant figure in the early years of the tournament because he was a consistent presence from professional ball. He became a sort of ambassador for Grand Junction to the larger baseball world. "He was the first big-name speaker we ever had at the banquet," Suplizio said, "and his presence helped pave the way for others of his caliber to come to Grand Junction." Gomez is far from the only big name now. The list of tournament guests and banquet speakers is about as talented a list of players and managers from the last half century that one could compile. The local organizing committee recognized early on that the banquet tradition was a good way to convince people there was something special going on in Grand Junction.

Other celebrities and former ballplayers occasionally visit the JUCO World Series, but it is the banquet that kicks off the week in style. It is held at a time when anticipation has been building since the district tournaments decided the qualifying teams. Those players and coaches have only been in town for a short while, and the local civic clubs that serve as their hosts are still getting to know the visitors. Meanwhile, fans can mingle and take a look at the diamond stars for the week ahead and get primed for the tournament experience. Recently, fans and participants can see display cases in the lobby of the current banquet venue, the Two Rivers Convention Center (named for the Gunnison and Colorado rivers that join south of town), that highlight the JUCO World Series' history. It is another means to appreciate the memories while preparing for the anticipated entertainment ahead.

University of Utah football coach Jack Curtis was the first banquet speaker in 1959, when Bookcliff Country Club held the event. A group of major league scouts made a presentation in 1960, and baseball connections have been in place ever since. There were big names in the early years—Stan Musial in 1964, Lefty Gomez first was a featured speaker in 1965, and Duke

Snider in 1967—but the roster has only strengthened over the years thanks to Sam Suplizio's deep baseball roots. Of all the roles Suplizio has played in the JUCO World Series' illustrious past, his big-league connections that have helped bring in such outstanding banquet guests is one of the most taken for granted. It has become perfectly natural to expect all-time greats: Willie Mays, Tommy Lasorda, Bob Gibson, Joe Torre—and because of Suplizio's sweet-talking, they don't even charge a fee. Controversial George Steinbrenner even donated $25,000 to the NJCAA when he spoke in 1990.

The event moved to the new Mesa Junior CollegeStudent Center later in the 1960s, then for a time to the Ramada Inn Convention Center, and ultimately to the Two Rivers Convention Center downtown, which has seating for 1,200 people. The first time the event sold out was for Steinbrenner's speech in 1990. Tickets are now sold out each year in advance and cost $35.

Frank Torre, who was inducted into the JUCO Hall of Fame in 1991, became a sort of successor to Gomez. He attended ten national tournaments during the 1970s and 1980s, though he wasn't the banquet speaker until 1986. "So many people had told me about the nice people in Grand Junction, and of course George (NJCAA director Killian) and Sam (Suplizio) convinced me that I should be in Grand Junction watching a great baseball tournament," Torre said in the official program that year. "When I did attend my first tournament, it was everything they said it would be. People are great, many fans attend the games, and it is just a super community effort."

Those sentiments are shared by many banquet speakers and other prestigious guests that visit Grand Junction, and it creates a relationship that helps project a first-class image to a tournament that, for much of its life, has been held in a time zone without a major league baseball team. By definition, the JUCO World Series is not professional. But the tradition of bringing in pro players, managers, and officials gives the opening of the weeklong tournament an annual boost.

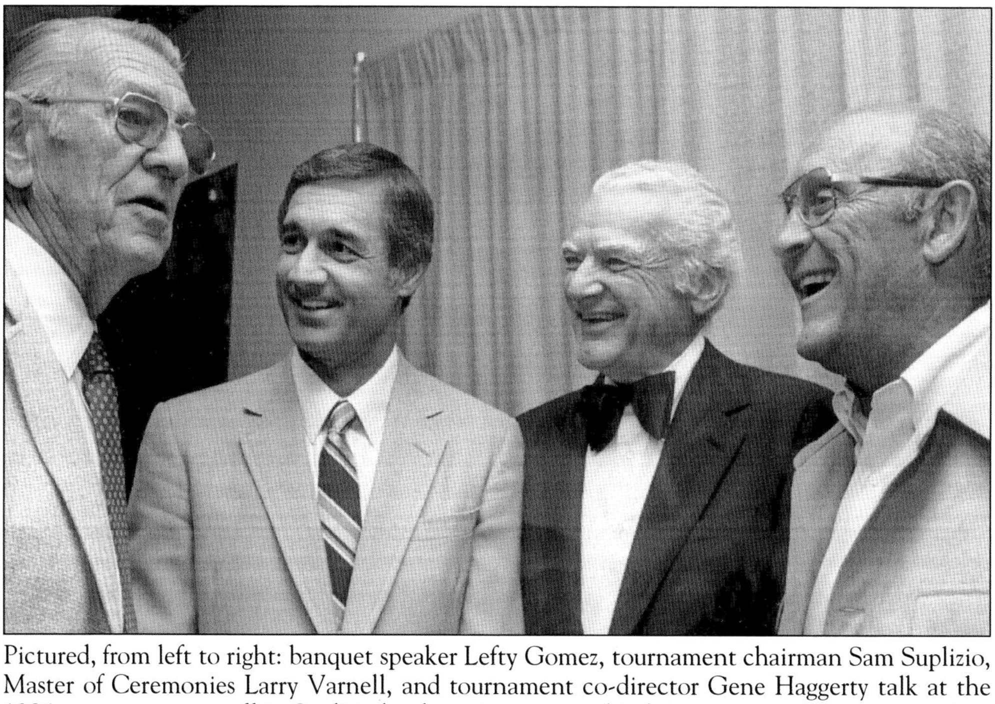

Pictured, from left to right: banquet speaker Lefty Gomez, tournament chairman Sam Suplizio, Master of Ceremonies Larry Varnell, and tournament co-director Gene Haggerty talk at the 1984 pre-tournament affair. Suplizio has been instrumental in bringing many big-name speakers to Grand Junction, while Gomez was a frequent visitor in the early years and a four-time banquet speaker. Varnell has come from Denver numerous times to MC the banquet.

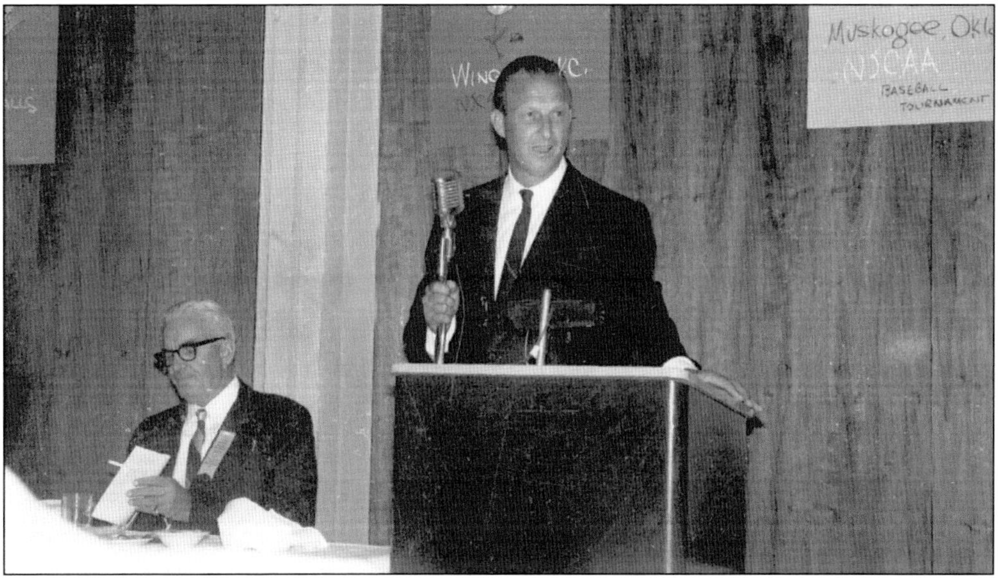


St. Louis Cardinal Hall of Famer Stan Musial addresses the audience at the 1964 JUCO banquet in front of team banners.

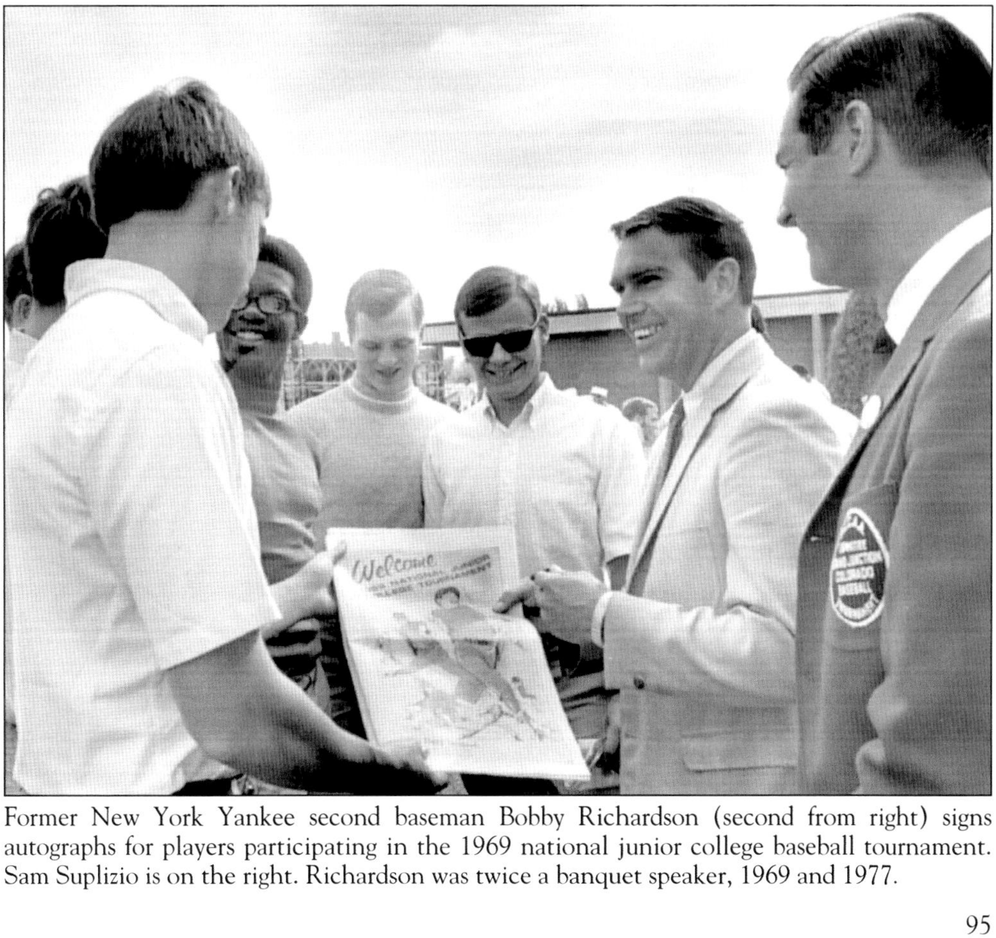


Former New York Yankee second baseman Bobby Richardson (second from right) signs autographs for players participating in the 1969 national junior college baseball tournament. Sam Suplizio is on the right. Richardson was twice a banquet speaker, 1969 and 1977.

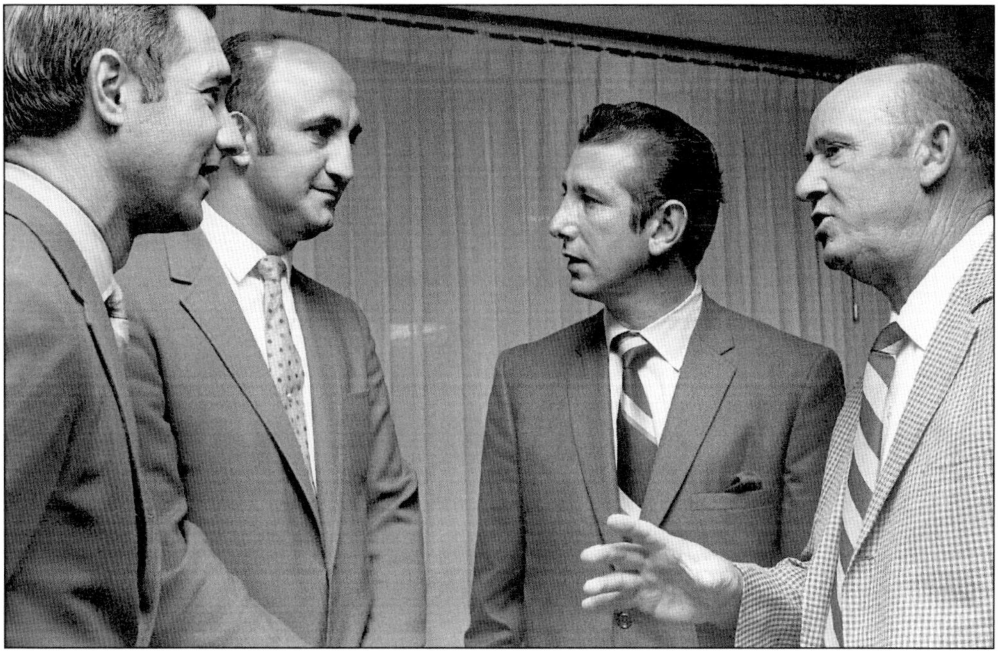

Four veteran baseball men, from left to right, Sam Suplizio, Frank Torre, Billy Martin, and Joe Gordon talk at the national junior college baseball pre-tournament banquet. Martin was the banquet speaker in 1970, and Torre was a frequent visitor to Grand Junction in the 1970s and 1980s.

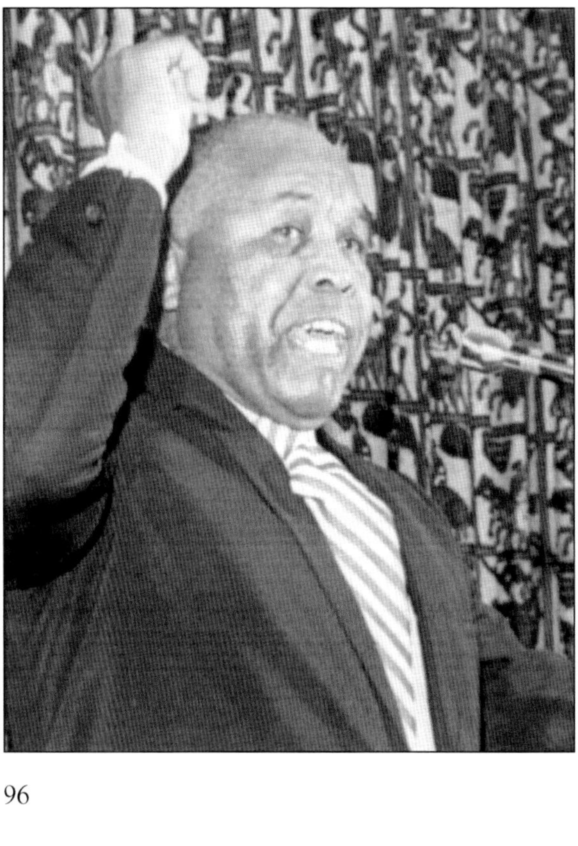

Former American League umpire Emmett Ashford was the 1971 banquet speaker. He was the second umpire to perform the duties. Jocko Conlan, who was elected to the Baseball Hall of Fame by the veterans committee in 1974, addressed the audience in 1963.

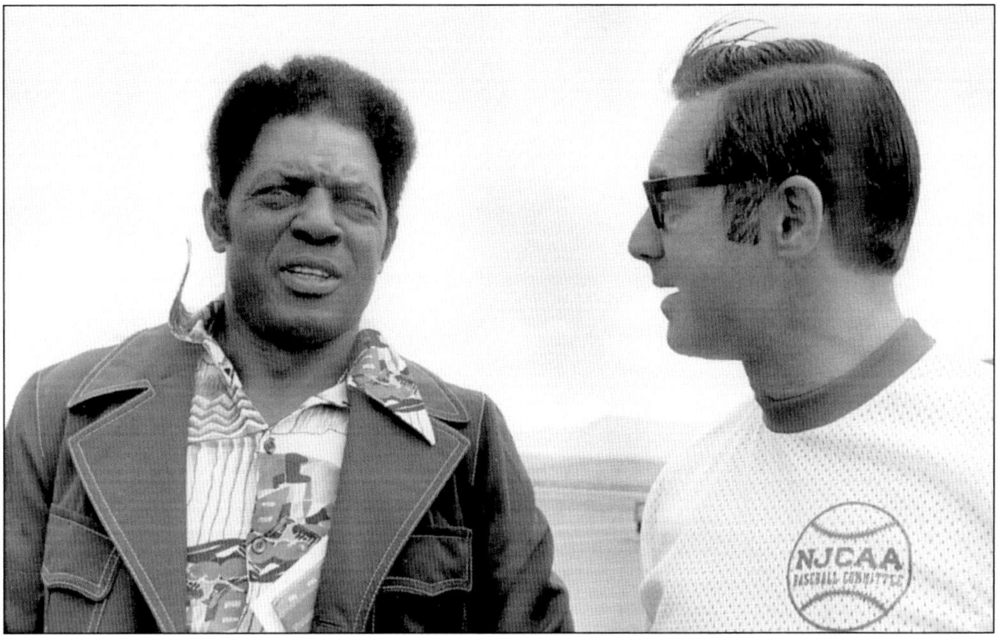


Willie Mays was the banquet speaker in 1975, and to accommodate the increased demand he spoke at two different venues. Here, he talks to tournament chairman Sam Suplizio. Being able to get some of the greatest ballplayers ever, including the likes of "The Say Hey Kid," has given the tournament prestige over the years.

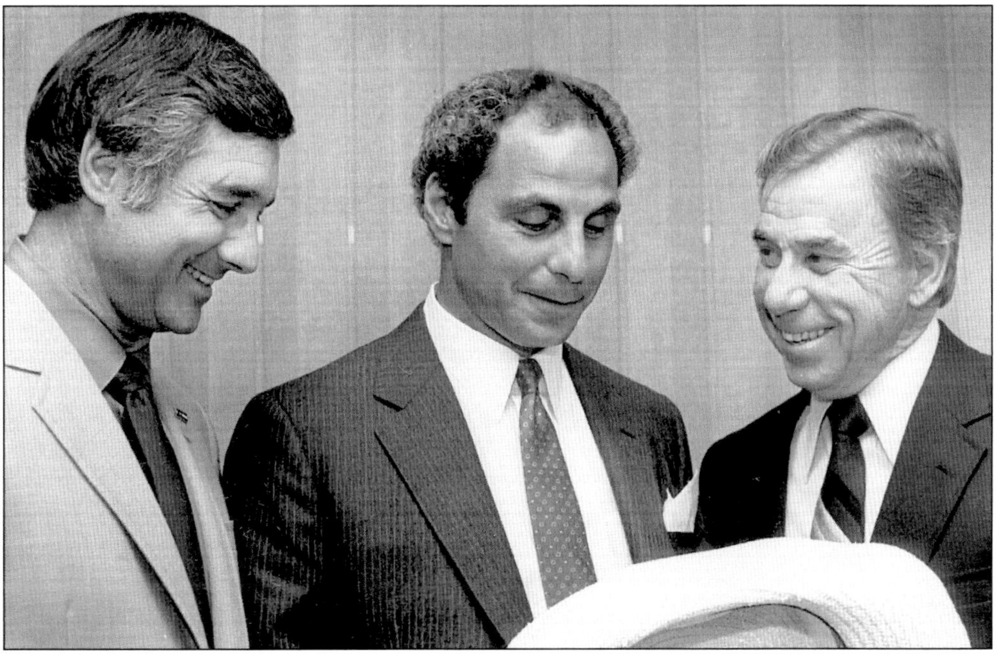

Banquet speaker Sal Bando (center) and former Brooklyn Dodgers shortstop Pee Wee Reese (right) experience western hospitality from Sam Suplizio in 1982. Bando spent the final five years of his big-league career with the Milwaukee Brewers and Suplizio served as a part-time Brewers coach during their American League pennant-winning season in 1982.

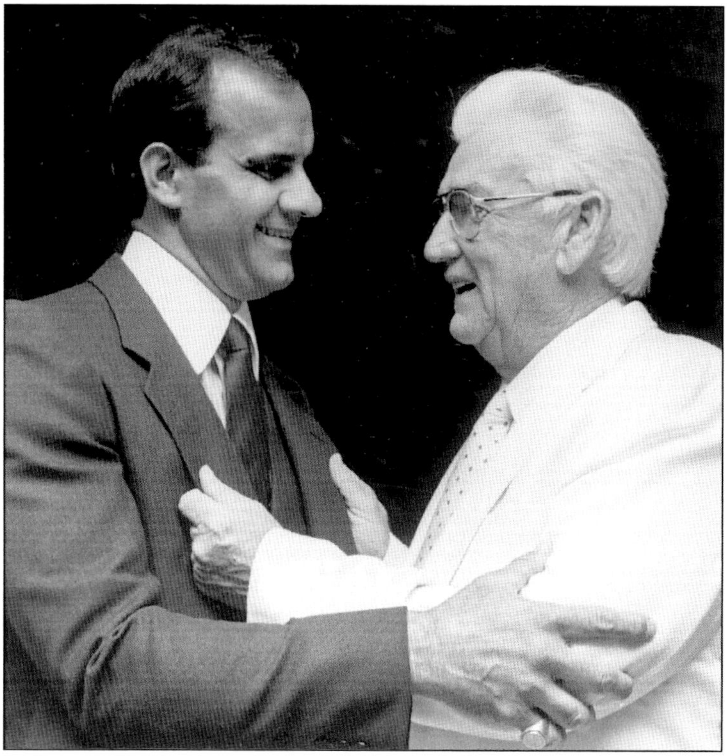

Delgado (LA) coach Louis Scheuermann gives banquet speaker Joe Torre a tug on the lapels prior to the 1985 JUCO World Series. Torre, a former National League MVP who has since gone on to become one of the most successful managers in New York Yankees history, had then been most recently manager of the Atlanta Braves.

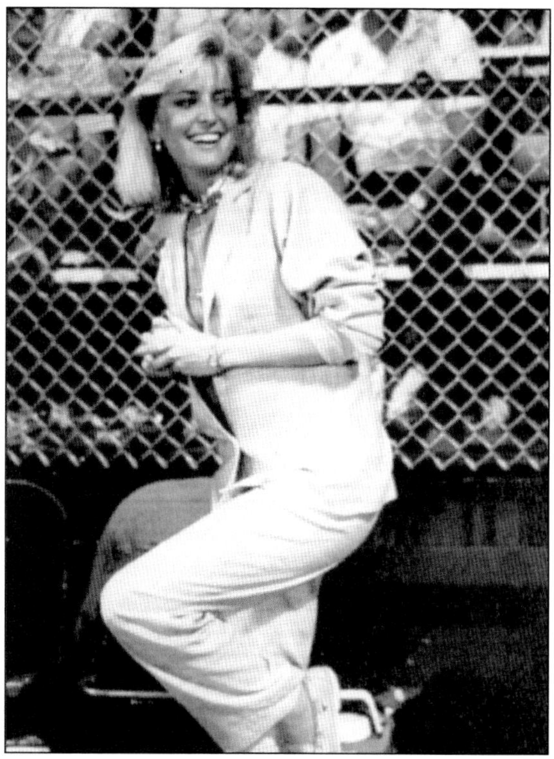

Not all visitors to Grand Junction have baseball connections. Miss America Charlene Wells of Utah threw out the ceremonial first pitch of a game during the 1985 tournament.

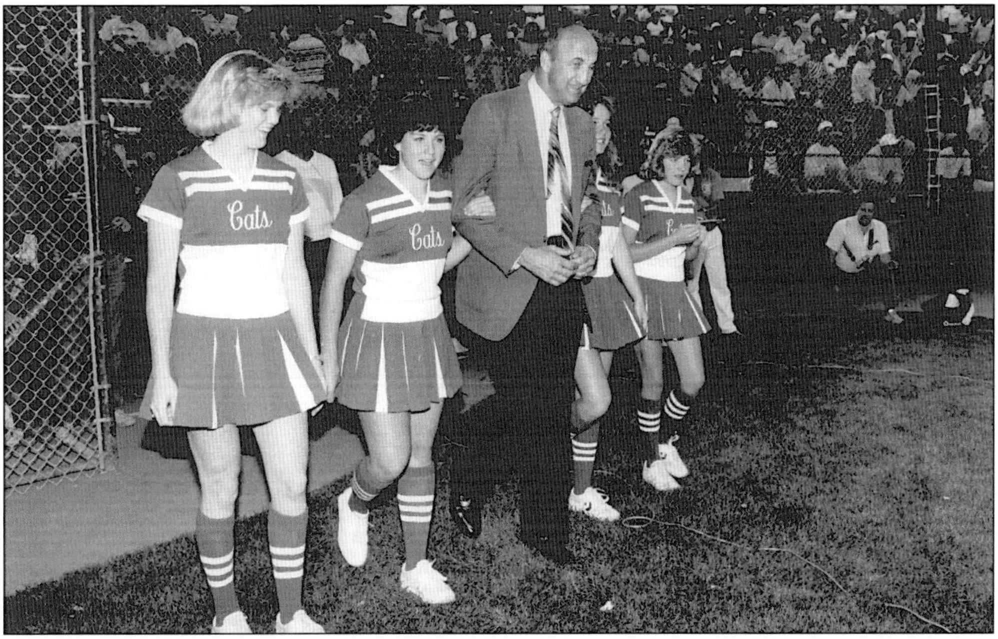

Frank Torre is escorted onto the field by cheerleaders from Fruita Monument High School during the 1986 JUCO World Series.

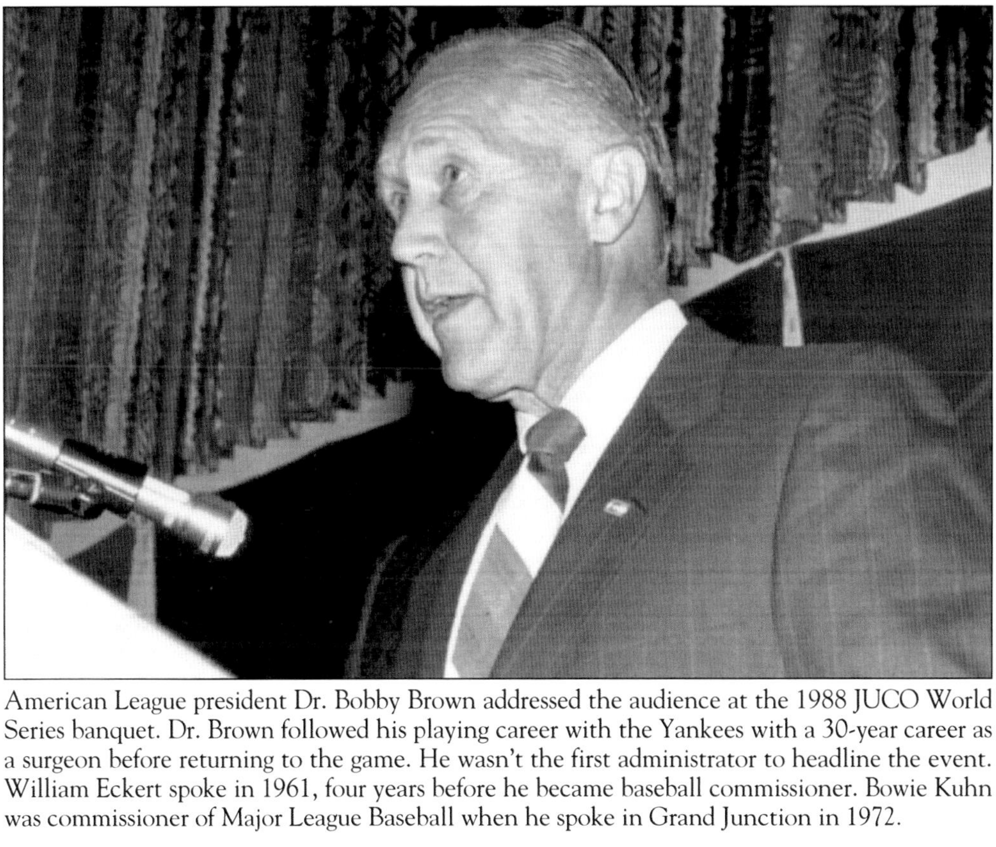
American League president Dr. Bobby Brown addressed the audience at the 1988 JUCO World Series banquet. Dr. Brown followed his playing career with the Yankees with a 30-year career as a surgeon before returning to the game. He wasn't the first administrator to headline the event. William Eckert spoke in 1961, four years before he became baseball commissioner. Bowie Kuhn was commissioner of Major League Baseball when he spoke in Grand Junction in 1972.

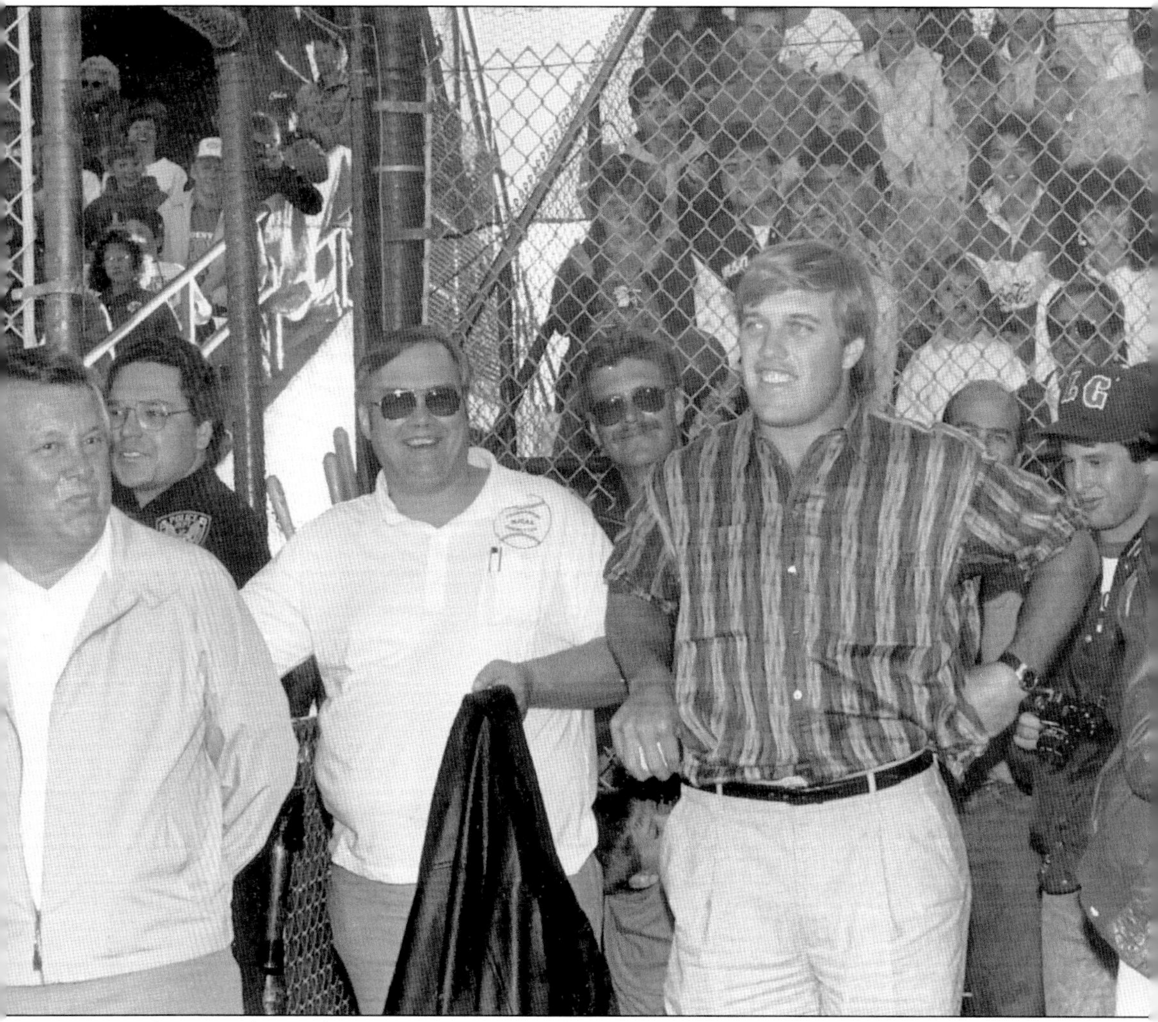

It only seems fitting for a great sporting tradition that is held in Colorado to invite the most popular man in the state to throw out the first pitch. The JUCO World Series did just that in 1989, to the obvious delight of the fans, when Denver Broncos quarterback (and former minor league baseball player) John Elway made the trip over the Rockies from Denver. Elway wasn't the first two-sport star to have connections with Grand Junction and Colorado. Craig Morton, who later quarterbacked the Broncos to Super Bowl XII, and Mike Epstein, a University of California football star who went on to a nine-year American League baseball career, both played on the 1962 Grand Junction Eagles. Morton also was a Cal student when he spent that season in Colorado. He attended the 1979 JUCO banquet to present some awards.

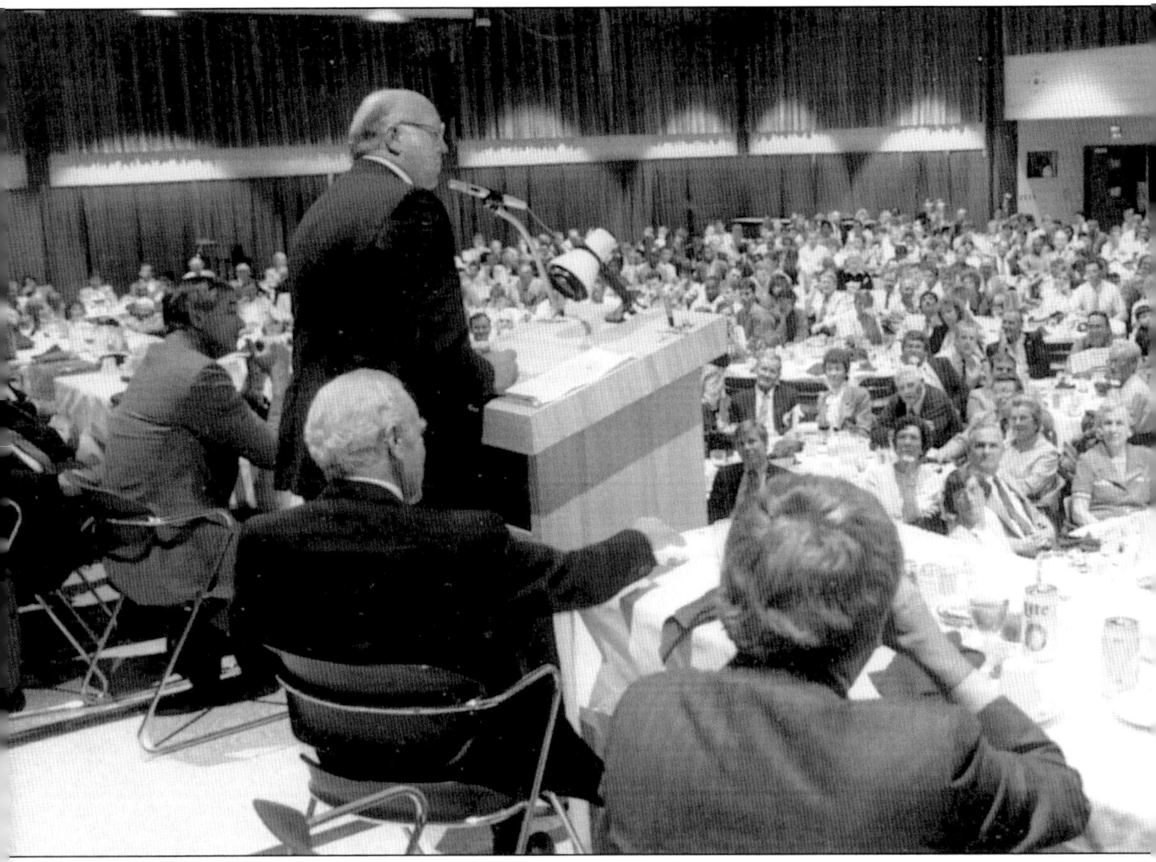

Marv Throneberry has several claims to fame from his playing days. He was part of the trade that sent future home run king Roger Maris from the Kansas City Athletics to the New York Yankees. Throneberry later found himself as the starting first baseman for the hapless New York Mets in their inaugural 1961 season. After his career ended, he became perhaps best known for his part in the famous Miller Lite beer commercials of the late 1970s. He spoke at the 1987 JUCO World Series banquet at the Two Rivers Convention Center in downtown Grand Junction. The banquet hall seats 1,200 people and is regularly full for the annual pre-tournament speaker and JUCO Hall of Fame inductions the night before the games begin.

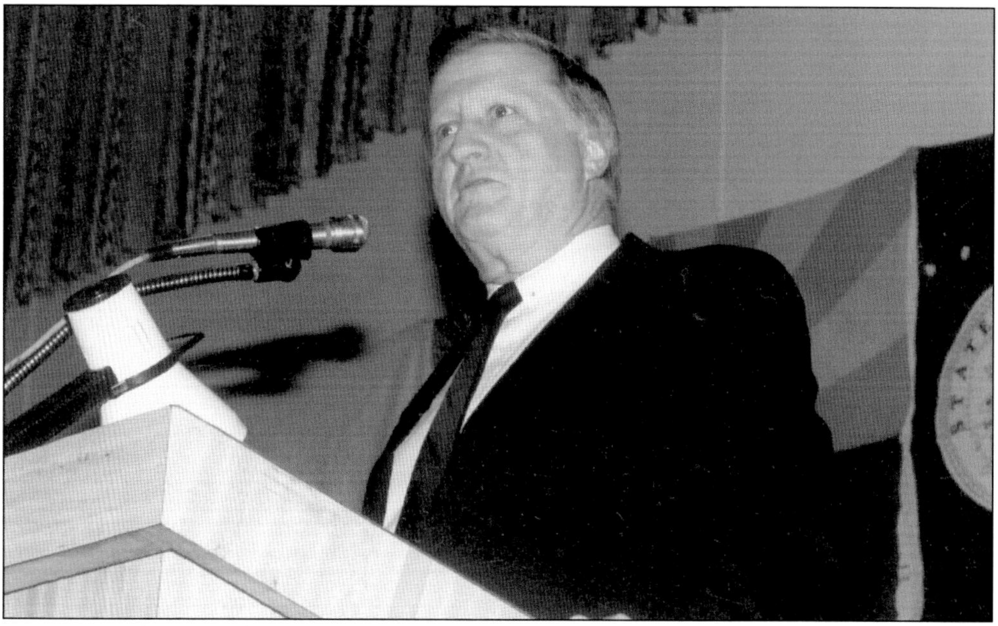

Controversial New York Yankees owner George Steinbrenner showed his soft side while at the 1990 JUCO World Series. Although he had a reputation for being a no-show as a speaker, he did arrive, his talk was well received, and he donated $25,000 to the NJCAA. His speech was the first time that the Two Rivers Convention Center had been sold out for a JUCO banquet speaker. Sadly and ironically, the man with whom Steinbrenner will always be linked in the imagination, his on-again/off-again manager Billy Martin, was slated to be the banquet MC and introduce his former boss in 1990. "As close as George and Billy have been, and as good a friend as Billy was to Grand Junction and the JUCO World Series, it is rather fitting that George is our (1990) guest speaker," said Sam Suplizio at the time. He said that Martin, the 1970 banquet speaker himself, used to go fishing near Grand Junction and loved the region.

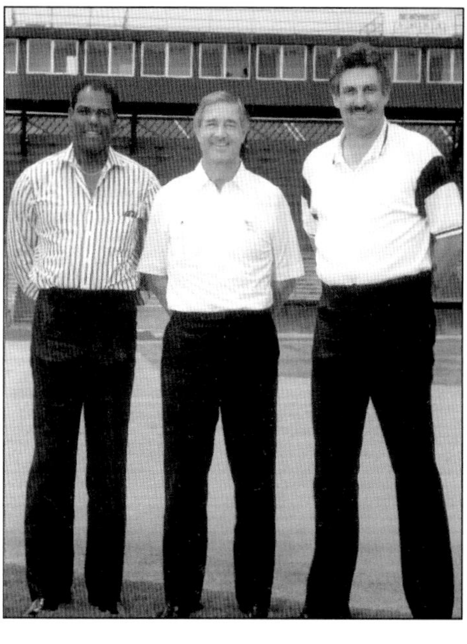

St. Louis Cardinals pitching legend Bob Gibson (left) headlined the 1991 JUCO banquet, and Rollie Fingers (right), still sporting his famed handlebar mustache, joined him as a banquet guest.

Former St. Louis Cardinals and Kansas City Royals manager Whitey Herzog signs autographs at the 1992 banquet. Herzog, a teammate of Sam Suplizio in the Yankees farm system, is one of several people best known as big-league managers that have spoke at the JUCO pre-tournament affair. Herzog also was the headliner in 2002. Bobby Winkles (1983 and 1989), Buck Showalter (1996), Tommy Lasorda (1997), Davey Johnson (1998), and Bobby Valentine (2003) have also stood behind the Two Rivers Convention Center podium.

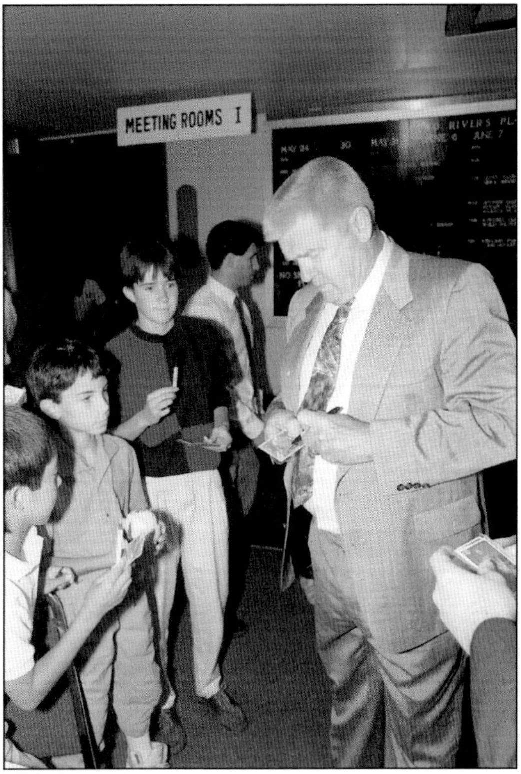


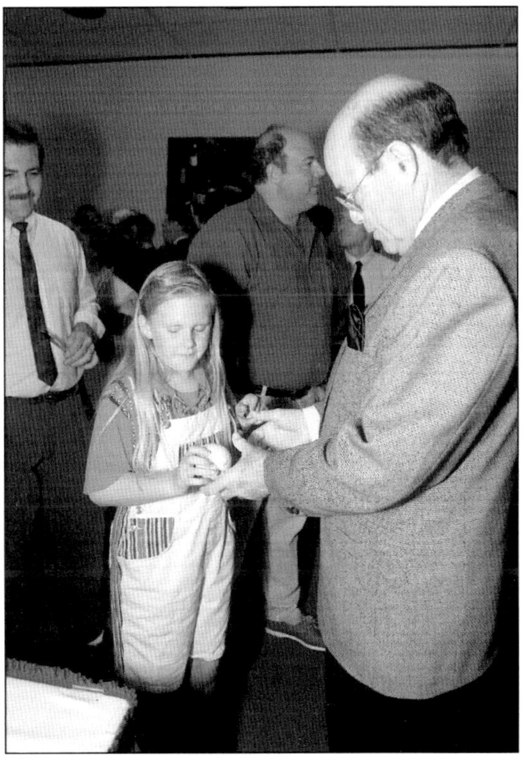

Noted philanthropist, broadcaster, and ballplayer Joe Garagiola signs autographs during the 1993 JUCO World Series banquet, where he was speaker.

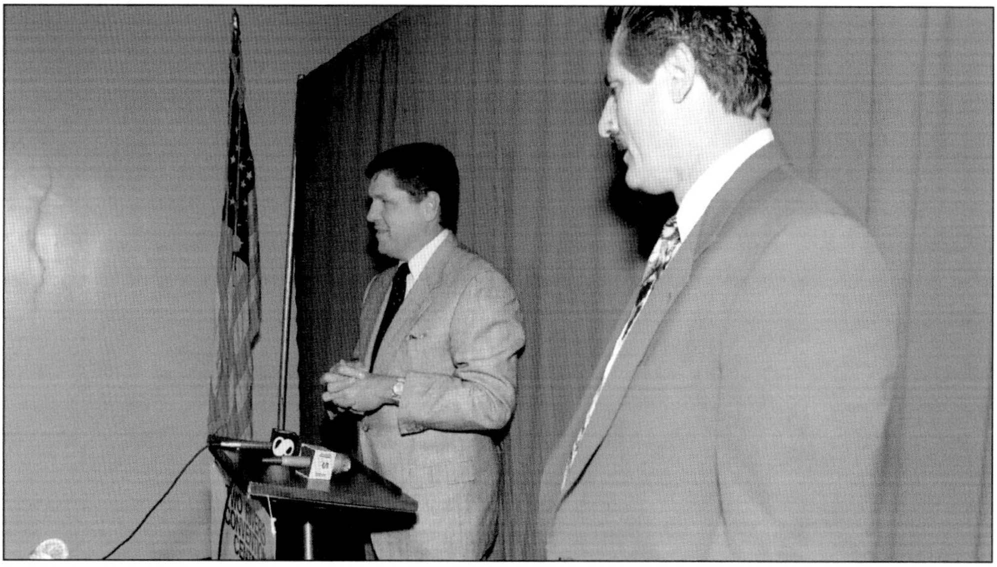

The 1994 banquet's featured speaker had a long history with the town of Grand Junction, although newer residents might not have known about it since the connection occurred prior to his Hall of Fame big-league career. Tom Seaver (left) was part of the Alaska Goldpanners back in 1963, when the semipro Grand Junction Eagles and the Goldpanners would play summer games against one another. Seaver pitched at Lincoln Park Stadium that year as he and the rest of legendary manager Red Boucher's Goldpanners were on their way to the National Baseball Congress World Series in Wichita, Kansas. Sam Suplizio, then playing for and managing the Eagles, still had some pop in his bat and managed to rough up Seaver at the park that would eventually contain his name. The Goldpanners took Suplizio with them to Wichita and the Grand Junction ballplayer did well enough to win tournament Most Valuable Player honors. The Eagles and Goldpanners were two of the best semipro programs in the West. They both were instrumental in the switch from town ball talent to elite college players that transformed that level of baseball during the 1960s and 1970s. Seaver, part of the 1963 NBC World Series champion squad, was joined at the 1994 banquet by guest Rollie Fingers (right), making his second appearance in four years.

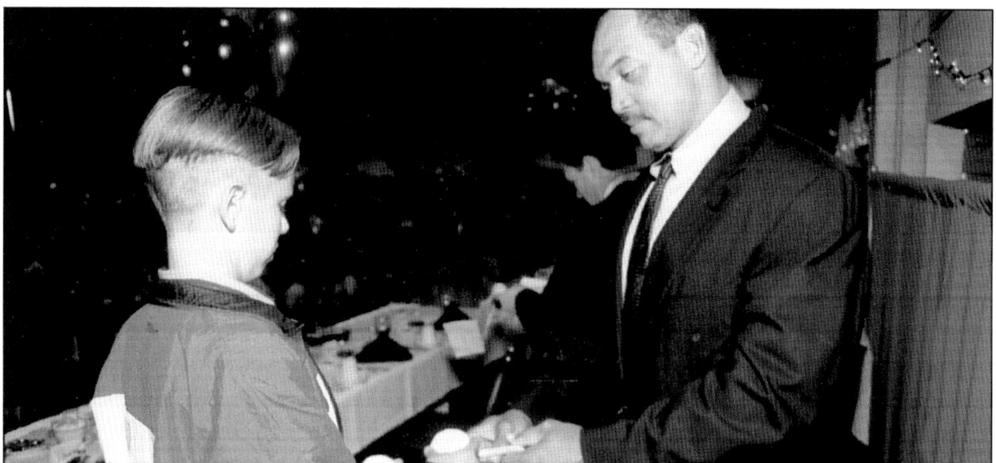

"Mr. October" became "Mr. May" when he spoke in Grand Junction in 1995. Here, Reggie Jackson signs autographs.

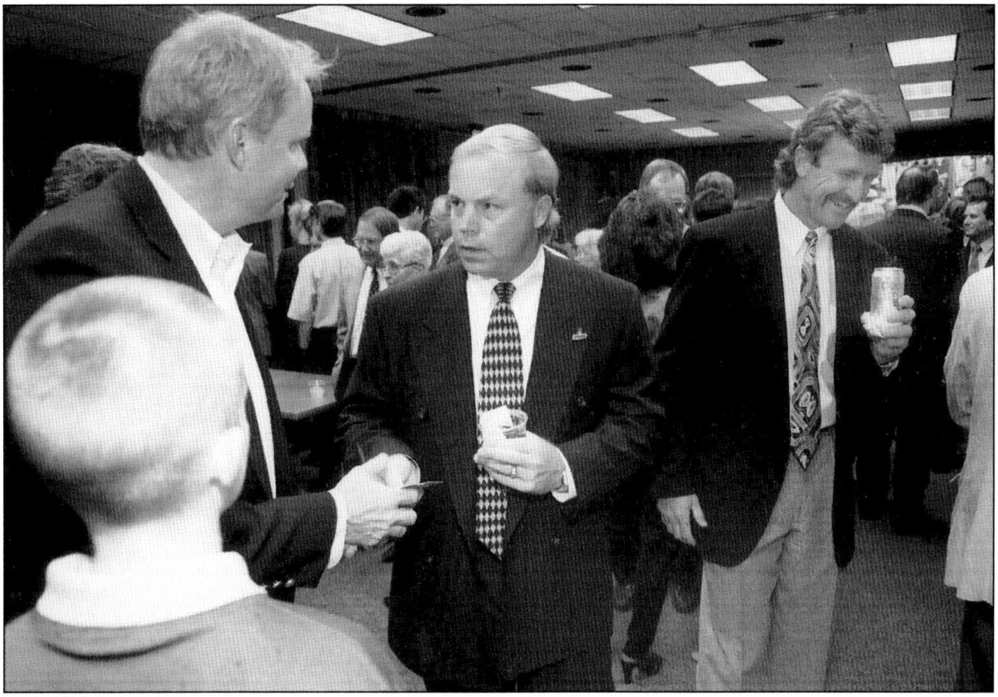

The 1996 banquet speaker Buck Showalter (center) was joined by Milwaukee Brewer star Robin Yount (right), with whom Sam Suplizio had worked as a coach in the 1980s with Milwaukee.

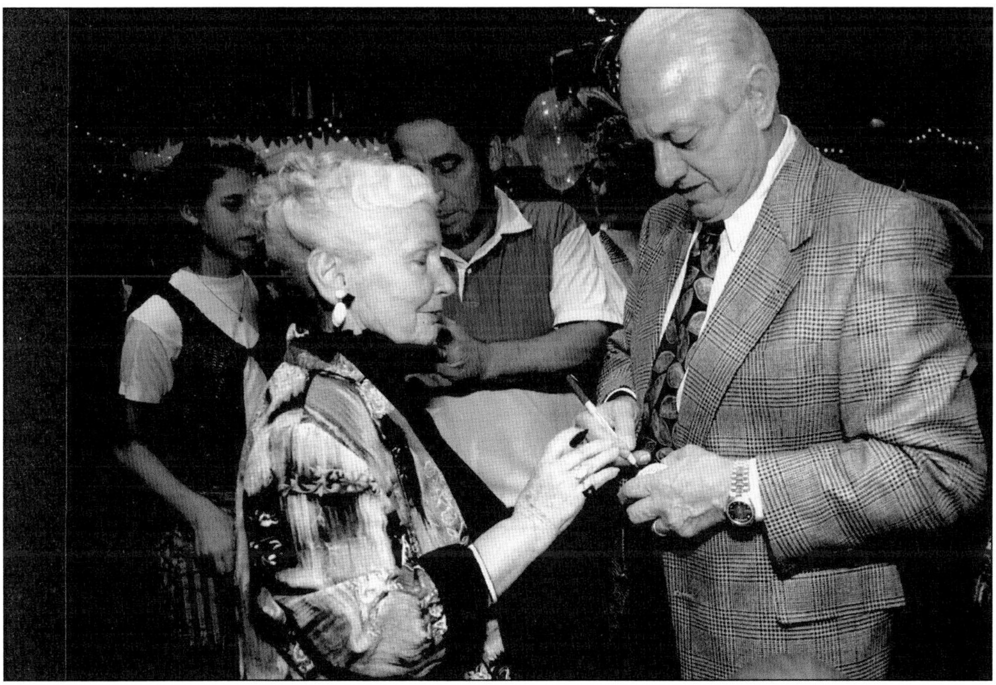

Fresh off managing the U.S. baseball team's gold medal triumph at the 2000 Sydney Olympics, the beloved Tommy Lasorda spoke at the JUCO banquet the following year.

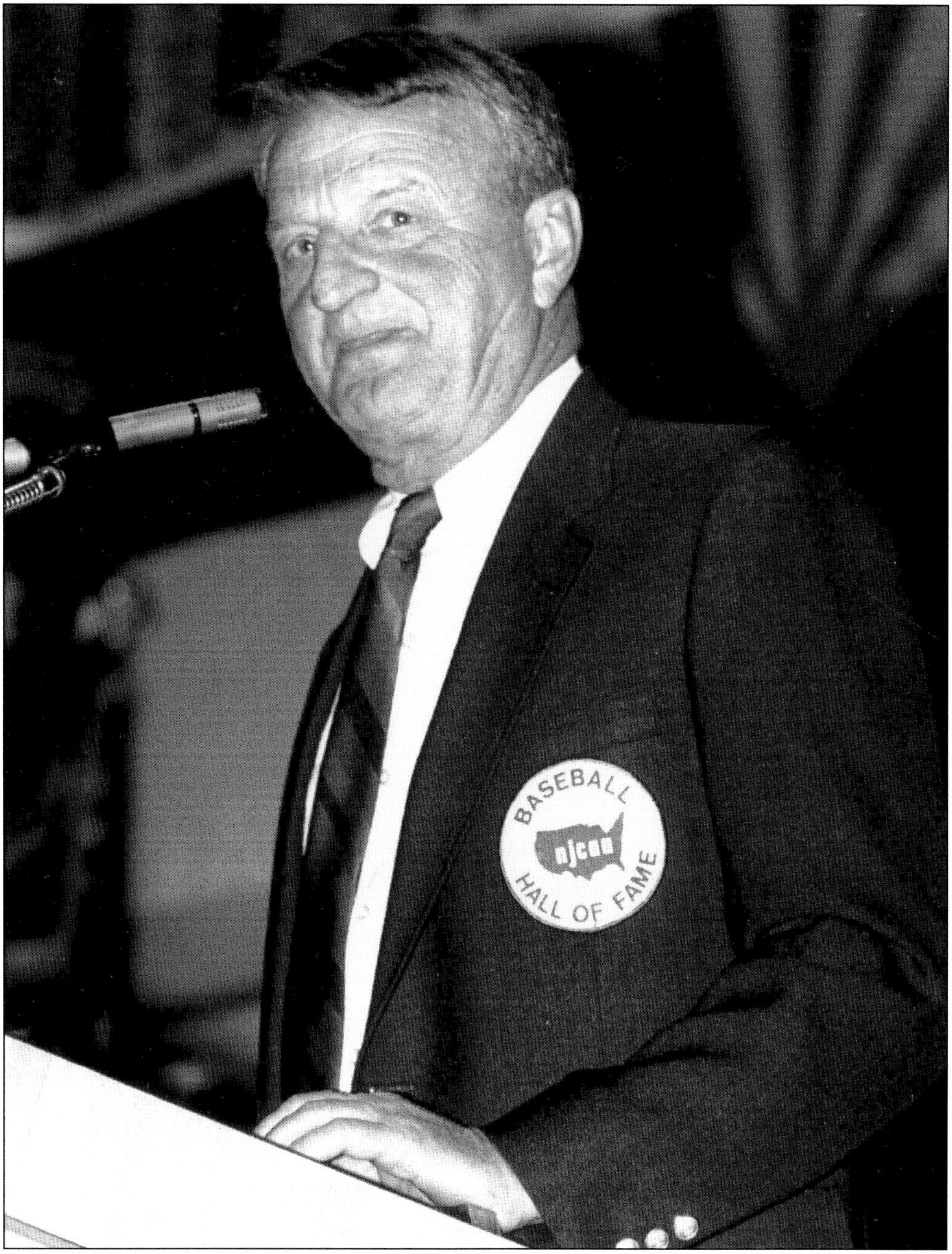


George Killian is hardly a guest in Grand Junction; he's more like a citizen. The executive director of the National Junior College Athletic Association is the only person that has held that post since it was initiated in 1969, but he plans to step down in the summer of 2004. During his time as basketball coach and athletic director at Erie County Technical Institute (currently Erie Community College) in the 1950s, he became more involved with the fledgling NJCAA. In 1969, when the Board of Directors approved the hiring of a full-time director, Killian was an obvious choice. He has been a staunch advocate to keep the tournament in Grand Junction whenever threats arose that made it appear the tournament could be in danger of leaving.

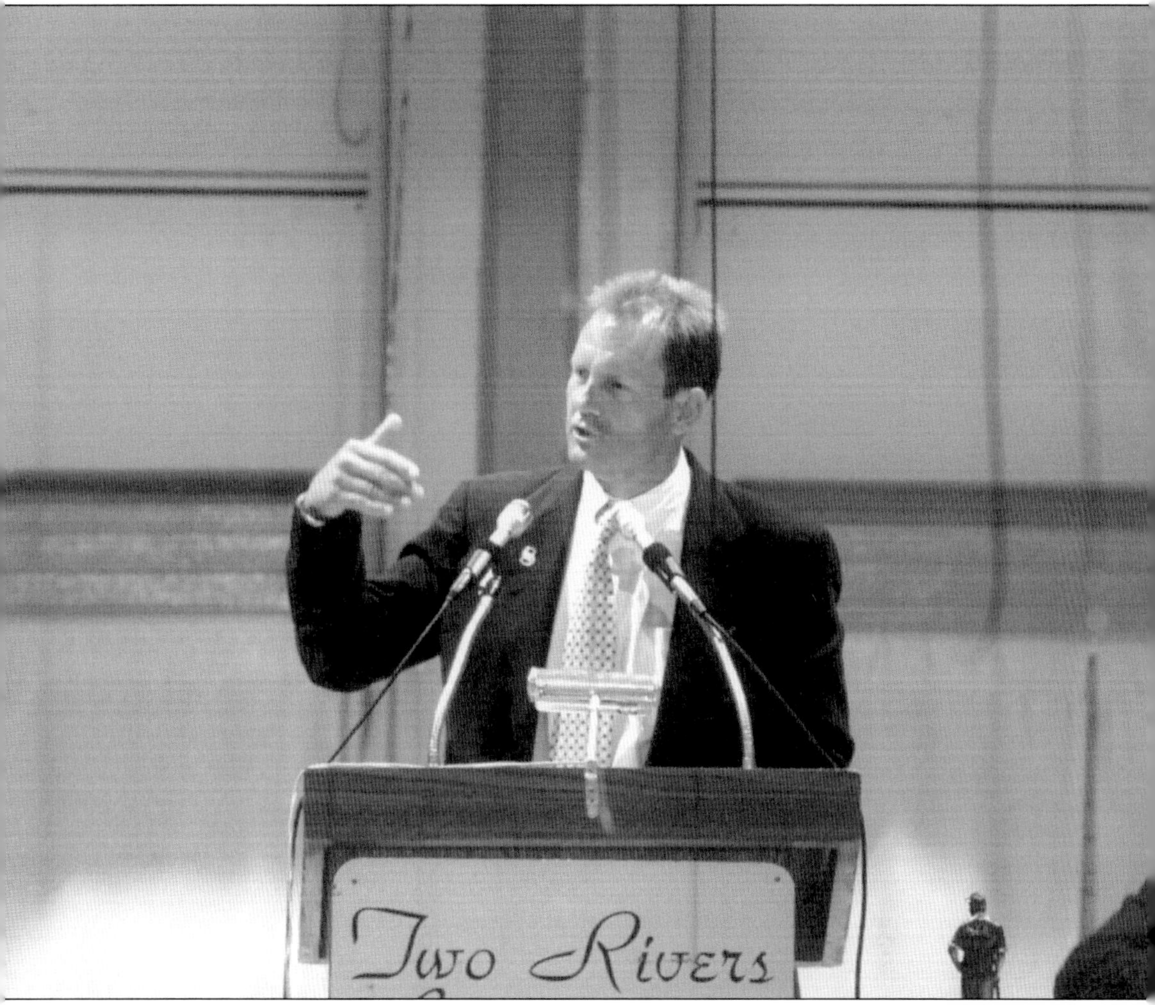

A member of the renowned 1999 Baseball Hall of Fame induction class that included Robin Yount and Nolan Ryan, George Brett delivered the pre-tournament talk at the 2000 JUCO banquet.

**Banquet Speakers:**

1959: Jack Curtis
1960: Presentation by major league scouts
1961: William Eckert
1962: Eddie Stanky
1963: Jocko Conlan
1964: Stan Musial
1965: Lefty Gomez
1966: Ed Doherty, James Gallagher, Hugh Finnerty
1967: John McHale
1968: Duke Snider
1969: Bobby Richardson
1970: Billy Martin
1971: Emmett Ashford
1972: Bowie Kuhn
1973: Bob Howsam
1974: Lefty Gomez
1975: Willie Mays
1976: Whitey Ford
1977: Bobby Richardson
1978: Ernie Banks
1979: Eddie Stanky and Lefty Gomez
1980: Carl Erskine
1981: Tom Gorman
1982: Sal Bando
1983: Bobby Winkles
1984: Lefty Gomez
1985: Joe Torre
1986: Frank Torre
1987: Marv Throneberry
1988: Dr. Bobby Brown
1989: Bobby Winkles
1990: George Steinbrenner
1991: Bob Gibson
1992: Whitey Herzog
1993: Joe Garagiola
1994: Tom Seaver
1995: Reggie Jackson
1996: Buck Showalter
1997: Tommy Lasorda
1998: Davey Johnson
1999: Paul Molitor
2000: George Brett
2001: Tommy Lasorda
2002: Whitey Herzog
2003: Bobby Valentine

# SEVEN

# *Baseball is a Funny (and Fun) Game*

1993 JUCO World Series banquet speaker Joe Garagiola is known, among other things in baseball, for his book titled "Baseball Is a Funny Game." The former catcher and broadcaster wrote a humorous look at the national pastime in his 1960 classic. Garagiola has always had the good sense to take the game seriously as a sport but on the lighter side to acknowledge that it also is fine entertainment. It seems fitting to end this book, with all due respect to Garagiola, by amending his title here to include "fun" along with "funny," and show some of the images that help make Grand Junction's rendition of the national pastime such an enjoyable experience.

The oddities and pageantry and the social gathering at a ballpark are all part of baseball, both on the diamond and off. Spend some time at Sam Suplizio Field and you will begin to see why the JUCO World Series has lasted so long at this site. You will see all the joy and heartache that the game inspires on the field. You will also see the humor and silly fun it inspires on the other side of the foul lines. You will also find some wonderful traditions specifically created in Grand Junction. There's the annual Memorial Day fireworks. Or the three chairs on the field in front of the backstop reserved for committee members to watch the game (and watch it closely if they don't want to get hurt! They've been known to scatter on a foul ball hit straight back.). High school kids gather underneath the bleachers in a mass of hormones during the tournament, as the beginning of summer arrives, while the slightly more mature college students might graduate to sitting in the bleachers with the rest of the adults enjoying the park as a reunion site. Mud rubbing is also part of JUCO. Before the tournament, ball shaggers are charged with rubbing the shine off the more than 500 balls that will be used in the tournament to get them game ready. They use Blackburne's Baseball Rubbing Mud with porous mud marketed specifically for this purpose.

The final chapter of this book is devoted to some of the funny and fun moments at the JUCO World Series that help make this such a grand tradition in this corner of the world. Enjoying the National Pastime on Memorial Day weekend is a local tradition that Grand Junction can be proud of.

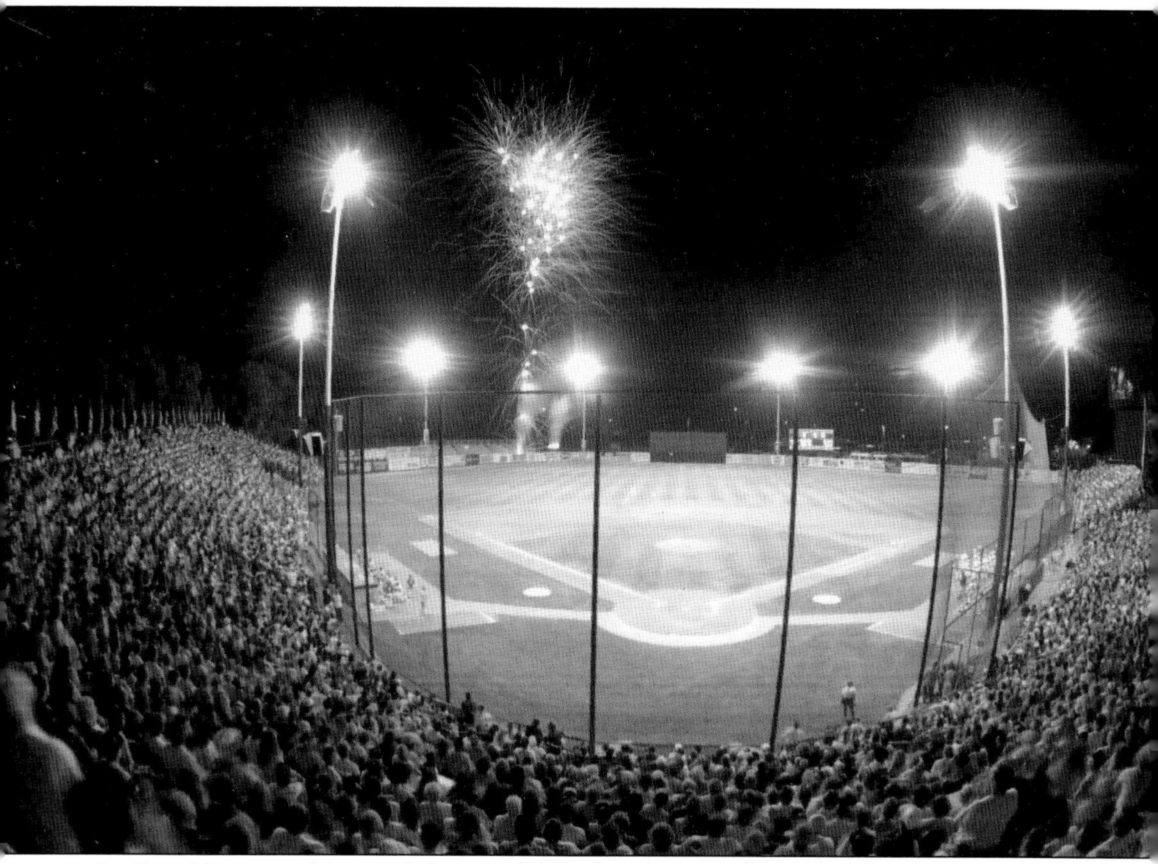

In Grand Junction, Memorial Day is celebrated with fireworks and baseball at a packed Sam Suplizio Field. After the night game is over on the holiday, fans stay in their seats, players sit at the top of the dugout, and this American community joins together for a spectacular light show. It is one of many ways that the JUCO World Series tradition has developed over the years.

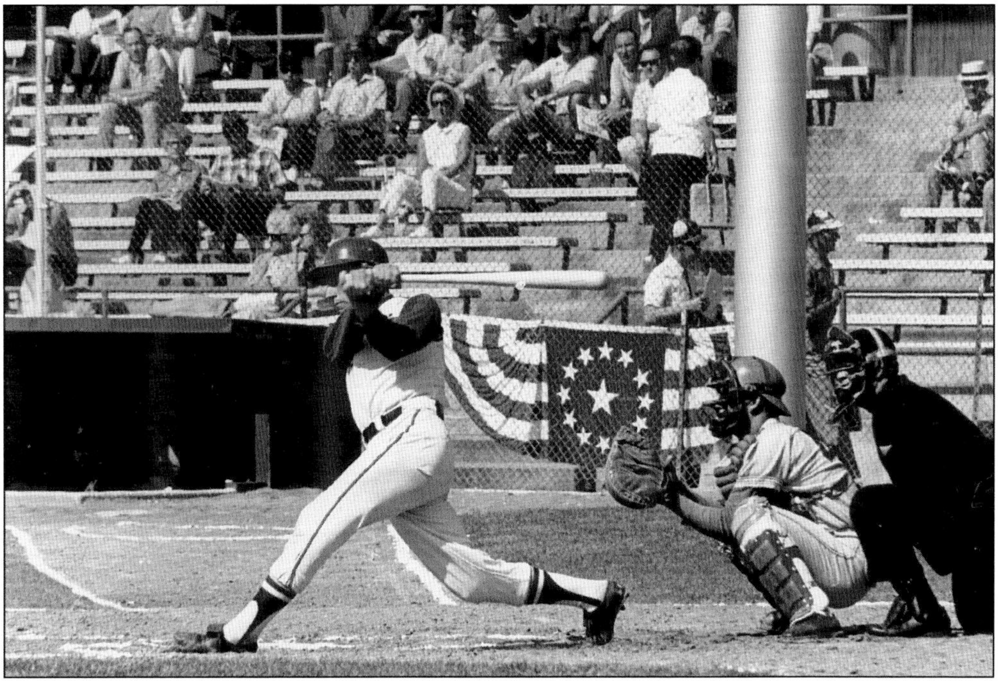

Baseball is pageantry. Red, white, and blue can be readily found at Lincoln Park and has been part of this Memorial Day tradition for many years, from the bunting that appears at field level (*above*) to the multiple American flags and state flags that fly across the top of the bleachers representing the year's participating teams (*below*).

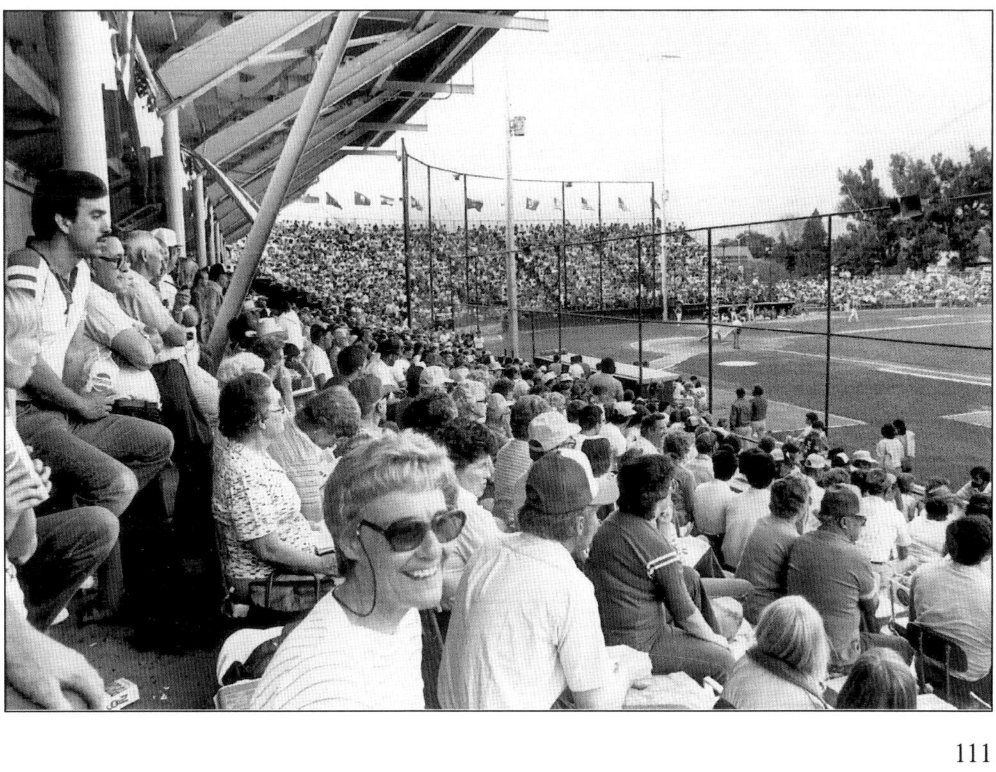

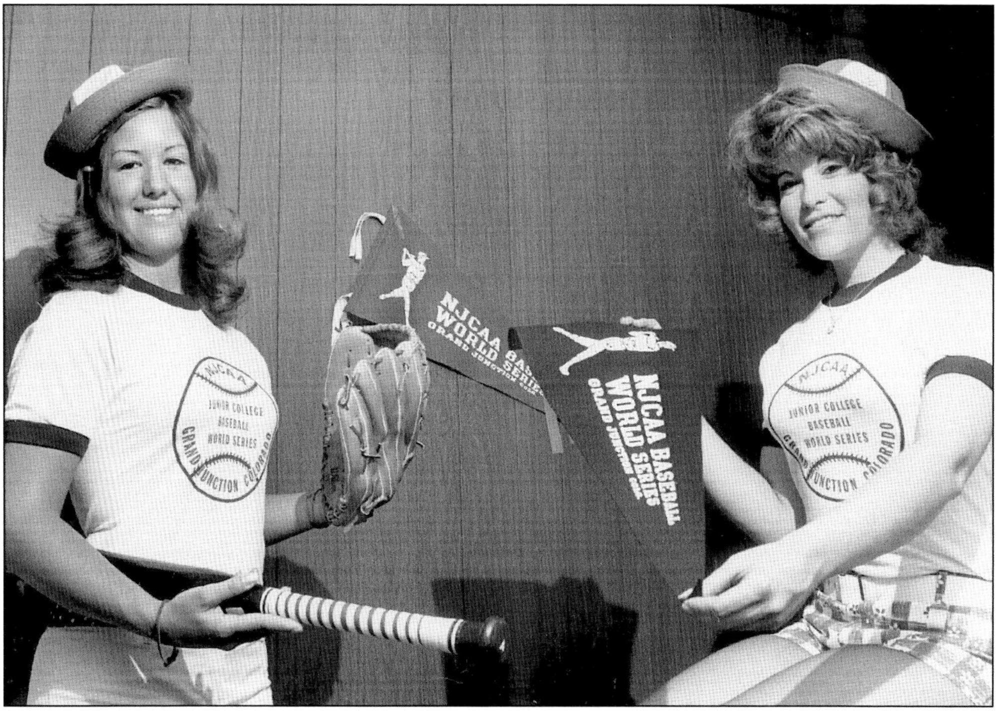


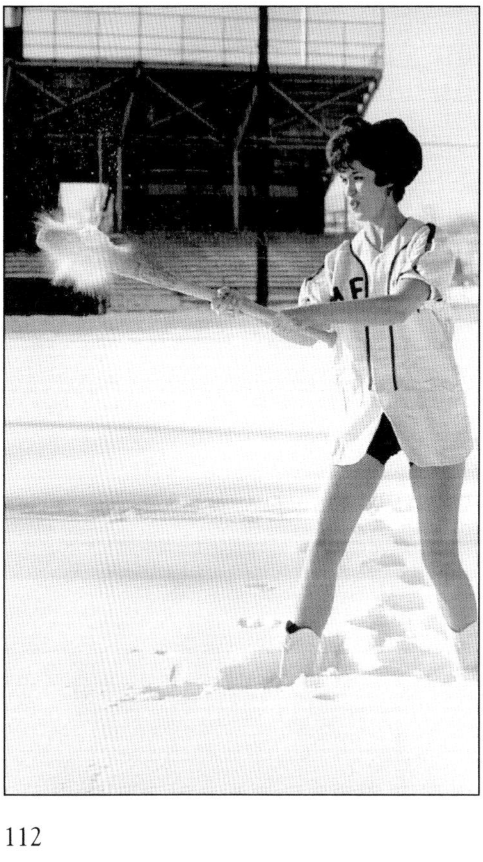

Baseball is advertising. Odd advertising has always gone with baseball. These two young women helped promote the tournament in the mid-1970s by showing off JUCO pennants (*above*), while this woman (*left*) in the 1960s braved the Colorado winter to show that it's never early to start thinking about baseball season.

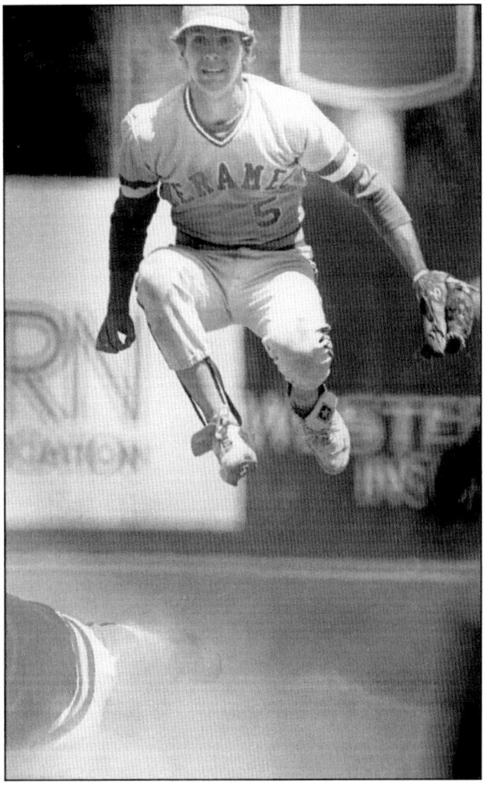

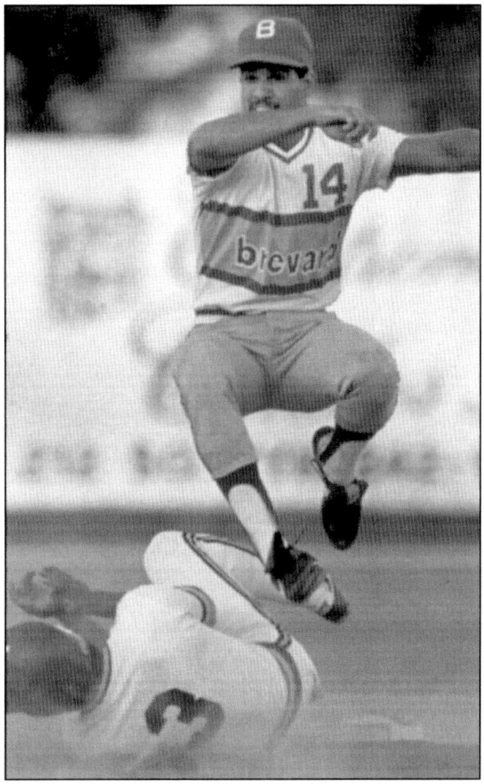


Baseball is acrobatics. Laz Balsera of Brevard (FL) Community College (*left*) and Ted Williams of Meramec (MO) both go airborne to make the force play at second base during the 1986 JUCO World Series. Ted Williams—blessed with a great baseball name—made the all-tournament team that year. Brevard's uniforms are a good reminder that in fashion, the baseball world is no different than anywhere else. Not all duds remain in style forever.

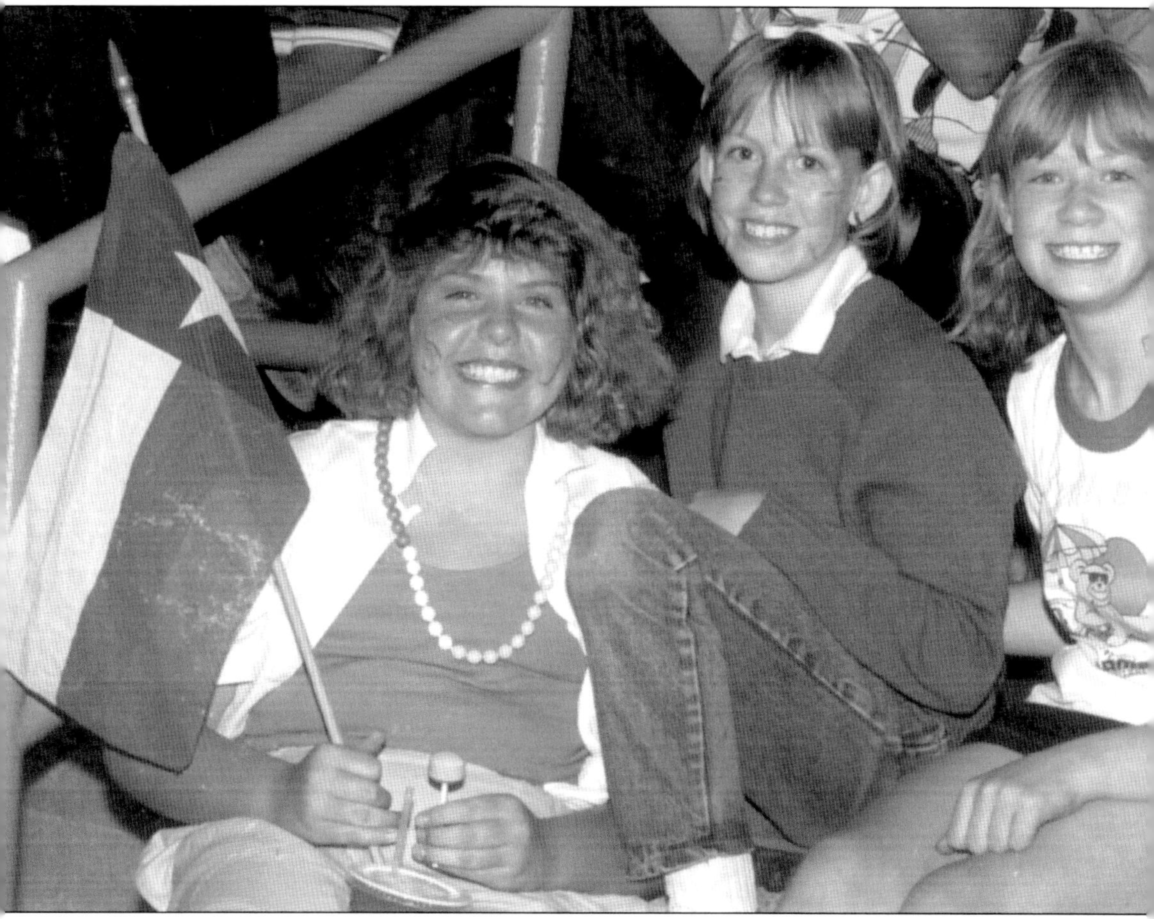

Baseball is root, root, rooting for your team. And nobody has brought upon so much rooting either for or against it than the New York Yankees of the JUCO world, the perennial power from San Jacinto-North (TX). These three girls, Kim Collins (left), Taryn Newman (center), and Julie Moran, have their game faces on in support of the Gators during the 1987 championship game, a 2-1 San Jac win. But another group of fans arose during the mighty Texans' dominant 1980s run: the "Gator Haters." They simply organized themselves with T-shirts and became a known entity at Lincoln Park. "I really enjoy Grand Junction, the people, I even love the Gator Haters because they are part of the atmosphere," San Jac coaching legend Wayne Graham told JUCO program editor Ray Coca in 1991. San Jac still has its supporters and detractors, and one thing is for certain: everybody in town picks a team to root for each year.

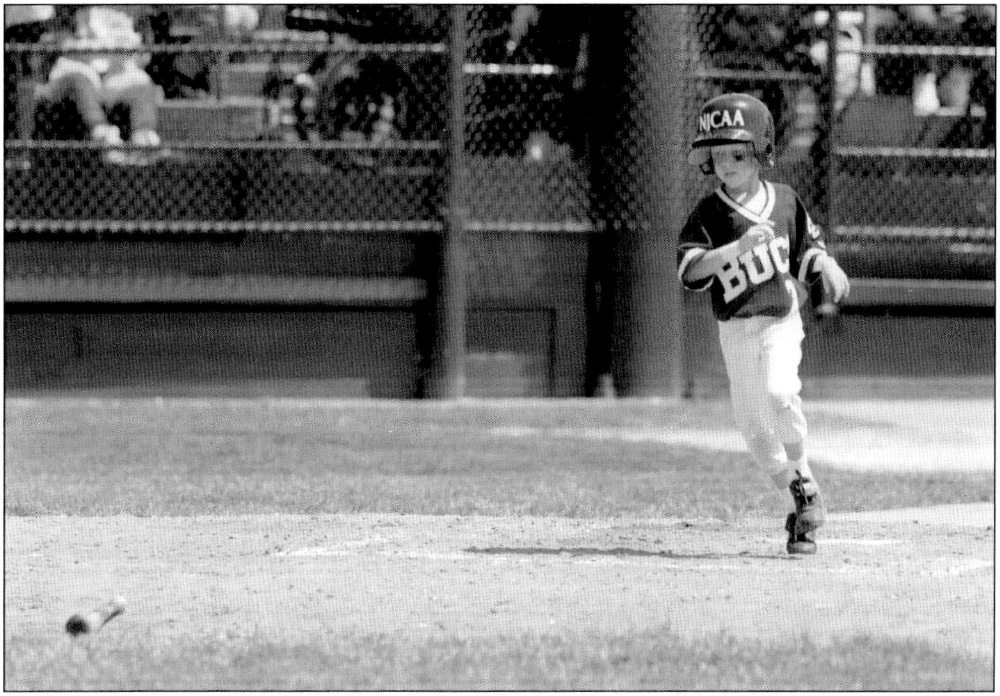


Baseball is hard work. Just ask these young people performing essential bat boy duties (*above*) and selling soft drinks to fans in the hot sun at the start of summer (*below*).

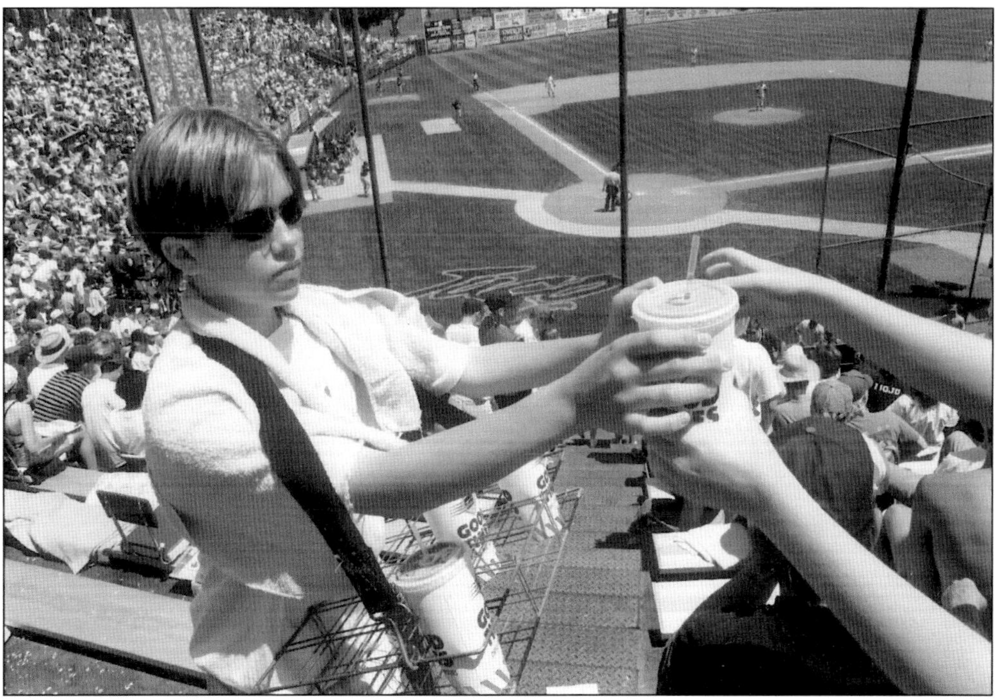

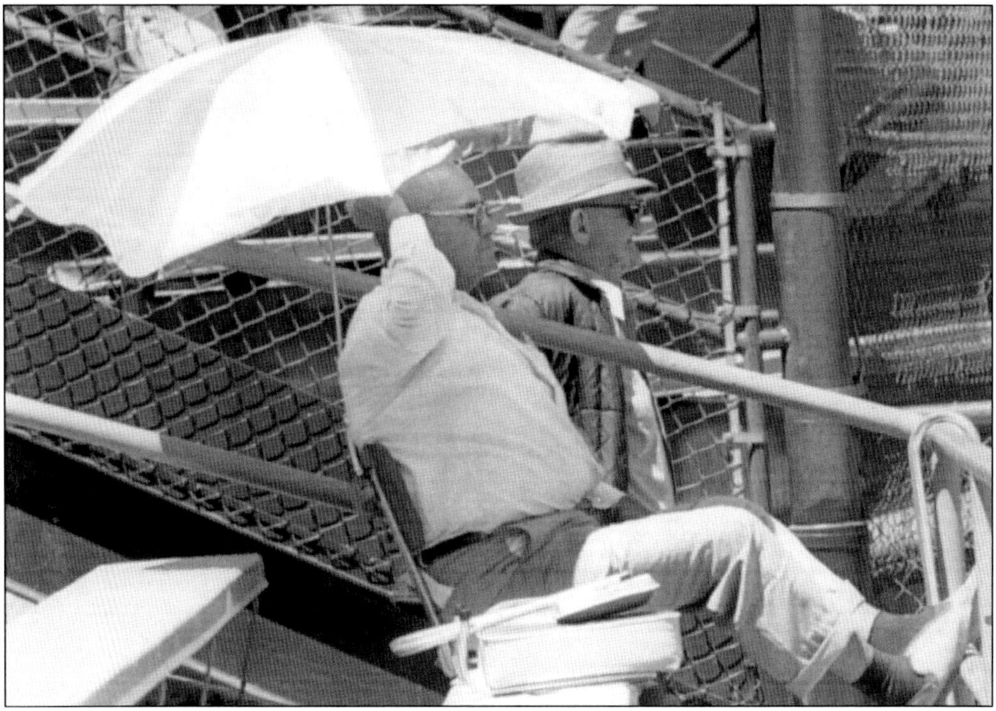

Baseball is leisure. Just ask these two fans trying to keep cool during a midday game in the 1980s (*top*) or these two men taking a break on the still-unfinished permanent bleachers behind home plate in the early years (*bottom*).

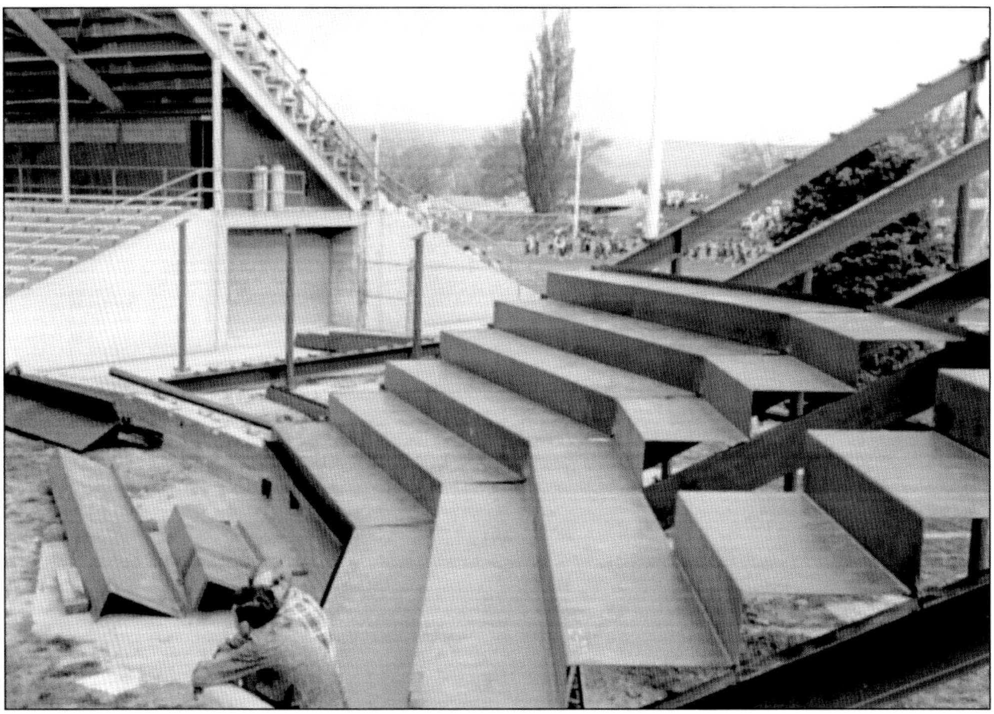

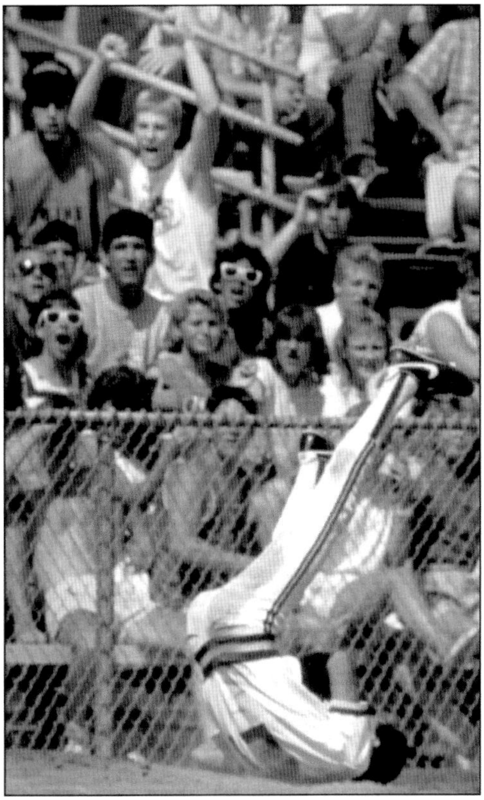

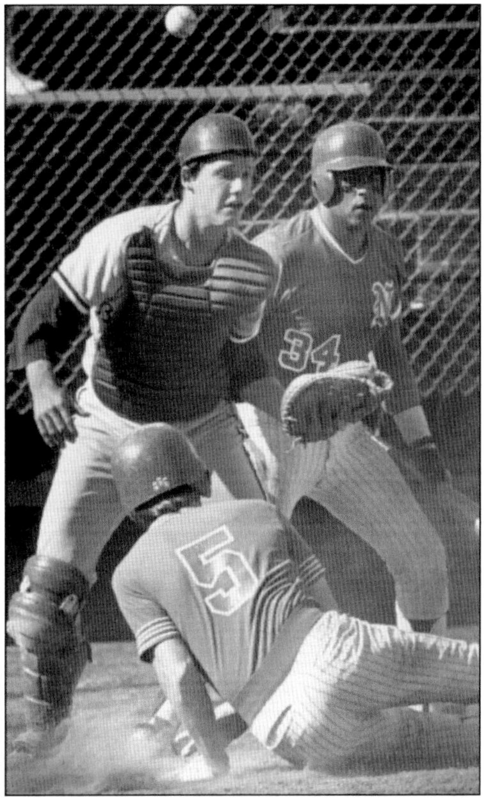

Baseball is bloopers. That is clear here as David Vasquez of San Jacinto makes a head-over-heels catch (*left*) and Todd Walsack of Brookdale (NJ) Community College can't find the handle on the ball (*right*). Both plays occurred in 1986.

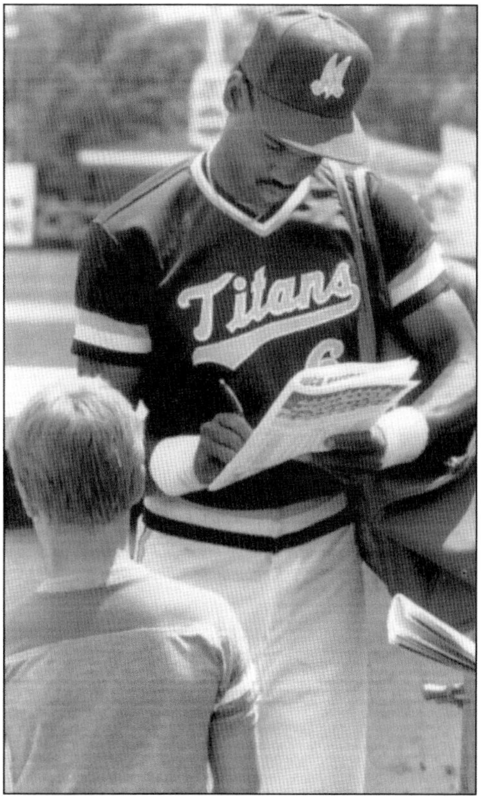


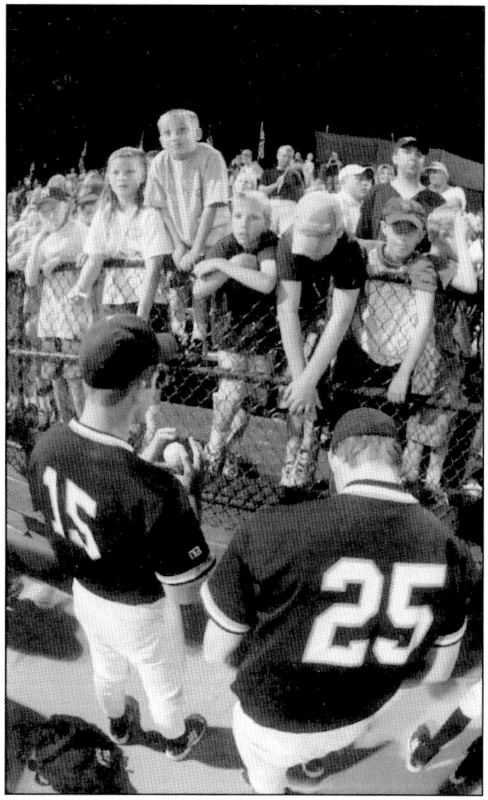


Baseball is autographs. One of the enjoyable traditions at JUCO is young fans getting autographs from the players at every conceivable opportunity during the tournament. Here, players from County College (NJ) of Morris (*above left*) Cowley County (KS) (*above right*), Columbia State

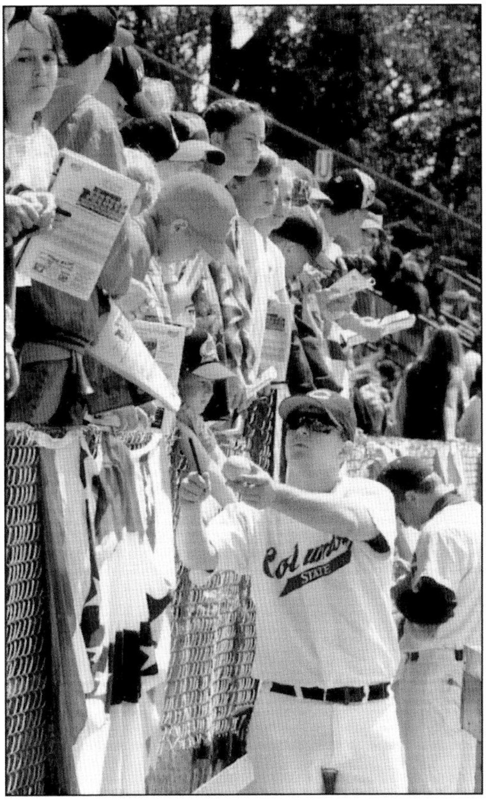

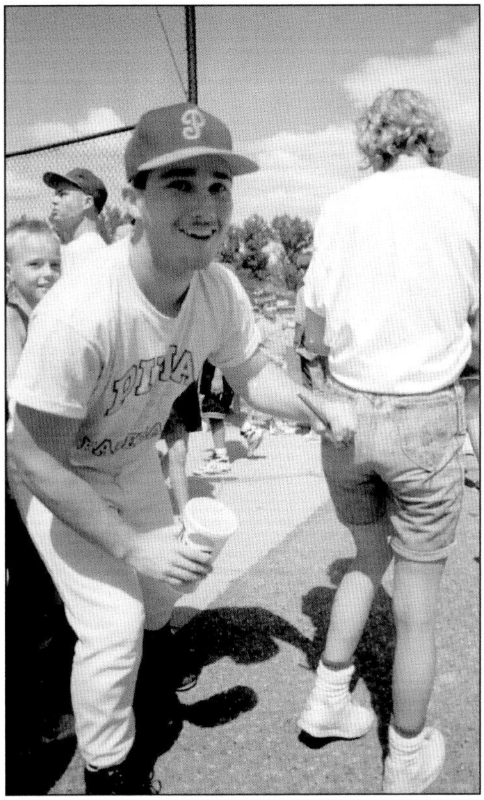

(TN) Community College (*above left*), and Pima (AZ) Community College (*above right*) take part in the tradition. When a team is eliminated, kids flock to the dugouts in hopes of grabbing a generous player's batting glove or hat or sweaty wristband.

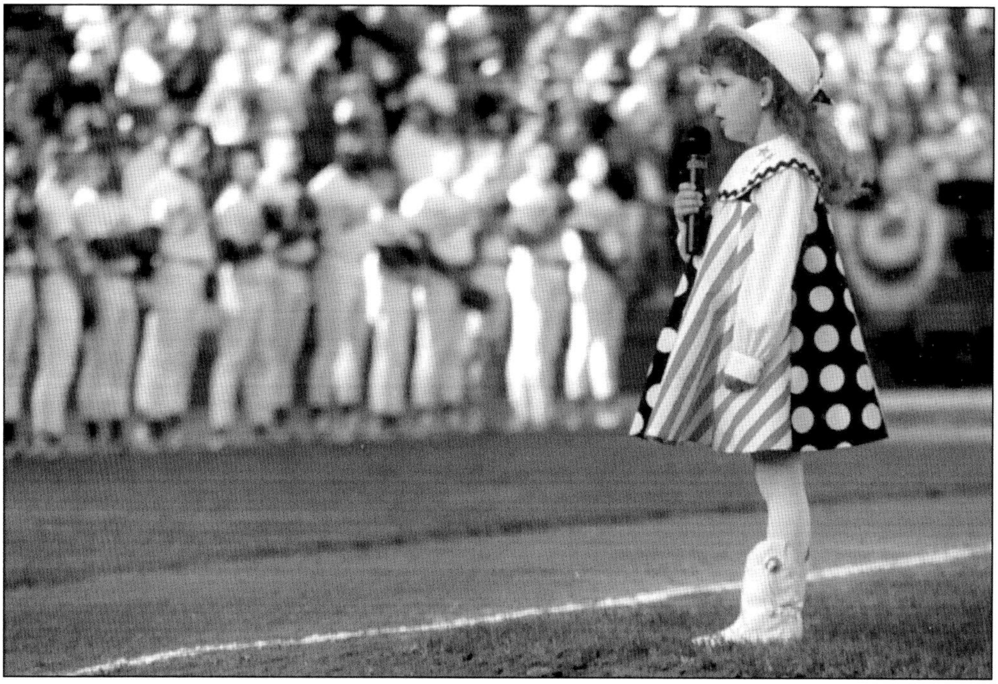

Baseball is kids. Sometimes, even the people wear red, white, and blue, as this national anthem-singing girl did in 1993.

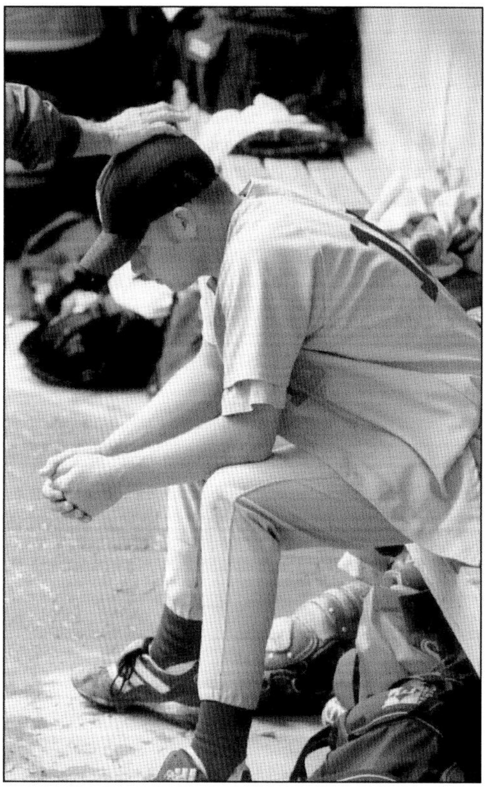

Baseball is dejection. As this player from Scottsdale (AZ) Community College discovered in 1997. One could also mention that baseball is colorful nicknames, and the Scottsdale Artichokes would certainly be near the top of that list.

Baseball is concentration. Coaches come in all shapes and sizes, but they all keep their eyes on the action when they reach Grand Junction.

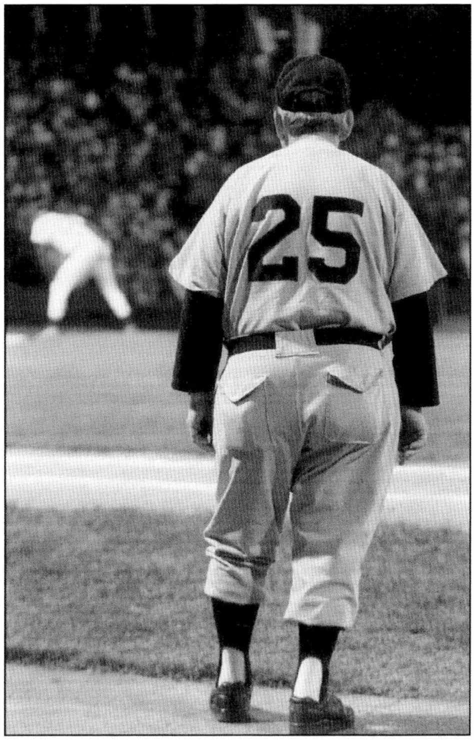

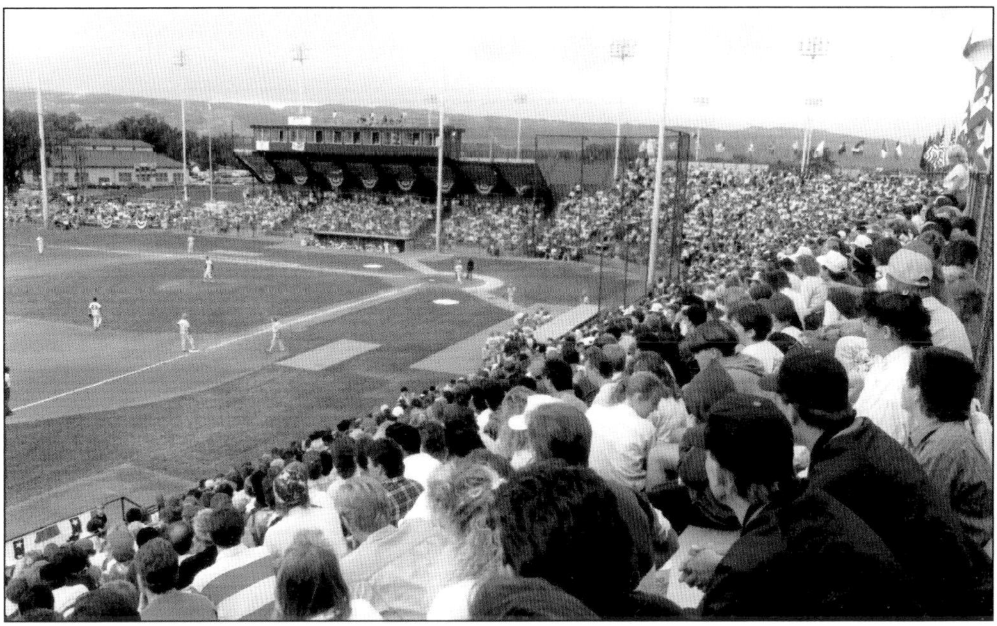

Baseball is scenery. Especially in Grand Junction, Colorado, where fans down the left-field line (above) can look west to the majestic Colorado National Monument. Fans along the right-field line and behind home plate don't have it too bad either. They can peer out over the left fielder and see Grand Mesa. By now, more than four decades since a national baseball tournament first arrived on the Western Slope, the JUCO World Series has become as much of a fixture of the landscape as these natural wonders.

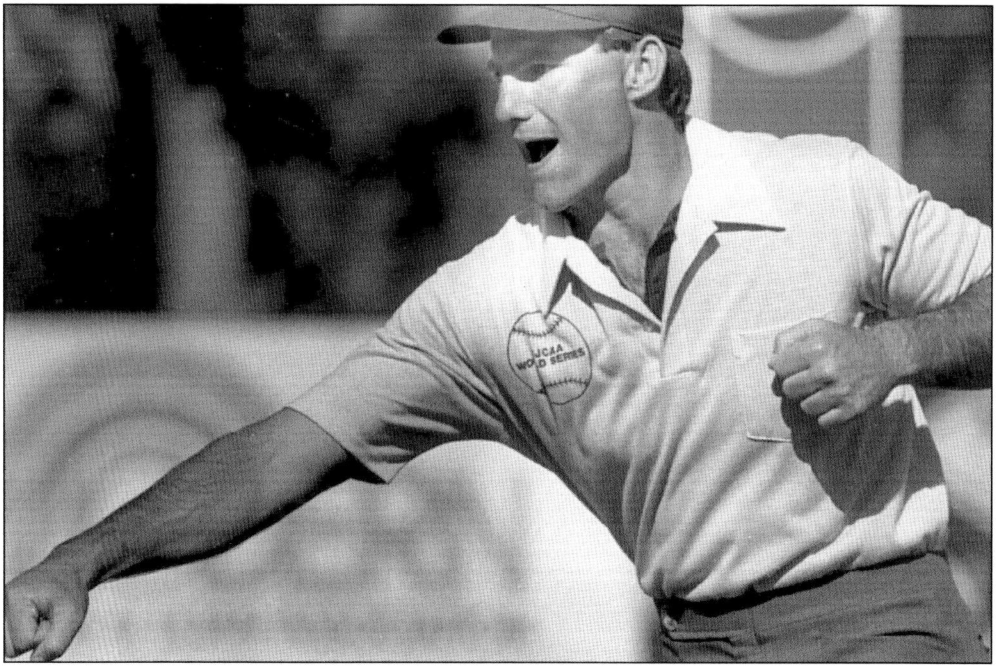

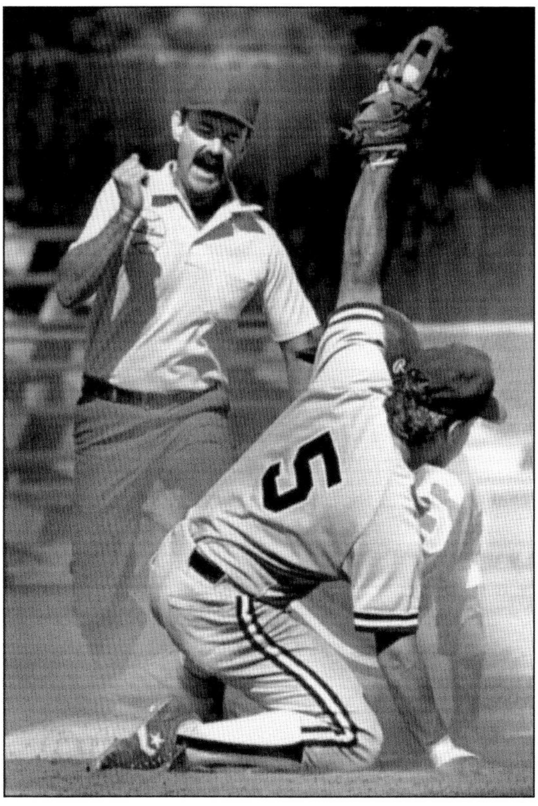

Baseball is umpires. The men in blue are vital to the game, whether we like to admit it or not. JUCO has acknowledged that with two banquet speakers (Emmett Ashford and Jocko Conlan) and a Hall of Fame inductee (John Toppi). Here are four JUCO field arbiters performing their jobs with gusto, a good eye, and precision: Kelly Nutt (*above*), Mike Bullen (*left*), Bud Schoepflin (*opposite, top*), and Toppi (*opposite, bottom*).

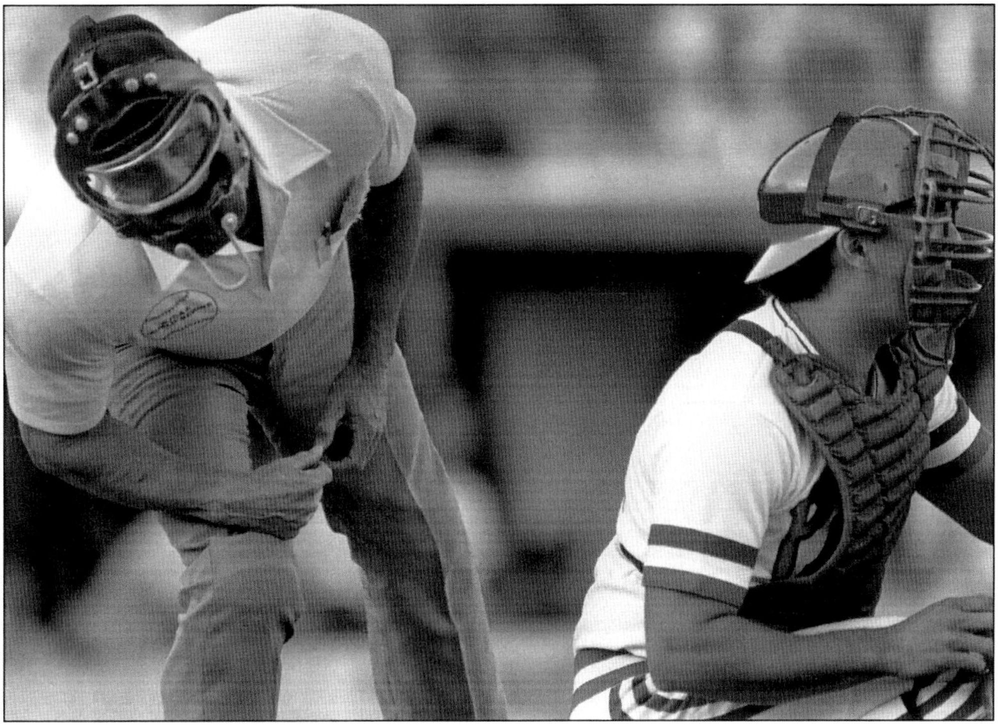

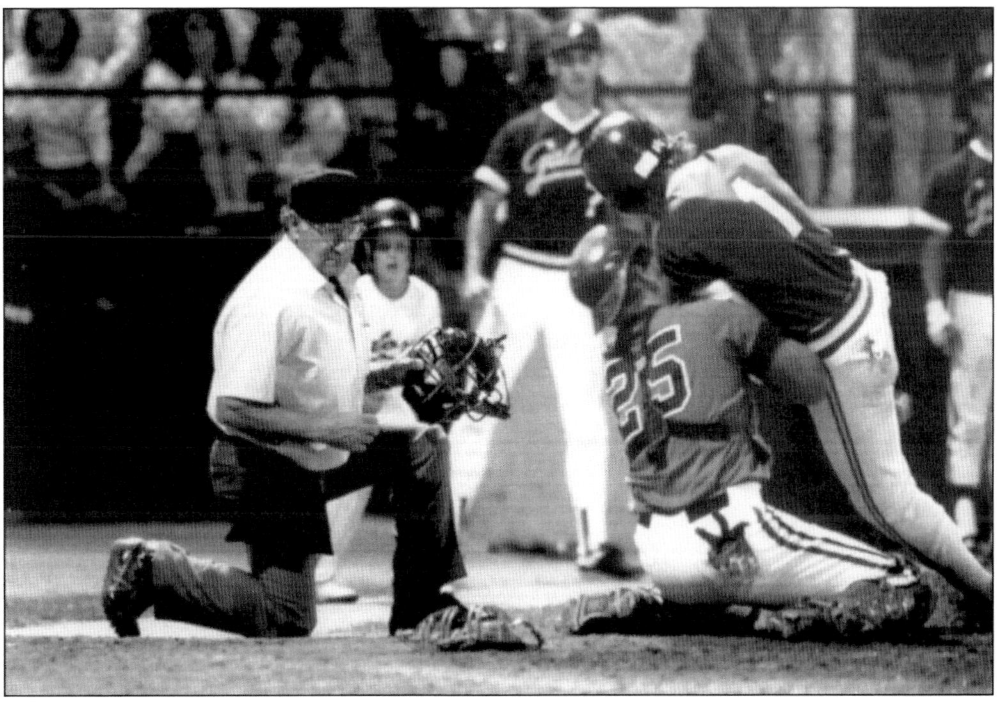

# *Appendix A*

**Tournaments at a Glance, 1958–2003**

| Year | Champion | MVP |
|---|---|---|
| 1958 | Cameron College, Lawton, OK (Tournament held in Miami, OK) | |
| 1959 | Paris Junior College, Paris, TX | Glendell Baker, Paris |
| 1960 | Phoenix College, Phoenix, AZ | Mickey Lee, Tarleton State (TX) |
| 1961 | Wilmington College, Wilmington, NC | Ronnie Durham, Wilmington |
| 1962 | Phoenix College, Phoenix, AZ | Lee McFarland, Phoenix |
| 1963 | Wilmington College, Wilmington, NC | Ken Widman, Long Island (NY) |
| 1964 | Miami-Dade Junior College, Miami, FL | Mack Gendreau, Mesa JC (CO) |
| 1965 | Phoenix College, Phoenix, AZ | Tom Burgess, Phoenix |
| 1966 | Nassau CC, Garden City, NY | Joe Arnold, Miami-Dade (FL) |
| 1967 | Bacone Junior College, Muskogee, OK | Gerald Pirtle, Bacone |
| 1968 | Glendale CC, Glendale, AZ | Otis McCowan, Glendale |
| 1969 | Panola Junior College, Carthage, TX | Doug Ault, Panola |
| 1970 | Mesa Community College, Mesa, AZ | Larry Patton, Columbia State (TN) |
| 1971 | Mesa Community College, Mesa, AZ | Jim Otten, Mesa CC |
| 1972 | Mesa Community College, Mesa, AZ | Greg Snowden, Mesa CC |
| 1973 | Ranger Junior College, Ranger, TX | Donnie Moore, Ranger |
| 1974 | Meramec CC, Kirkwood, MO | Steve Viefhaus, Meramec |
| 1975 | Yavapai College, Prescott, AZ | Neil Fiala, Meramec |
| 1976 | Central Arizona College, Coolidge, AZ | Jim Morley, Central Arizona |
| 1977 | Yavapai College, Prescott, AZ | Dan Townsend, Yavapai |
| 1978 | Ranger Junior College, Ranger, TX | Jim Mick, Ranger |
| 1979 | Middle Georgia College, Cochran, GA | Tommy Dunbar, Middle Georgia |
| 1980 | Middle Georgia College, Cochran, GA | Greg Geren, Cleveland State |
| 1981 | Miami-Dade CC South, Miami, FL | Curtis Morgan, Seminole (OK) |
| 1982 | Middle Georgia College, Cochran, GA | Kal Daniels, Middle Georgia |
| 1983 | McLennan CC, Waco, TX | David Turner, McLennan |
| 1984 | Southern Idaho, Twin Falls, ID | Shell Scott, Southern Idaho |
| 1985 | San Jacinto College North, Houston, TX | Randy Randle, San Jac |
| 1986 | San Jacinto College North, Houston, TX | Brian Deak, Yavapai |
| 1987 | San Jacinto College North, Houston, TX | Bill Losa, San Jac |
| 1988 | Hillsborough CC, Tampa, FL | Chris Hanks, Southern Idaho |
| 1989 | San Jacinto College North, Houston, TX | David Evans, San Jac |
| 1990 | San Jacinto College North, Houston, TX | Randy Brown, San Jac |
| 1991 | Howard College, Big Springs, TX | Frank Rodriguez, Howard |
| 1992 | Essex CC, Baltimore Co., MD | Mike Peters, Essex |
| 1993 | Yavapai College, Prescott, AZ | Kevin Pitts, Triton |
| 1994 | Galveston College, Galveston Island, TX | Jose Rosado, Galveston |
| 1995 | Middle Georgia College, Cochran, GA | Brian Davis, Middle Georgia |
| 1996 | Northeast Texas CC, Mt. Pleasant, TX | Robert Vaz, NE Texas |
| 1997 | Cowley County CC, Arkansas City, KS | Travis Hafner, Cowley CO |
| 1998 | Cowley County Community College, | |

| | | |
|---|---|---|
| | Arkansas City, KS | Josh McMillen, Cowley CO |
| 1999 | Grayson County College, Denison, TX | Matt Gawer, Grayson CO |
| 2000 | Grayson County College, Denison, TX | Adam LaRoche, Seminole (OK) State |
| 2001 | North Central Texas College, Gainesville, TX | Blake Justice, N. Central TX |
| 2002 | Central Arizona College, Coolidge, AZ | Gabe Mayorga, Central Arizona |
| 2003 | CC of Southern Nevada, Las Vegas | Tyler Coon, Southern Nevada |

# *Appendix B*

**Major Leaguers That Played in the JUCO World Series**

| Player, College, (JUCO) | Years Played |
|---|---|
| Jim Brenneman, Mesa (CO) | 1960–61 |
| Floyd Weaver, Paris (TX) | 1961 |
| Pete Loverich, Mesa (CO) | 1961 |
| Paul Dicken, Manatee (FL | 1963 |
| Oscar Zamora, Miami-Dade (FL) | 1964 |
| Barry Lersch, Mesa (CO) | 1964 |
| Gary Gentry, Phoenix (AZ) | 1965–66 |
| Tom Robson, Phoenix (AZ) | 1965 |
| Kurt Bevacqua, Miami-Dade (FL) | 1966–67 |
| Rich Folkers, Ellsworth (NC) | 1966 |
| Bob Stinson, Miami-Dade (FL) | 1966 |
| Gerald Pirtle, Bacone (OK) | 1967 |
| John Grubb, Manatee (FL) | 1968 |
| Ron Cash, Manatee (FL) | 1968 |
| Dave Moates, Manatee (FL) | 1968 |
| Rick Krueger, Grand Rapids (MI) | 1968 |
| Steve Foucault, Southern Georgia, | 1969 |
| Pat Darcy, Mesa (AZ) | 1969 |
| Roy Staiger, Bacone (OK) | 1969 |
| Doug Ault, Panola (TX) | 1969–70 |
| Larry Harlow, Mesa (AZ) | 1970 |
| Jim Otten, Mesa (AZ) | 1970–71 |
| John Tamargo, Miami-Dade (FL) | 1971 |
| Dave Collins, Mesa (AZ) | 1972 |
| Bill Nahorodny, St. Clair (MI) | 1972 |
| Rick Langford, Manatee (FL) | 1972 |
| Donnie Moore, Ranger (TX) | 1973 |
| Pat Putnam, Miami-Dade (FL) | 1974 |
| Neil Fiala, Meramec (MO) | 1975 |
| John Butcher, Yavapai (AZ) | 1979–80 |
| Tommy Dunbar, Middle Georgia | 1979–80 |
| Otis Nixon, Louisburg (NC) | 1979 |
| Craig McMurtry, McLennan (TX) | 1980 |
| Earnie Riles, Middle Georgia | 1980 |
| Jeff Treadway, Middle Georgia | 1980 |
| Jack Howell, Pima (AZ) | 1981 |
| Nelson Santovenia, Miami-Dade (FL) | 1981 |
| Keith Miller, Seminole (OK), | 1981–82 |
| Jose Tolentino, Seminole (OK) | 1981–82 |
| Kirby Puckett, Triton (IL) | 1982 |
| Kal Daniels, Middle Georgia | 1982 |
| Steve Peters, Seminole (OK) | 1982 |
| Mike Devereaux, Mesa (AZ) | 1982 |
| David Johnson, Baltimore (MD) | 1982 |
| Lance Johnson, Triton (IL) | 1982–83 |
| Alex Diaz, Middle Georgia | 1982–83 |
| Mike Fitzgerald, Middle Georgia | 1983 |
| Jay Buhner, McLennan (TX) | 1983 |
| Ken Patterson, McLennan (TX) | 1983 |
| Dwight Smith, Spartanburg (SC) | 1983 |
| Ray Stephens, Middle Georgia | 1983 |
| Jeff Reboulet, Triton (IL) | 1983 |
| Shawn Hillegas, Middle Georgia | 1984 |
| Jim Leyritz, Middle Georgia | 1984 |
| Kevin Ritz, Indian Hills (IA) | 1985 |
| Gil Heredia, Pima (AZ) | 1985 |
| Mike James, Santa Fe (FL.) | 1985 |
| Jonathan Hurst, Spartanburg (SC) | 1986 |
| Curt Schilling, Yavapai (AZ) | 1986 |
| Doug Lindsey, Seminole (OK) | 1987 |
| Rick Wilkins, Florida CC | 1987 |
| Rheal Cormier, CC of Rhode Island | 1988 |
| Chad Curtis, Cochise (AZ) | 1988 |
| Jessie Hollins, San Jacinto North (TX) | 1989 |
| Albie Lopez, Mesa (AZ) | 1990 |
| Garey Ingram, Middle Georgia | 1990 |
| Kelly Stinnett, Seminole (OK.) | 1990 |
| Shane Halter, Seminole (OK) | 1990 |

| | |
|---|---|
| Frank Rodriguez, Howard (TX) | 1991 |
| Mark Grudzielanek, Trinidad (CO) | 1991 |
| Matt Lawton, MS Gulf Coast CC | 1991 |
| Jason Dickson, Northeastern OK A&M | 1991 |
| Steve Kline, Allegany (MD) | 1991 |
| Paul Lo Duca, Glendale (AZ) | 1991 |
| Chad Fonville, Louisburg (NC) | 1992 |
| George Arias, Pima (AZ) | 1992 |
| Ryan Franklin, Seminole (OK) | 1992 |
| Rafael Carmona, Indian Hills (IA) | 1993 |
| Lou Collier, Triton (IL) | 1993 |
| Keith Foulke, Galveston (TX) | 1993 |
| Jose Rosado, Galveston (TX) | 1994 |
| Donzell McDonald, Trinidad (CO) | 1994 |
| Eric Gagne, Seminole (OK) | 1995 |
| Joe Nelson, Seminole (OK) | 1995 |
| Travis Hafner, Cowley County (KS) | 1997 |
| John Lackey, Grayson Co. (TX) | 1999 |
| Brandon Lyon, Dixie (UT) | 2000 |

# *Appendix C*

**JUCO Hall of Fame Inductees**

1982
Jay Tolman, Mesa JC, Grand Junction, CO
Martin "Pug" Marich, Phoenix College, Phoenix, AZ
Homa Thomas, Northeastern Oklahoma A&M, Miami, OK

1983
Demie Mainieri, Miami-Dade Community College-North, Miami, FL
Bill Griffin, Panola JC, Carthage, TX
Martin Dittmer, Ellsworth JC, Iowa Falls, IA

1984
Walter "Bus" Bergman, Mesa JC, Grand Junction, CO
Pat Daugherty, Indian Hills CC, Centerville, IA
LeRoy Wheat, Broward CC, Ft. Lauderdale, FL

1985
Sam Suplizio, Grand Junction, CO

1986
Jack Allen, Ranger JC, Ranger, TX

1987
Floyd Jacobson, Wilbur Wright College, Chicago, IL
Russ Frazier, Louisburg JC, Louisburg, NC
George E. Killian, Colorado Springs, CO

1988
Herb Boetto, Glendale CC, Glendale, AZ
George Cook, South Georgia College, Douglas, GA
Bob Wynn, Manatee JC, Bradenton, FL

1989
James T. Gallagher, Major League Baseball, New York City
Negial King, Bacone JC, Muskogee, OK
David Rowlands, Harry S. Truman College, Chicago, IL

1990
William J. Brooks, Wilmington College, Wilmington, NC
Kenneth C. Farris, Mississippi Gulf Coast CC, Perkinston, MS
Charles J. Ross, Community College of Beaver County, Monaca, PA

1991
James LeRoy Dreyer, Blinn College, Brenham, TX
Charles P. Greene, Miami-Dade Community College-South, Miami, FL
Richard A. Lessmann, St. Louis Community College-Meramec, Kirkwood, MO
Frank J. Torre, Palm Grove Garden, FL

1992
Bruce C. DuBois, Nassau Community College, Garden City, NY
Eugene F. Haggerty, Grand Junction, CO
Robert Symonds, Triton College, River Grove, IL

1993
Ronald W. Christopher, Wingate JC, Wingate, NC
Thomas M. Hofmann, Grand Rapids JC, Grand Rapids, MI
Richard E. Reimer, Grand Junction, CO

1994
H. David Chamberlain, Monroe CC, Rochester, NY
Bill Frazier, Gulf Coast CC, Panama City, FL
Duane S. Dykstra, Grand Junction, CO

1995
Wayne L. Graham, San Jacinto College-North, Houston, TX
Howard C. Roey, Florida Community College, Jacksonville, FL
Robert Ned Sapp Jr., Middle Georgia College, Cochran, GA

1996
Steven Bazarnic, Allegany Community College, Cumberland, MD
Rex L. Bradley, Louisville, KY
Joseph Dondero, Nassau Community College, Garden City, NY
Dale Hollingsworth, Grand Junction, CO

1997
James E. Frye, Mesa Community College, Mesa, AZ
Paul MacLaughlin, Lincroft, NJ
Lloyd Russell Simmons, Seminole Junior College, Seminole, OK

1998
Richard B. Butler, Waco, TX
Richard J. Croch, Port Huron, MI
Rich R. Mathews, Centerville, IA

1999
Tilman M. Bishop, Grand Junction, CO
Edward R. Sylvia, Housatonic Community College, Bridgeport, CT
Harry H. Tholen, Santa Fe Community College, Gainesville, FL

2000
Earnest G. Myers, C.S. Mott Community College, Flint, MI
Rick Zimmerman, Odessa College, Odessa, TX
Elliott Oppenheim, Community College of Baltimore County, Dundalk, MD

2001
Hurst F. Otto, Grand Junction, CO
Billy M. Crowder, Westark Junior College, Fort Smith, AR
Gene D. Hanson, College of Lake County, Grayslake, IL
Richard R. Symonds, Oakton Community College, Des Plaines, IL

2002
Barry A. Glinski, Quinsigamond Community College, Worchester, MA
Claude J. Kracik, Lincoln Land Community College, Springfield, IL
Stephen Cohen, North Hennepin Community College, Minneapolis, MN
Wayne Nelson, Grand Junction, CO

2003
John Toppi, Phoenix, AZ
James C. Painter, Columbia State Community College, Columbia, TN
Ronald "Gene" Creek, Lake Land College, Mattoon, IL

# *Appendix D*

**Mesa JC All-Tournament Selections, 1959–1974**

Eldon Miller, C, 1959
Randy Dow, 1B, 1960–1961
Pete Lovrich, P, 1961
Mike DerManual, 3B, 1963
Tex Tolman, OF, 1963
Bucky Hakes, 1B, 1963 (honorable mention)
Bobby Andrews, SS, 1964
Jerry Chick, C, 1964 (honorable mention)
Mack Gendreau, P, 1964 (Tournament Most Valuable Player)
Barry Lersch, P, 1964
Bill Brill, 1B, 1966
Larry Linville, OF, 1966
Dick Allred, OF,1968
Ralph Dick, OF, 1968
Bob Engle, C, 1969
Mike Hall, P, 1970
Al Torrey, 3B, 1970
Bob Blaser, SS, 1974
Mike Higgins, OF, 1974

Coach Bus Bergman and the Mesa team won the Homa Thomas Sportsmanship Award in 1974.